From Being to Living

François Jullien

From Being to Living
(De l'Être au Vivre)

a Euro-Chinese lexicon of thought

Translated by
Michael Richardson & Krzysztof Fijalkowski

Los Angeles | London | New Delhi
Singapore | Washington DC | Melbourne

Los Angeles | London | New Delhi
Singapore | Washington DC | Melbourne

SAGE Publications Ltd
1 Oliver's Yard
55 City Road
London EC1Y 1SP

SAGE Publications Inc.
2455 Teller Road
Thousand Oaks, California 91320

SAGE Publications India Pvt Ltd
B 1/I 1 Mohan Cooperative Industrial Area
Mathura Road
New Delhi 110 044

SAGE Publications Asia-Pacific Pte Ltd
3 Church Street
#10-04 Samsung Hub
Singapore 049483

Editor: Natalie Aguilera
Assistant editor: Eve Williams
Production editor: Katherine Haw
Copyeditor: Leigh Mueller
Proofreader: Sharon Cawood
Indexer: Michael Richardson
Marketing manager: George Kimble
Cover design: Wendy Scott
Typeset by: C&M Digitals (P) Ltd, Chennai, India
Printed in the UK

© Editions Gallimard 2015

Translation © Krzysztof Fijalkowski and
    Michael Richardson 2020

First published 2020

Library of Congress Control Number: 2019933912

British Library Cataloguing in Publication data

A catalogue record for this book is available from the
British Library

ISBN 978-1-5264-9166-4
ISBN 978-1-5264-8729-2 (pbk)

At SAGE we take sustainability seriously. Most of our products are printed in the UK using responsibly
sourced papers and boards. When we print overseas we ensure sustainable papers are used as
measured by the PREPS grading system. We undertake an annual audit to monitor our sustainability.

Contents

Contents

Translator's Introduction

In this book, François Jullien sets up a series of oppositions in order to conceptualise what he calls the *écarts* (divergences) between European and Chinese ways of thinking. It is important to realise that these are not dualisms, and for this reason Jullien insists on their *divergent* and not *different* character. It is not, therefore, that European thought and Chinese thought are different in kind from one another in the sense that they represent differences of sensibility that can be overcome by seeking to understand one another from the perspective of the same. A European cannot 'understand' China in these terms any more than a Chinese can 'understand' Europe: there is no 'Chinese mind' to be deciphered. Rather, over the course of their different histories, European thought and Chinese thought have taken divergent paths based upon concepts that were established in ancient times and continue to condition, if not determine, what it is possible to think in different contexts. In the European context, these concepts were first developed in ancient Greece, most especially in the philosophy of Plato and Aristotle, while Chinese ways of thinking are grounded in the various schools of its ancient philosophy (Confucianism, Taoism, Mohism and so on). The distinction – the point of divergence – lies in what has been given priority: following the concerns of Plato and Aristotle, Western thinking has been overwhelmingly concerned with the question of Being, whereas Chinese thinking concerned itself principally with that of living. Jullien insists on the importance of recognising this divergence, the result of a branching off of ways of thinking that has occurred over the course of their respective histories, failing which we are in danger of reducing all thinking to a single model, which will be that of the European. The question here is whether Chinese thought, like all other divergences, is being chiselled away by processes of globalisation, reduced to a universalism under the sway of the hegemony of Western ideas.

In exploring this complex and difficult issue, Jullien's language can often seem opaque and it presents considerable difficulties for the translator. This is especially so for certain words which cannot easily be rendered in English. Most problematic is the distinction drawn throughout, and extensively explored in the chapter we have entitled 'Surge versus Settled'. The words Jullien uses here are 'essor' and 'étale'. *Essor* means, according to the *Larousse*, 'an action from a bird when it takes flight; figuratively, a sudden movement, progress'. It can be translated by 'flight, rise, development, becoming self-sufficient'. *Étale* means 'what neither rises nor falls; a ship that is completely still; the moment when the tide turns'. As a verb, how-ever, it normally means 'to exhibit in a sale, to display, to show all one's cards'. Translations for the first alternative are given as 'slack, steady, becalmed'; for the second, as 'to display, lay out, spread, show off'. In pre-vious works, we tended to translate 'essor' as 'springing up' but here 'surge' appeared to us as more appropriate. This is because Jullien is in general less concerned with emergence (in the sense of a plant that starts to put forth shoots) than with the forward movement that occurs within a continuity, due to factors that have developed over time and created a sense of tension. In setting this *essor* against the *étale*, he emphasises the dynamism of this movement in opposition to what is established to such an extent that it is taken for granted and not questioned. It responds to periods of calm and achievement when we tend to become complacent. However, things have only become 'settled' in anticipation of the turning of the tide, as the final chapter of the Chinese book of changes, the *I Ching*, expresses it: not a conclusion but a moment of incompletion or transition.

Another term that presents difficulties is *modélisation*, by which Jullien is referring to ideas of planning or designing which dominate policy decisions in the West: in order to set up a business, for instance, we today need a business plan worked out in detail in advance, even though everyday contingencies in the actual running of the business will inevitably make most of what is planned redundant or ineffective. Ancient Chinese thought, in contrast, emphasises 'maturation', by which we do not plan in advance but assess situations in the full range of their possibilities, allowing them to develop on their own terms whilst seeking to impel them towards the result we would like.

Perhaps the most difficult of the oppositions Jullien establishes for English-language speakers to grasp is that of *disponible*, set up in Chapter III in opposition to 'freedom'. Ordinarily, this word would be translated as 'availability', but to do so may lead to confusion, since the proliferation of mobile phones and other modes of today's communication systems has made the idea of constantly 'being available' a contemporary reality. This is not the sort of availability that Jullien means, however; indeed, in some ways, it is even its very opposite since this form of availability is imposed and often leads to closure (people using their mobile phones while being oblivious to what is going on all around them). In using the word 'disponi-ble', he is referring to means of remaining open to possibilities, of being responsive to everything that may happen. To exemplify this notion, Jullien refers to a novel by the French twentieth-century author André Gide, *The Fruits of the Earth* (1952), which concerns the adventures of a young man advised to experience the world in its fullness without being worried about the duties of family, society or nation. He should therefore be 'available' or receptive to the contingency of the world, open to whatever may come. To express this notion, it has therefore seemed to us more easily understanda-ble for an English-language audience to translate this term as 'receptive'.

*****

Acknowledgements

The translators would like to thank Noémi Lemoine-Blanchard for her help.

A time comes in one's work (a moment of life, perhaps?) when it is appropriate to start bringing its various threads together. Or we might say, have a look through our projects as a gardener does when surveying his garden to reflect on what is growing, what has taken and what hasn't, in what state his plants are and what parts of the plot need to be reworked, what should be pulled up and replanted, and finally what its overall shape is.

When it comes to a philosophical project, it will be a question of establishing the state of its concepts and how effective they can be.

Concepts have taken root here where Chinese and European thought have come into contact with one another. I might alternatively express this as Chinese thought-language and European thought-language because thought, if it isn't determined by language, nonetheless exploits its resources. The concepts I am presenting here have been conceived as a result of this encounter whilst at the same time serving to conceive it – in other words, to make it possible. The difficulty is that, as they encounter one another, these languages and thoughts must produce tools. Indeed, without these tools, there would have been no encounter – the result is therefore also its condition. For how are we to think between *thoughts – that is, without continuing to be blocked from one side or the other, but in freeing oneself from one* by means of *the other so allowing them to* interpret and borrow *from one another? I shall therefore proceed by passing in turn via one and then the other, from one side but also from the other side, consequently in a lateral way, but without falling in with either of the two, qua hinc qua hac, as the Latin says, or as is said more familiarly in French, 'cahin-caha', or 'haltingly'. Yes, from here to there, via zigzags and in a way that is conducted haltingly; this approach isn't brilliant but if we are to avoid the ordinary illusion, that of laying claim to an impossible projection (of an immediate translation between these languages and thoughts), this is the only logical way if we want gradually to develop the necessary conditions from which the other may, on both sides, gradually be comprehended. Wouldn't any other approach, right from the start, simply mean projecting the categories and biases of our own language and thinking (that remain unthought) onto this elsewhere of language and thought? Could an* effective *encounter then take place?*

In other words, I don't believe it is possible for a Westerner to begin by 'introducing' Chinese thought directly or head-on. I don't believe it can be summed up or that a chart could be drawn up or some handy digest made of it. We can't even begin by giving its history. For then we would still inevitably be dependent, without being aware of the fact, on the implicit choices of our own language and thought. In the end, we'd never be able to offer anything but a more or less unfaithful facsimile of what we had already thought. A displacement hasn't occurred; we haven't left home. We haven't left 'Europe with its ancient parapets'.[1] The only strategy I can therefore see by which to emerge from this aporia is to organise the confrontation step by step, laterally as I've said, by means of successive sideways steps, by gaps and disturbances that link together, by de- and re-categorising, link by link, going from one concept to the next, to form a lexicon progressively – in other words, as we go along.

Hence, we will here be concerned with conceptual divergences *along the fault lines of a too hastily accepted generality, rather than with concepts confident in their generality. This will enable us to open up the 'between' that is between these languages and thoughts. Consequently, it won't be a matter of 'comparing', of seeking to identify resemblances and differences in order to characterise either thought (empty, as well as impossible, identifications), but of organising a confrontation between these languages and thoughts, by allowing a reciprocal scrutiny to be effected, from which a* reflection *of one through the other can result, one that takes place simultaneously on both sides. Difference arranges, in accordance with the Same and the Other, but the characteristic of divergence is to* disturb. *This leads to a probing, through the distance opened up, of how far such divergence can go in putting thought back in* tension, *thereby setting it back to work. Equally, these concepts are prospective and not retrospective: they don't take stock of two past traditions, but – by inviting a dissidence into the heart of philosophy and, consequently, by reconfiguring the field of what is thinkable – they gradually call for thought by making good use of resources available on both sides, so once again becoming extricated from one as well as from the other. This means cost (work), but also taste, passion,* drive, *'gaiety' ('Gay Science': against what is too often depressing in Sinological erudition). Having recovered its initiative, thought can once again take risks.*

A concept is a tool. *Each concept forged here, being placed in relation to an* other *(versus* the other*) which appears at first sight to be its equivalent or what takes its place, might prove through divergence to be its contradiction or antonym. These concepts thereby 'unfold' thought – in other words, they take apart its marked and fixed 'folds'. As a result, they no longer have a specific usage or course assigned to them that is fixed in advance. On the other hand, due to one oblique approach or another, they gradually reveal a comprehensive network of fault lines that is to be explored. This is between what is revealed to be the prominence of the* subject *at the heart of European thought and what the Chinese regard as something that we in Europe only know how to speak of, in a feeble and too restrictive way, as a 'situation'. This word is too restrictive because it doesn't truly loosen us from the perspective of the subject – an alternative will need to be constructed. These concepts are vagabonds, useful for anything – they swiftly cross the traditional fields of history, morality, politics or aesthetics, going from first philosophy to management theory. Moreover, they are theoretical and practical, or rather they begin by unmaking the opposition of 'theory' and 'practice'. I would argue that this means that they are* strategic. *By taking advantage of the resources of both languages and both systems of thought, they serve to conceive a strategy of* living *and* thinking.

What is the perspective that gradually emerges from this development, and what history does it reveal? A way out of the 'question of Existence' gradually comes into view which reveals at the same time *an entry point into the thought of* living *by following the mesh I am spinning, thread by thread, between the thought-languages of China and Europe. For we cannot 'leave' (deconstruct) without entering somewhere else (to discover). How then is living to be approached when it isn't understood in terms of how European thought, or at least most of its philosophy, has conceived it – that is, in terms of 'being' and therefore of knowledge? In other words, how can we arrive at 'living' if we allow it to be set up as an object of thought, so that it becomes that thing in which we are engaged from the outset and from which therefore we have no distance? Since it is also true that to live is the only thing to which we can aspire.*

Note

1   An allusion to Rimbaud's *Le Bateau ivre* [trans.].

1

Propensity (vs Causality)

1 In order to think about things we have needed to separate Being and becoming – does this 'we' only mean the Greeks? And when I speak of 'things', it is of course lives as much as things that are at stake, and it applies as much to natures and behaviours as well – its indetermination gives the term its most general sense. From an initial gesture which seems to be controlled by the approach of the mind, we have decided between the *static* and the *dynamic*, states that are either stable or shifting, with the latter even being regarded as contradictory due to the fact that it changes. Not that the inevitability of language inescapably stabilises things (in France, this is the Bergsonian question), but we can consider the *situation* on the one side and its *evolution* on the other. This precludes us from seeing things in their configuration at the same time as in their transformation. We never get sufficiently close to that (but it is precisely not a 'that', because no part of it can be isolated) at which (through which) we nevertheless know that the real is formed or extended, but which is precisely not the 'real' (*res*: the substantial 'thing'), in other words what *is carried out*. This means that we leave their inseparability, and not so much the passage from one to the other, in a black hole: things become *constituted* from their *evolution*. This can also be read in the opposite sense: they evolve through what constitutes them. To assume olden terms, the event lies in the structure.

Propensity seems to me to be the most appropriate term to deal with this lack: it designates and defines this inseparability. It would be the term that most closely approaches what is unthinkable, in order to express how things are driven by what they 'are' and that they 'are' due to what drives them; how inclination is implied in the disposition and how, *at the same time*, the inclination itself constitutes the disposition – how the evolution is therefore not only contained in the configuration, but forms a union with it and is mingled in it. I've found some support for this in *shi*, a term from ancient Chinese thought that has not been conceptualised very much but has passed into use in the most diverse fields, from strategy to the theory of power, from aesthetics to how history as well as first philosophy is considered. I am amazed that in text after text, in the same context, it is variously translated by 'situation' or by 'evolution', by 'condition' or by the 'course of things'.

For at what point – one never completely clarified by intelligence – do the two meet up to the point of finding themselves in communication, and even, it could be said, equivalent to one another? 'Tendency' would be too biased towards evolution to be usable, since it does not make the situational sufficiently clear. As well as being too genetic, it too often carries psychological baggage. In 'propensity', on the other hand (the term is somewhat strange, but Leibniz was aware of it, for this was also what he wanted to think), let's admit not that things 'are', but that they 'lean', that they split themselves according to how they are inclined, and that this is what constitutes their 'advance': they are constantly toppling over due to their *weight and hanging quality* (the Latin *pendere*), in one way or another (the situational), and to *pro*-duce their future by this momentum and drive; that they are taken forward to reconfigure themselves due to the sole fact that they are always, not a 'being', but an inflection. Always: the world is made only from the fact that everything, always, 'leans' towards what is 'ahead' in a certain way – *pro-pendere* – producing its renewal.

In using this vocabulary, we may be thought to be lapsing into some materialist and deterministic theory as it has been developed in a recurrent way in Europe since antiquity, but this is precisely not so – and this is what the thought of *propensity* can bring us that is new, in beginning to shift us from what we have been conditioned to accept. The interest of this concept, or rather of how it needs to be made into a concept, is that it takes us out of the regime of causality and therefore of 'explanation', a regime that has reigned supreme over European knowledge, to introduce us to a constant *implication*. The Greeks thought from 'cause' and 'principle', the cause as primary and as a principle (*arché* ἀρχή – *aitia* χ, the two preliminary terms of Aristotle's vocabulary). We enter into the 'thing', in other words, through the 'cause', *causa*, the former supporting the latter's truth, and we 'account' (the well-known *logon didonai* of the Greeks) for any being whatever by something outside of itself – which is sufficient to disclose, at least in a symbolic way, this *ex-* of ex-plaining. 'To know' is 'to know the cause of things', *rerum cognoscere causas*, as the Latin sententiously puts it in a formula that would dispel the mystery of the world by setting it out within this explanatory regime. God himself (this was already self-evident to Plato) is set forth as 'first cause', that to which one cannot go back and from which everything is linked and becomes 'understandable' (or else, in the *Phaedon*, the 'Idea' is 'cause').

2 The idea of *causality* thus contains an effect of intelligence or clarity, and in this respect it leads back to everything with which the Greeks marked the whole of reality (the division 'causing/caused' enables it to be recognised as 'real'). Such is the causal *link*, one that as such is archetypal, to the extent that the role of the understanding is really to establish relations and 'link together', so that one is considered to be external to the other one at the same time as it can produce it (therefore 'fire is what causes water to boil'). This has so dominated European thought that we have not emerged from this framework and explanatory regime, which acts as a powerful lever, especially in the realm of physical knowledge, in a way that remained unsuspected until our modernity – the only exceptions to this being Hume and Nietzsche, an exception that makes them great. This is to such an extent

that our modernity, for one part, is really formed by how we try to extricate ourselves from this yoke and linkage – for what if these had no other justification than our 'habit' alone? To try to emancipate the mind from the great impetus of causality (as is already the case in physics), but especially in a way that meta-physics is destroyed by it, the latter having too credulously believed it was able to rest its edifice on this artifice.

Some Chinese thinkers from the end of antiquity (those who are called late Mohists) had also thought about causality and had even inscribed it at the head of their *canon*, but at the same time we note what an odd place they hold in the heart of Chinese tradition. They appear close to the Greeks in their interest in science, physics and optics, as well as in their need for definition and the rigour of refutation, and they never considered the *tao*, the 'way'. To what extent did they diverge from the logic of processes that, according to the premise of the 'way', has dominated Chinese thought? In any case, we can *glimpse* in their work the possibility of a form of thinking that Chinese tradition as a whole hasn't developed (they probably belonged to the milieu of artisans, or 'technicians', rather than that of court 'councillors' and literati) – and so their texts have been transmitted to us only in fragments, having been recovered in China only at the dawn of the twentieth century, rediscovered at the time that European thought was being encountered. We should try to understand why this *possible* glimpse of causality was not taken forward and developed in the Chinese context of thought. And why another prevailed, which didn't seek to explain the world, to respond to its great questioning, but delicately attempted to detect its slightest propensities so as to marry their inflections and thereby place itself in phase with the world's 'functioning'. In so doing, it turned away not simply from what we call physics but also from metaphysics. Having no need to posit a God as the 'cause' of the world, it also had no reason to consider Freedom as the 'cause' of the subject's will.

To think in terms not of causality but of propensity isn't simply about leaving a regime of *explanation* for one of *implication*, or to pass from an external reason to one that is internal and in tune with immanence. More broadly, it also effects a shift from clarity through 'cutting out' (elements) and uncoupling (what is opposed), that of Being and its construction, into a logic that is both *continuous* and *correlated* and, as such, involves processes that are indefinitely interwoven. For it must be understood that the *processural* should be radically separated from what we have traditionally conceived as 'becoming', which is always understood within the shadow of Being and as its derivation or perdition. Indeed, becoming is either degeneration, in prey to its corruption, Being sinking from the peace of identity into temporal movement, or it is, on the contrary, as a 'potential', *dunamis*, extended towards an end and aspiring towards realisation (Aristotle's *energeia*). But *propensity* signals towards a deployment which is not driven by any loss or marked by a vocation. It continues, and it doesn't lean towards what is ahead (the 'towards', *zu*, of accomplishment and destination), so true is it that what orients and induces its extension, and so effects its renewal, is only the way in which the situation is inclined to 'tilt'.

Hence, the mode of intelligence called upon to grasp propensity isn't 'liaison' ('synthetic': that of Kantian understanding), but let's call it *discernment* (the frequent meaning of *zhī* 知): detecting a 'priming' of transformation in each thread or fibre of the situation (the ancient notion of *jī* 幾 in the Chinese *Oracle of Changes*). This means examining phases and stages rather than analysing states, so that the mutation to come is already perceived to be at work in the present as *lineaments* (the notion of *xiàng* 象). This has been called 'contextual' intelligence, one that both branches out and is globalising, since one needs to detect how, at each instant, the configuration is propelled to shift in a certain way, and to do so in accordance with relations and variations that together form, by their effect of coupling, what we call 'situation' – *situation* being the term we need to think afresh. Henceforth, we won't be content with following the singular causation of an effect, since everything is always a play of correlated factors, worked by its polarities, from which a modification follows (is secreted) and by which the barely emerged tiny possibility will probably become more and more pronounced until it effectively activates itself.

3 Yet entering a logic of propensity means that the great European scenario of *choice* and its Freedom capsizes all at once, notwithstanding its sublimity. When it comes to ethics, the Greek question is that of the cause of my action. Therefore, so as not to become trapped in a determinist explanation, I will have to pierce its rationality by presupposing some 'declension' – but which might be fortuitous (*clinamen*) – such that its own cause will 'prevent the indefinite succession of causes', as Lucretius said, and give way to the possibility of the will. As soon as I do as the Greeks did and cut out and isolate a particular segment in the course of my behaviour, to which I assign a beginning and end and which I call an 'action' (*praxis*) that will subsequently only know succession through a plurality of addition ('an' action – 'some' actions), I cannot fail to question the origin and reason for such a unity of 'action' being constituted as an entity; I cannot fail to question whether I have performed this action, isolated as it is, according to an internal or external causality, which does or does not depend on me, 'willingly' or 'against my will', *ekôn / akôn* ἑκών / ἄκων, a first splitting of morality from responsibility. Indeed, Greek tragedy had already been grappling with this question before philosophy: when Ajax throws himself on his sword (in Sophocles), did he do so from his own volition or was he tortured by a madness that came from elsewhere, a divine *atè*?

The fact that the West became so attached to Freedom and made it its ideal reveals its anxiety about the capacity each of us has to be our own cause, independently of any external determination – in other words, to find our cause within our 'self', to be *causa sui*, as Spinoza (in the first words of the *Ethics*) put it. Yet, as soon as we cease to think in terms of an isolatable, atomisable Being (or action), and start thinking in terms of a continuous course (of what I thus call my conduct: 'the course of the world', 'the course of conduct', *tiān-xíng, rén-xíng* 天行, 人行, is what the Chinese parallel says), the question can only become that of by what uninterrupted inclination, in what forms my incessant affective interaction with the world (*xiàng-gǎn* 相 感), am I in the process of bending the value of my behaviour – am I raising or debasing it? Such a propensity isn't, however, deterministic (the opposite of our freedom which, as such, doesn't change anything). The element of choice and initiative gets diluted during this process so that it becomes imperceptibly selective: in the end, this 'choice' is only the manifestation of its 'leaning' and finally its toppling over – of the order of the result. And the question that then arises is: how can this anticipation of behaviour be promoted and defined so that, from it, the morality of my conduct will then ensue by its propensity? In other words, how are we to deploy the slightest 'priming' of morality discovered within myself (like my reaction to what is 'unbearable', which I experience when suddenly coming across a misfortune that has happened to someone else, as in the *Mencius*) and 'cultivate' this inclination towards the good – in the same way as 'water inclines downwards' – by favouring its conditioning? For it is when behaviour in its entirety is finally no more than the expression of this moral propensity, when virtue has become spontaneous and requires no further constraint and effort (*Zhong yong*, § 20), that one has attained 'wisdom'.

Yet this also applies when it comes to the understanding of history. Rather than atomising it in events whose sequence will be sought out by successively finding each cause, one should, according to Braudel, follow its slow duration over a long period and according to its driving force and in its 'comprehensive propensity' (named *dà shì* 大势 by Wang Fuzhi)[1]. Montesquieu, already ill at ease with a standpoint of causality that encouraged assigning and therefore divided things up too much, implied the same thing when he dealt with a 'general cause', which he corrected afterwards to 'principal bearing', to illuminate the familiar 'grandeur and decadence of the Romans'. For history isn't formed from an indefinite teeming of causes that are impossible to inventory and that we retrace back to an arbitrary point, but from propensities that are always universal, that are considered on a more or less vast scale and that will increase and then reverse – or rather that, while they are growing and expanding, are already beginning discreetly to go into reverse. This means we can only fix them in an artificial way when 'this' has started. Salient events are themselves modifications; declared situations are never anything but transitions.

And so today, when the term 'crisis' is on everyone's lips and would express the truth of our time, indeed, one would beneficially be seized with such a doubt: when did the 'crisis' in Europe begin? Do we have to invoke its 'causes' analytically? But, since it did begin one day, we tell ourselves, it will also come to an end on another day. Every discernible beginning calls for an equally settled end, like any segment with two extremities... Yet we get tired of this theatre of raising and lowering the curtain, of this facile and bland and reassuring imagery – the idea that, whatever the misfortune, there is light at the end of every 'tunnel'. How are we unable to *see* this *comprehensive propensity*, according to which the economic and political *potential* of the world is subject to a continuous modification, like a ground swell that the situation carries to all points, and above all from the West to the Far East? And then this inflexion will experience others that are already taking shape.

Note

1   Wang Fuzhi (1619–92), a philosopher, historian and poet during the early Qing dynasty [trans.].

II

Potential of Situation (vs Initiative of the Subject)

1 What European philosophy has promoted, and that in the end has retro-spectively constituted its fate, is what has come to fix its point of departure in a self-subject (an observation that unfortunately is too banal for us to be able to think about adequately). This means that, when I think, I start by thinking not from the world or from 'things', as the Greeks did, but from an 'I' which thinks: the subject passes itself off as the first object and as sufficient of itself. Any 'world' comes only later and as a consequence of it. The first features of this 'I think', an insular *cogito*, appear in Saint Augustine, but it was Descartes who knew how to draw back the curtain and so brought into view what Hegel would call the 'land of truth'. The philoso-pher, who begins by 'doubting', discovering as he does so how uncertain and insecure his thought is, is obviously secondary compared with this initial 'I' on whose rock he has been able to roost in order to make a start. Or, rather, this doubt is itself essential since it is from this 'I' of 'I doubt' alone that I discover that I cannot doubt, no matter how insistent my doubt may be. Yet from what did Descartes *right from the start* unknowingly cut himself off due to this hyperbolic doubt, which from the outset believed it could embrace everything, and from which we certainly wouldn't fail to find the world and every thing in its place once more? He would later recover this in his own terms, but only by being dependent on this initial *ego*. This meant that from this moment he would no longer be entirely able to think but would only be able to do so within this *fold* of the subject. By means of this masterstroke, didn't Descartes immediately and definitively cast out what was unthought?

The response has often been – even while it has been solemnly condemned – that what Descartes from the start radically cut out was the Other, defin-itively missing the joint origin of the You and the I, of the Other and the subject, and so he isolated himself in his solipsism. It's true that from the start Descartes turned away from Hebraic scrutiny – but is this the only thing that would be lost in beginning as he did? I fear that he may have lost something else, something that, while 'God' remained to furnish some sup-port for the status of the Other, from this point could only be considered on the margins and could only fall back into the fragmentation of empiricism. This is therefore something that in Europe we haven't been able to recover, except by cobbling it together. I have myself only been able to recover it under the unsophisticated form of 'situation' that I earlier advanced. *Subject* or *situation*: this is where European thought, without knowing it, has also forked off. For if, as it returns to this decisive place of the *cogito* in order to wash its hands of its mistake, but with little sense of repentance, modern philosophy has since been so strongly attached to restoring and magnifying the great Other, it has perhaps paid insufficient attention to what it has put to one side, although in a less obtrusive way because it hasn't even known how to grapple with it. This means that we in Europe have always thought about the One, the Subject, to the detriment of this small other, which has remained nameless and faceless; and that we can envisage what we call, as best we can, 'situation' only by means of an unsatisfying hasty adjustment and stop-gap solution.

Subject *or* situation: this opposition is strangely illuminated quite differently in Chinese thought. Just think about what we call 'landscape'. On the whole, this is simply the natural and initial mode of 'situation'. Its notion was discovered during the Renaissance in Europe, when the classification of the subject began to take shape and was subsequently developed so magisterially by Descartes: landscape is the 'part of the land', as the dictionary still says, 'that nature presents to an observer', who delineates it according to his perspective so that this horizon modifies itself in step with how he is positioned. The Subject, in other words, is *in the presence of* the landscape, which is external to him and remains autonomous; he is not implicated in it. Yet China speaks not of landscape but of 'mountain(s)-water(s)', *shān-shuǐ* 山水. At the same time, this is what extends towards the high (the mountain) and the low (water), towards what is motionless and remains unmoveable (the mountain) and what never stops billowing or flowing (water), or towards what has form and is three-dimensional (the mountain) and what by nature is formless and married to the form of things (water), or towards what offers itself directly to sight (the mountain) and something whose rustling comes from various directions to the ear (water) …

Another example we might note is what Chinese refers to as 'wind-light', *fēng- jǐng* 风景 which indicates what on the one hand is constantly passing and animated but that we don't see (the 'wind'), and what on the other hand brings visibility and favours vitality ('light'). In saying, or rather doing, this, Chinese thought-language always names a correlation of factors, entering into interaction and being constituted in polarity. Any 'subject' isn't absent but rather immersed in it: from the outset, it is part of this field of tensions that is established and from which it cannot be detached. In other words, it doesn't emerge in an autonomous posture, one that is exemplified by the self-sufficient 'I think'. But nor does it project its point of view onto the world by unfolding it like a panorama, from the height of its overhang, so that it is presented as an object ('thrown' 'before' him: 'ob'-'ject'), one which his sight will stumble upon and that he can sovereignly 'ob-serve'. The landscape is therefore not approached from the initiative of a subject, as the celebrated Cartesian beginning instituted it, but is conceived as an investment of capacities reciprocally at work, which is revealed to be both opposed and complementary, at whose heart 'some' subject is implicated. *Situation* would thus designate, in a preliminary way, this web of unlimited implications at whose heart each one is originally seized upon, whose configuration is outlined through various tensions and from which only by abstraction can one exempt oneself.

2 This makes it possible for us to deploy such thought about the situation by going back to the Chinese term with which I started, and which, taking apart the opposition between the static and the dynamic (also translated as 'condition' or 'evolution', *shi* 势), began in the *Art of War* of Ancient China by designating the *potential* to be taken advantage of *in the situation*. The divergence opened up at the outset is twofold here: on the one hand, the situation is immediately thought of as invested capacity; on the other hand, it is initially approached not in a speculative way but according to the use or function that follows on from it. Moreover, if I translate the Chinese term in this way, it is particularly with reference to European physics which teaches us to calculate, under a theorem of this name, according to the accumulated mass of water and the incline of the slope opened up below it, with what strength this water will rush down. Yet we find exactly the same image at the start of the *Sunzi*: the good general is said to be one who is organising his troops like water accumulated at the top of a slope and in which a breach is suddenly opened – its passage will then carry along everything in its path. Strategy, in other words, is simply a matter of knowing how to make good use of the situation by progressively bending it like a slope in developing its favourable *propensity*, and doing so in such a way that the effects rush down of their own accord and without having to be forced.

Once the situation is revealed as not simply a frame, or even a context, but as an active *potential*, it is at the same time reconfigured in its relation to a 'subject'. The strategist will no longer be someone who makes a plan in accordance with his objectives and *projects* it onto the situation, thus appealing to his understanding in order to conceive of what should be and then to his will in order to make it accord with the facts. This 'according' can imply force – the 'understanding' and the 'will' being the two master faculties of the subject of the European classical age. But the real strategist would be the one who knows how to *discern*, at once to detect and to unleash – directly from the situation itself in which he is engaged, and not in such a way that he would ideally reconfigure it in his mind – the favourable factors, the 'contributing' factors as they say. Following this and without others even noticing it, he will continually gain in *propensity* and turn the situation to his advantage.

This means that efficacy doesn't strictly come from me, the subject who has conceived and willed the initiative, who has constructed a plan and then implemented it according to the time-honoured theory–practice relation from which Europe hasn't extricated itself, but that, if I have been able to diagnose the potential in my favour by means of distributing factors, and then gradually to exploit them, then it advances *directly* from the situation itself. From this point, the situation won't constitute that stubborn and resistant idea on which I must impose the plan that I earlier erected, but becomes a mine whose veins I'll explore, a field of resources whose furrows I shall follow like a network of various opportunities, on which I will learn to become a 'surfer'. To be able to 'surf' or, as they say, respond to the 'contributing' factors, one day it will be necessary to pay close attention to this imagery asserted by experience, *experientia reclamante*, an imagery of what is supple and *fluid* rather than active or heroic, and introduce it into the field of our reflection. This is why the *Sunzi* begins by teaching us to 'evaluate' ('calculate', the ancient meaning of *ji* 计) the potential of the situation invested between the adversary and me. I do this by identifying, item by item, how favourable or unfavourable are the directions towards which the factors that conjoin in it are leaning (what direction offers the best relation between the prince and the general, or between the prince and the people, and so on; or which side has the best spies, and so on). Therefore, instead of erecting a plan, I trace a diagram of factors and vectors at play, the lesson being that, before engaging in combat, I must tip over the potential of the situation onto my side: as a result, when I finally engage in the combat, I have *already* won; the enemy is *already* defeated.

3 Yet, if I return to the European lexicon, 'situation' designates 'the entirety of circumstances in which one finds oneself' – as though that were sufficient. But 'circumstance(s)' *fragment* the situation into infinite pieces due to its plural which slices up and juxtaposes (spatially, temporally, aspectually, etc.). *Circumstance* is therefore a feeble notion, ranked in the final ablative case in Latin and whose European semantics is enough to reveal at once its secondary and composite status. 'Circum'-'stance' (in the same way, *péri-stasis* περί- στασις in Greek; *Um-stand* in German): the circumstance is what 'stands' 'around'. But around what, if it is not precisely the perspective of a sovereign Subject that predominates from the start? Thus, far from being as neutral as it appears, 'circum-stance' is a term that wrongly both stabilises and peripheralises, the subject being represented in it as an island against which the moving flow of circumstances will strike. Thus, as Clausewitz noted, circumstances are inevitably a source of 'friction'. They occur unexpectedly against the plan that was put together ahead of time, and this means that it will gradually stumble and fall short. Yet to think of the situation as a potential takes exactly the opposite path from this negative and turns it around. Instead of the causal circumstance arising as an obstacle that causes the derailing of the template, the very evolution of the situation and its constantly renewing dynamism (something strongly expressed by the term *shi* 势) mean that, since no mind has been restricted by any projection, I can continue to take support as I incline this *quality of situation* to my advantage and gradually make use of it.

The consequences can easily be deduced at an operational level, and concerning any 'management'. Henceforth, there will be no further preoccupation with 'chance' or 'luck', or with having to worry about gods and fate or with casting runes, or counting on a 'stroke of genius' (the other large hole made in our rationality of the subject: when we give up all of the plans drawn up in advance and react directly to what arises circumstantially): the victory is always simply the result of the potential of the situation in which one is engaged, or, as Sunzi tersely says about war, that it 'doesn't deviate', *bù tè* 不忒. This means, at the same time, that the battle is won even before combat has started; while the beaten troops are those 'which seek victory only at the moment of combat', hoping to snatch success. From this, it is finally inferred that the (true) good strategist is the one whose strategy is not even noticed and therefore whom no one thinks of 'praising'. He has been so well prepared beforehand, in how to detect the favourable factors and continually making the potential of the situation evolve to his advantage, that, when victory is achieved, everyone judges the success 'easy' and without merit, so much does it appear to have been brought about naturally by the situation and so to have been decided in advance. This 'without merit' is the great merit, which leaves the Subject of glory disappointed – we can appreciate why China has not conceived any epics.

In any case, there's already enough here to begin to make clear what a situation is by detaching it from the status of the accidental as well as from the circumstantial. Yet, to express it at first negatively, I am not 'in' a situation as I am in a place – a 'site' – nor am I even like the captain at his helm, to take up again an otherwise well-known Cartesian comparison. Nor is the situation of the order of an 'accident' in relation to the essence, or substance, of a subject-Self. Moreover, it's really the grammar of our languages, in Europe, its constricting system of rection and prepositions, and above all its morphology of cases, which arranges the circumstantial into compartments, as the final complement. But in this I am always implicated in a tensile field of various factors and vectors, due to the *situational* inherent in the fact of existing. By the very fact of their correlation, these factors and vectors are necessarily in a process of transformation, which also means that I am at the heart of a continual relation of interaction which, as such, constitutes 'myself' in response. The autonomy or independence of the subject is no longer an absolute predicate, but has an extension only as a margin of manoeuvre according to which we adaptively manage our conduct, therefore without radically breaking away from an 'intention', a 'pure' one, abruptly transcending anything given, whether it be one's 'good' or 'bad' will.

This will give us a better understanding of why Chinese thought is alone in having a clear strategic conception. It is because it thinks in terms of *actualisation* and *configuration* (the notion of *xing* 形), of *propensity* and the *potential of situation* (the notion of *shi* 势), and also (which is what lies behind these notions) in terms of flow and energy, the *qi* 气, and not of Being or Acting, which go together as a pair. At the beginning of the nineteenth century, Clausewitz could only note the failure of (European) thought in its thinking about war, since he acknowledged that it was a phenomenon that is 'living and reacting'. However, it isn't constituted solely from an insular subject, but is one that involves an adversary *from the outset*. Yet this is precisely what China, thinking in terms of polarity, found it 'easy' to think about. This also enables us to understand why the foundational book of Chinese culture should be the *I Ching*, the *Book of Changes*, a 'book' that lacks *logos* or *muthos* and is without a sustained discourse, as well as containing neither a narrative nor a message. From the beginning, it is composed of only two types of features (— and – –) that are full and broken, hard and malleable, *yang* or *yin*, representing the polarity at work. These are superimposed in figures which, transforming themselves into one another, symbolise so many situations that read themselves, feature after feature, in their evolution. This is to reveal – the ancient fruit of the mantic – how each situation is borne by its own nature to topple over, by nothing but the play of its factors (the only internal relation of these features) in a 'fortunate' or 'ill-fated' way. In order to interfere in this play of energies, to get in phase with these figures, it will still be necessary to testify to what, opening up a breach in our vocabulary, I can't find a better word to express this than receptivity (*disponibilité*), which begins to express a vacancy of the initiative and the will. This means that, just as the ontology of Being that serves as a basis of knowledge needs to be taken apart, so we will have to try to undo the ontology of the Subject that provides a basis for Freedom.

III

Receptivity (vs Freedom)

1 *Receptivity* is an under-developed notion in European thought. It is mainly concerned with goods, property or functions. Conversely, it has barely taken shape in proximity to a subject-self. At most it draws on a sentence in André Gide: 'I held that every new thing should always find the whole of us wholly available' (1952: 65). Hence this notion doesn't belong to the order of morality any more than it does to psychology; it isn't prescriptive (or if it is, what it prescribes cannot be clarified) or descriptive (or explanatory) and cannot therefore be thought of either as a virtue or as a faculty. Yet these are really the two great pillars or referents on which we in Europe have erected our conception of the Subject. The notion of it therefore barely exists and it is left in a state of a vague injunction, or else it lapses into subjectivism and facile anxiety, which is precisely what taints the Gidean subject. In short, it hasn't entered an effective construction of our interiority. It can be approached in a familiar way, the term being slipped into the banality of our phrases as a call to common sense – and even per-haps we would now not know how to do without it (according to the Gidean notion of availability or 'receptivity'); the fact is, nonetheless, that we barely go beyond this. The possibility that, following this thread, a fully fledged category could be elaborated that would be ethical and cognitive at the same time hasn't been put together.

Then why has it been so under-developed? Wouldn't it be precisely because, in order to promote *receptivity* as both an ethical and cognitive category, we would need (finally emerging from that old tandem of morality and psy-chology, and virtues and faculties) profoundly to modify the very conception of our *ethos*? Discreetly, without warning, slipped incidentally between our sentences, this muted notion nevertheless starts a revolution. It undermines the structure according to which we represent ourselves: the subject is now implicitly rather than directly conceived. In the process, it calls for a more profound and complete reversal, one that is more ahead of its time than so many of the reversals of values that are announced. For the subject, it is in fact a question of nothing less than the letting go of its initiative as a 'subject' – one which from the outset presumes and projects, chooses, decides, places a focus on ends and gives itself means. Yet, if it momentarily lets go of this power of mastery, as receptivity invites it to do, it is because it then fears that this initiative over which it prevails forms an obstacle and may be untimely; that it closes off the 'opportunity', locking it in a sterile confrontation with itself and making it no longer accessible. But *accessible* to what? To be precise, it doesn't know 'what'. If the subject lets go of its own prerogatives, distrusts its ownership and 'privacy', it is because it senses that the privilege it confers on itself, which it attaches to itself, encloses it within limits it can't even suspect.

In this, it will already be understood that this won't constitute a category 'of renunciation', a kind of invitation to passivity, but rather of what is contrary to solipsism (on the part of the subject) and its activism. Nor is it a matter of relying on another power (or another Subject) – in other words, of transferring mastery to God, as Quietists effectively do. No, this letting go that is the characteristic of receptivity is a taking hold, even one that is more dexterous because it is fluid, unrestricted and uncurtailed: the notion is strategic at the same time as it is ethical. A 'taking hold' that is all the more effective because it isn't located, isn't specified and isn't essential. It is all the more continually adapted insofar as, no longer having a goal, it is never disappointed or even deprived; it is neither re-routed nor fragmented. It is a far more complete 'taking hold of' – or rather it doesn't recognise limits or extremities – precisely because it no longer has a track to follow, goal to satisfy, quest to fulfil, or object to seize. For this taking hold by letting go is no longer oriented; it *no longer projects*. It is without a looming shadow, is no longer driven by intentionality, and consequently holds everything in equality. Its harnessing is wide open because it doesn't expect to harness anything.

Indeed, the term should be understood according to the resource that reveals its composition. In French, the *dis* of *disponibilité* (availability or receptivity) not only means the erasure of any opposition[1] but also the diffraction in every direction of the 'position', and consequently its very dissolution. If any determination is negation, as Spinoza's adage says, then any position is at the same time the loss of other possibilities. Any *position* is an im-position. Yet, if to arrange is to adopt a certain order and arrangement, receptivity, by rendering those ductile due to the compossibility (Leibnitz) it opens, withdraws all of the particular modality that fixes and focuses from it. The 'openness' it expresses is no longer a pious vow, some substitute of the monk dreaming of being released from confinement through an unveiling – a theme that is verbose today. It is effectively incarnated in behaviour and in attitude or, more rigorously still, as I've said, in *strategy*. In comparison, 'virtues' and 'faculties' can in fact no longer appear after this except as dispersion and loss: specifying one in relation to the other, they each affirm themselves to the detriment of the others. By claiming autonomy from the outset, their self-affirmation still has an element of force. Yet receptivity mixes (includes) this plurality of their diversity into the same, and equal, potentiality. In the same way, neither congealing nor opposing anything, it remains apart from effort and confrontation.

Knowledge, no longer being oriented, becomes in receptivity a *vigilance* that cannot be reduced by any form of hoarding – or the good, no longer being codified or assigned, becomes a capacity to embrace and exploit indefinitely which, because it is without exclusion or hardening, is also without loss. By promoting the autonomous figure of the subject and its internal structuring of thought as emerging from its faculties as properties (and therefore apart from the flow of the world), we appreciate how Western thought has hindered such a capacity of 'opening up', except when it deals with it through reprisal and compensation on a mystical level. It would be better to think about such receptivity without allowing it to slip into quietism, to conceive of this opening as a means of *operating*. This would mean no longer separating ethics (or the theoretical) on the one hand from the strategic on the other. Or doing what Chinese thought universally does – that is, separating wisdom and effectiveness. Even if it is in its infancy in European thought and has been left in the margin of its theorisations, in China *receptivity* is actually revealed to be the very *ground* of thought.

2 What's striking, as soon as we enter Chinese thought, is the realisation that what I understand here by *receptivity* – far from going against authorised cognitive approaches, which are founded on our faculties – constitutes its very condition, or that, far from having remained an embryonic notion, worth almost nothing except as a familiar injunction (conceded as a safety valve for our strictness, like a necessary leniency and entrusted as an aside), receptivity is, before all virtues, the very principle of the Sage's conduct. But it is a non-principle 'principle', because to erect receptivity as a principle would be to contradict it for the same reason that receptivity is a disposition without a definite disposition. This is something all Chinese schools of antiquity agree upon (what I call *grounds of understanding* of thought), even if they may approach it from different directions. Indeed, I'd be quite prepared to sum up the teaching of Chinese thought in this way: someone is wise when he gains access to receptivity – nothing more is needed. This is why Chinese thought amazes us by its anti-dogmatism (for which ritualism provides a social compensation).

This is how it is expressed in the motto from the *Analects* of Confucius (IX, 4), which was one of my starting points in a previous work, and highlights the point:

> No ideas, no necessity, no position and no self. These are the four things the master didn't have.

What is evident in Chinese (I call it 'evident' because this is not questioned) is that 'to have an idea' – or, better, to advance an idea – means *already* to leave others in the shade; it means to privilege one aspect of things to the detriment of others, and at the same time to sink into partiality. Every idea advanced is at the same time a bias about things, and this prevents us from considering them in their entirety, on the same level and on equal terms. We have entered preference and prevention. In fact, we need to read the motto in its sequence. If we advance an 'idea', we then impose a 'necessity' (a certain 'one should' projected onto behaviour); consequently, the fact that we maintain this 'one should' results in an arrested position in which the mind becomes bogged down and no longer evolves. From out of this blockage into a 'position', a 'self' finally appears: a *self* fixed in its rut and presenting a character. This 'self', being fixed in its 'position', has lost its receptivity. Yet the motto is also circular: from the fact that behaviour is fixed in the 'self', this self advances an 'idea', one which becomes established as 'necessity', and so on.

Mottos along these lines abound in the *Analects* of Confucius: the good man is 'complete' (II, 14) – that's to say that he doesn't lose sight of comprehensiveness, doesn't allow the field of possibilities to narrow in any way. He 'aims to be neither for nor against', but 'inclines' to what the situation calls for (IV, 10). Or, as Confucius says about himself, 'there's nothing I can or cannot do' (XVIII, 8). The Sage, in other words, keeps every possibility open, not excluding from it any *a priori* and remaining in the *compossible*. This is why he is without character and cannot be described: his disciples don't know what to say about him (*Analects*, VII, 18). Or when the Sages are classified in categories – the intransigent ones, on the one hand, who refuse to soil their hands even a little for the good of the world, and, on the other hand, the obliging ones ready for some compromise to save it – what do we say of Confucius? Is he intransigent? Is he accommodating? Where should he be placed (what 'position' should be attributed to him) in this typology? We find this laconic response in the *Mencius* (V, B, 1): 'In wisdom, he is the moment': as intransigent as the most intransigent when it suits him, but equally as obliging as the most obliging when it suits him. He doesn't privilege either; the 'moment' is the only reference point. For 'wisdom' is without content that would orient and predispose it – or else it has no other wisdom, as it renews itself inexhaustibly, than to make itself receptive to the circumstances of the *moment*.

It can therefore be understood that the 'happy medium' – a boring topic if ever there was one, and that, in its banality, one would think arises from the wisdom of nations – finally emerges from its platitude. It assumes an unexpected relief. It becomes radical rather than trivial. It no longer exists in unadventurous and timid environments, half-way between oppositions and with a fear of excess ('you can have too much of a good thing', as the saying goes), thereby prudently avoiding venturing to either side or strongly asserting its colours. This is 'mediocrity' which isn't 'gilded', as they say, but which is dull, which is 'grey' (to quote Wittgenstein: 'Wisdom is *like cold, grey ash* covering the flowing embers' (Wittgenstein 1977: 64e). No, the happy medium, for anyone able to think with rigour about it (Wang Fuzhi), is to be able to do one *as well as* the other, in other words to be capable of going to either extreme. It is in this 'equal' of *equal access* to one as to the other that the 'mid-place' is to be found. We're told that to spend three years mourning for the death of one's father isn't too much, nor is drinking too much during a banquet – in neither case am I going too far (but going to the limit of each possibility, satisfying each demand completely). The risk is rather that, by becoming bogged down on one side, we close off the other possibility and thereby fail to see its circumstance. In contrast, receptivity keeps the fan completely open – without stiffening or avoidance – in a way that responds fully to each opportunity as it occurs, which means leaving nothing out nor changing one's own direction. As a consequence, no character or internal sedimentation stands in the way of this malleability.

Chinese thought has notably known how to perceive the difference between 'maintaining the middle ground' and 'holding on to the middle ground' (staying attached to it). If, on one side, there are people who, according to these conventional rubrics, wouldn't sacrifice a hair for the good of the world, and on the other side are those who are ready to wear themselves out for its salvation, a 'third man' (Zimo), holding the middle between these opposing positions, appears 'closer' (*Mencius*, VII, A, 26). But, since he 'is satisfied with this middle', 'without taking the variety of cases into account', he is able 'to hold only one possibility' and 'miss a hundred others' – and therefore just as much to 'despoil the way'. As soon as one holds (a position), a 'self' hardens, behaviour becomes bogged down, some imperative or 'one must' stabilises and one is no longer in phase: plenitude loses its amplitude and one no longer reacts to the diversity on offer. Receptivity, as an internal disposition without disposition, opening itself to this diversity, goes together with *opportunity*, which comes to us from the world as 'to its harbour': as Montaigne also says – but how far is it pushed in the disposition of knowledge? – 'someone who is receptive knows how to live appropriately'.

In China, this thinking about receptivity has made the *emptying of the mind* the very condition of knowledge: 'to know' in Chinese is not so much to *have an idea about* as to *make oneself receptive to* (see the *Xunzi*,[2] the 'Jiebi' chapter). An internal emptying occurs, not due to doubt eliminating prejudices, but by an abandonment or generalised disengagement taking place more at the level of behaviour than at that of the intellect. This results in the *letting go* that gives access back its amplitude. It is necessary to take care not to let one's mind become a 'purposeful' mind (*chéng xīn* 成心), as Zhuangzi also says. Having become taut and constituted, the activity of this *purposeful* mind is consequently paralysed and becomes immured in its own perspective, which unwittingly becomes a standpoint. For the first demand is, without further projecting any preference or reticence, to consider all things 'equally' (according to the watchword of his thought 齐, in the 'Qiwulun'). It is even, as Zhuangzi pertinently shows, because he knows how to make everything stand on equal terms and is in a position to go back to the undifferentiated, 'Taoist', grounds from which all differences arise that the Sage is able to welcome the slightest difference in his opportunity, without reducing or failing to notice it. Since the 'self' is no longer in the way (which is what 'to lose one's self' means, *wàng wǒ* 忘我), he can then listen to all the musics of the world, as diverse as they are, in their spontaneous 'thus', as they come, *to the will*, while accompanying their singular unfolding (*xian qi zi qu*, Guo).

3 Yet, while receptivity is a fundamental notion of Chinese thought, all Chinese schools agree about it without even suspecting its bias. On the other hand, it must be recognised that when it comes to European thought there is an awkwardness about taking hold of it: receptivity is recognised only indirectly and toils to discover its concept. Why, for instance, did Freud arrive at the rule of the 'evenly suspended attention', *gleichschwebende Aufmerksamkeit*, required of the psychoanalyst in the course of the cure – which also seems to me to signal towards this practical, or rather strategic, resource of receptivity – only to 'backtrack' or retreat, as he confides to us, and with reference to what he highlights as disappointments from his own experience (see his 'Recommendations to Physicians Practising Psycho-Analysis' of 1912 see Freud, 1958)? And isn't the formula even touched with contradiction: 'attention' *but* 'suspended'? The mind would be extended towards, but towards nothing in particular; it concentrates (attention), but on everything at once (which is the same as dispersion?). Or why did the 'openness' Heidegger extols as giving access to the truth (*Offenständigkeit*) need to be taken back, by brute force it seems to me, under the sign of Freedom, *Freiheit*? He made it clear that, being antepredicative and equivalent to 'behaviour' (*Verhalten*), it consists in a 'letting be', *Eingelassenheit* – in other words, in an 'ex-istant abandon'. By returning to our master category, didn't this constitute a betrayal of Freedom? In this major notion of European thought, I see, rather, 're-encapsulation', to make use of one of his terms for what his phenomenological analysis tended precisely to leave behind – and haven't a number of commentators been puzzled by it?

Or shouldn't we extend the divergence further and consider whether the European difficulty in thinking about receptivity cannot be properly understood except in relation to the notion of *freedom* – a rival notion which has prevailed in Europe and hindered its development? In the same way, when a number of contemporary Chinese intellectuals lay claim to an idea of freedom (*zì yóu* 自由, a term translated from the West) in relation to Chinese thought before Westernisation (notably when it is a matter of the *Zhuangzi*), arranging what I call 'receptivity' (*zì zài* 自在, as I would translate it into Chinese) under this term, it isn't a terminological dispute and is a matter of a logic of concepts. In fact, I'll extend this opposition to the point of reciprocal exclusion: because it has developed a thought of *freedom*, Europe has neglected this resource of *receptivity*, and the opposite is true for China. Aren't the two notions actually antagonistic to the point of contradiction, instead of being flatly synonymous, as is usually assumed? This is because freedom demands making an *intrusion* in relation to the situation in which the self is implicated and it is this emancipation which precisely elevates it into a 'Subject' with a claim to initiative. It requires that its power of negation (the power of the negative of which the subject takes advantage) extracts its element that allows it to leave its allotted conditions. In other words, freedom promotes this ideal *through a rupture* – not through an 'opening' – with the order of the world.

We should at this point distinguish the aspects of what the Greeks called 'freedom'. On the one hand is the possibility of doing what we please, as we like and without being prevented from doing so (what they called *exousia* ἐξουσία). I have no difficulty in recognising that this must commonly appear in various cultures, including therefore in China, and even that Chinese thought has particularly deployed and enriched this meaning (*xiāo yáo yóu* 逍遥游, the first phrase of the *Zhuangzi*: 'to evolve' comfortably and without shackles). On the other hand is what they called *eleutheria* ἐλευθερία which (already in Homer) was the condition of the free man in opposition to that of the slave (who loses, when he has been defeated, this 'day of freedom') from the outset. Yet what the 'Greeks' forged (or which forged them) was really this second experience, and above all at the political level, that of small cities resistant to the vast empire – at the fracture between two continents – and refusing to submit to the power of the Great King (the Greco-Persian wars); then by the deliberate founding of properly political institutions detached from the natural ties of kinship (democracy confronted with inherited family authority); then, when the City came apart, as the internal freeing of the individual by domination over his passions and above all over his 'representations', *phantasiai* (which assumed its fullest surge with Stoicism). Here, then, Freedom is the product of an invention (more than a 'discovery', as has been said so often) which is on the whole very singular, but which has been so assimilated in Europe that we forget its bias. This is so to such a point that classical thought was able to be set up as 'universal' in being based on the laws of freedom, which have been understood in terms of autonomy and as being part of a different order from those of natural laws. They are metaphysical rather than physical, and are erected as absolute.

As everyone knows, the opposite of freedom is servitude but it is receptivity that stands as contradictory to it: it unfolds a harmonious relation that is not of emancipation but of *integration* with the order of things. Or, if we can also find exemption in relation to the shackles of life in the world in Chinese thought, notably in the *Zhuangzi*, such a 'disconnection' is so much better at uniting us with the natural course of things (*zìrán* 自然), in that it isn't constituted as an ideal that has been erected through a cutting off and separation from the world. Instead of detaching us from it in order to make ourselves independent of it, such receptivity inserts us into it, by connecting us to its surge, impelling us to make use of its resources without challenging it. A *self* even has a better idea of how to conduct itself when it is uncoupled as a 'self' and becomes *implicated* in it as it responds to its *prompting* – which is immediate–immanent – and is freed from artificial agitations. Let's express things once more by standing back, and on a large scale: unlike the Greeks, China, with such a vast empire, wasn't brought into existence through a struggle for civic independence. Rather, it conceived politics as a simple continuation of family structures – their spontaneity has a regulatory vocation (under the figure of the father-king) that this political order reproduced – and did not detach itself from this.

On the moral level, too, it has called for a 'triumph over oneself', but has done so in order to return to the behavioural and social (strictly integral) norms that 'rites' are (according to Confucius' precepts: *ke ji fu li*). This is why it has conceived of this capacity which, in opening the position from all sides and not being enclosed in any one of them but holding all of these possibilities in equality, maintains the subject in an implicit (non-dogmatic) way which also puts it in phase with what comes to it from the world – from what it initially *trusts* in the world. It has therefore not needed a breaking open and empowerment of the Subject through Freedom.

Notes

1   The different etymology of the word 'availability' means that this sense is lost in English; indeed, its composition almost conveys an opposing meaning: the 'ability' to 'avail' one-self [trans.].
2   The *Xunzi*, the writings associated with Xun Zi (*c.* 312–230 BCE), a Confucian philosopher who stood in opposition to Mencius; in the English versions, the title of this chapter is given as 'Dispelling Blindness' or 'Undoing Fixation' [trans.].

IV

Reliability (vs Sincerity)

1 Sincerity is the response to freedom, such are the two demands placed on the constitution of an authentic subjectivity in Europe. The first reveals interiority as truth; the second frees us from all alienation coming from outside (including that within oneself). Sincerity would even initiate the great ethical division. Insofar as sincerity might be defined as 'to say what you think and not tell lies', we immediately see that Achilles is the 'simplest' of men and the most 'sincere', *alethes* ἀληθής; Ulysses is the cleverest as well as the most deceitful, *pseudes* ψευδής. From Achilles to Ulysses, in Homer: 'I detest those who hide one thing in their mind and speak of something else as much as I do the gates of Hades.' But the Greeks were too well versed in dialectical reversals and too adroit at cultivating enigmas to retain such an elementary cleavage (see Plato in *Lesser Hippias*). Did Achilles never lie? (Is this even possible?) And if he has lied, was it 'of his own volition' or in spite of himself? Yet isn't the one who lies of his own will, being wiser, superior to the one who lies without intending to? 'The best voice is that of those who sing out of tune because they want to rather than against their will' ... We soon find ourselves in an awkward position if we play with such arguments. The least that might be said is that the 'simplicity' of sincerity isn't simple, and Plato has no difficulty in authorising his legislator to lie when it comes to politics. Yet the question is radically modified, recovers its cutting edge, putting an end to these paradoxes and even assuming a dimension of the absolute, from the moment God appears in the background. The 'eye of Zeus' sees everything, so Hesiod tells us (we find the same thing in the Bible) – even if these figures of the divine have hardly anything in common, it is this fantasised power to probe hearts and behaviour that institutes 'God'. At once it becomes impossible to elude the eyes of god(s), as Plato recognised, and there is no 'reason for God to lie'. If, therefore, God is absolutely truthful, and at the same time that every falsehood that is committed is known to him, then to lie, for whatever reason, becomes a sin towards him: to lie to another is to lie to God; human subjectivity discovers its infinity in its transparent relation with the divine. If God hadn't been presented as transcendence, falsehood would not have been dramatised as experience. An unconditional condemnation of falsehood follows from this in Saint Augustine (in the *De mendacio*). From then on being conceived from the category of the will (when the will to delude is absent, falsehood is absent), falsehood contains in itself its own criteria of definition along with its exclusion of principle. There is no 'well-meant' lie, whether it be compelling or compassionate (as told to a

patient in a sickroom or to respond to the claims of desire, such as feigned orgasm). No compromise or tolerance is acceptable in this regard: the mouth which lies 'kills the soul' and, in the sacrifice it makes to temporal life, means that eternal life is lost.

This *dogma* of truth at any price is essential because it is the condition of possibility for an *unconditional* conceived at the level of practice, and this is actually the absolutism that Kant, following the example of Augustine, defended in his polemic with Benjamin Constant: if murderers ask me whether the friend I am hiding at home is there or not, I *must* tell the truth. If I don't, I am committing an injustice with regard to humanity *in general*, whilst also bringing into question the very principle of contract law. This is a *formal*, specifically rational, obligation, having nothing to do with the fact that a wrong is being committed in relation to the friend who is being unjustly pursued, a wrong that is only 'accidental'. Attached as a principle to his universalism, Kant maintains this untenable position, rejecting out of hand the argument according to which (since the notion of duty responds to that of law) the duty (to tell the truth) consequently ceases to apply when the law ceases to be worthy of respect. In fact, this judicious idea put forward by Benjamin Constant demands to be extended: one only has a duty to speak the truth to those who have a 'right to the truth'. The killer who has unjustly threatened this friend has thereby forfeited such a right.

Kant's theoretical blockage in this respect entails an unlikely deafness to the exigency, and consequently to the very experience, of morality. As such, it constitutes a symptom of the impoverishment of his universalism. It isn't refuted in the name of an unavoidable adaptation to circumstances that brings about a deviation from the divine law (according to the trivial argument that such a morality would be *de facto* impracticable, being too ideal, and that one cannot more or less fail to disguise one's thought in society). But this is not carried out alone but in relation to the other (and this relation comes first). This is the only rigorous way to support the strictly *situational* nature of a falsehood, rather than it being merely a matter of subjects. This means that it is not just the product of an introspective subject, something kept to oneself, but that it is essentially *relational*. This doesn't relativise it: to lie is to do so in a *double sense*. If I lie to the other it is because, unless wanting this to be falsehood for the sake of falsehood (to what extent is this possible anyway?), I suspect him of not being in a position to appreciate the truth. The child lies to his father because he doesn't think the latter can have access to his secret: the listening comes before what is spoken, and if I lie to myself it is because I have become incapable of understanding my own truth. There is therefore a co-responsibility for falsehood, which exists not only on the side of the one who hasn't dared to say something, but equally on that of the one who has not made himself receptive to what is said (reread the episode of the stolen ribbon in Rousseau: it is because a feeling of shame has started to weigh over him that Jean-Jacques hasn't dared to admit the truth).

2 It will therefore be beneficial, when confronting the European *fixation* on this sore point of falsehood, to lance such a theoretical abscess by taking a step back from it and so shifting our position. Indeed, if China, as can easily be seen, has not made a drama out of falsehood, or even seen it as a problem, it's because it has not isolated falsehood as a particular *act*, with specific – even the most iniquitous – features, overlapping the status of the word and the question of truth, and as such departing from the continuous course of behaviour. It is actually a divine and searching authority, celebrated from the first texts (the 'Lord on high', *Shang di*, in the *Shijing* or the *Shangshu*), which is said 'to approach you', but what is asked with respect to him is not to have a 'double spirit' (*wú èr ěr xīn* 无二尔心), in other words not to practise duplicity or to cheat: the relation to the word is not made explicit. Or if it is said not to be necessary to believe that, because one is alone, the spirits don't see you, the moral requirement involved, calling upon a 'return to oneself', *zì xǐng* 自省, concerns the non-deviation of one's behaviour: falsehood, as an intentional assertion contrary to truth, isn't as such a matter of concern.

Relationality is at the very origin of Chinese thought, and therefore also of its morality, since this is not only an issue for subjects: morality also arises from the phenomena of polarity and interaction, and 'existing as two' is fundamental (this is expressed by the notion of *rén* 仁 which is habitually translated as 'humanity': in its common written form, it designates mankind and the number two). *Contextuality* is therefore not simply circumstantial here: one does not denounce one's own father, Confucius insists. Ritual behaviour implies not just pretending but actually respecting forms, which also entails an internal investment, rather than opposing them: in visiting a temple, Confucius asked a question about each custom, even if he already knew what the response would be; he even expected that, one day, the prince would come out to thank him … Without either the erection of a principle of Evil, which is absent from Chinese thought, or a dogma of Truth, the conflict of truth and falsehood logically loses its cutting edge. The vocabulary is itself amazingly vague in this: 'to spread by wandering' says the Chinese (*sǎ huang*); 'to cheat' (*qī kuang*); 'to abuse' (*qi piàn*); 'to pretend' (*zhà*), etc. There is no uniform term isolating the fact (*pseudos*, *mendacium*, 'falsehood'), at once separating it as a particular action and giving it over to scandal, or at least to enigma, to thought.

It will therefore be understood why I am resisting rendering the very important term *xìn* (the key of man and the radical of the word 信) by 'sincerity', as Sinological tradition regularly does. For this term doesn't so much mean to *express what one thinks* – which can be cumbersome, rude or indiscreet (and do we really know 'what' we think, as if it consists of identifiable content?) – as to *maintain what one says*. The Confucius of the *Analects* distrusts 'smooth talkers' (*ning*) and only takes into account the conduct that is displayed. Even the Mohist *Canon*, which has a place apart in the thought of antiquity, defines this notion in keeping with sincerity ('the word is in tune with internal thought') and immediately comments: 'It isn't the adequacy of his words that impels others to take [them] seriously; it must be his conduct', 必其行也. From the outset, agreement between thought and word shifts to the accordance between speech and behaviour, and if the internal authority, as a moral authority, is constituted by self-reflection (*zi xing*), this doesn't have a vocation to tell 'itself', in trusting in the word's function (evidence of this cultural divergence is also provided by the difference, impelled as far as opposition, between the religious practice of confession and that, proceeding through political conformism, of self-criticism).

In place of an introspective sincerity seeking to go back to the depths of consciousness so as to find the most direct expression of an inner truth delivering the mystery of the unique in words that would be naked, blunt and uncensored, Chinese thought orients us towards what I'd call 'reliability', which refers to the even more central demand of 'viability'. Let's think about this *viable* life (what forms life): that beings and things are able to develop over the long term, in duration, *procedurally*, by correctly following their path, the *tao*. Here it's the 'in the long term' that becomes important: *reliability* is an effect of duration and consequently it dispenses with the word. Behaviour is judged *in the long term* and not in the instant in which a statement is made, and sincerity does not tolerate the slightest hiatus, least of all a temporal one, between the act of thinking and its expression. It occurs through directed and progressive consolidation as the days go by, even without thinking about it, without thinking about thinking about it.

3 *Reliability* We'll have to pause at this term to make it a principle that comes before both ethics and politics. If we fail to credit such silent *densification* and *probation* in the long term, our thinking about what we ordinarily call 'trust', which is merely its consequence, will forever remain destitute. The notion of trust is as crucial as it is banal, but are we able to grasp it? We know that it is the basis – the basis and the capital – of every human enterprise (we know this even more today when it comes to economic enterprise and its management), more determinant and decisive, eventually – even if in a less theatrical way – than the familiar external 'opportune moment', that imponderable *kairos* celebrated so much by the Greeks as the ultimate reason for success. Trust restores this ultimate determination of the course of things, this *fundamental* determination, within the human and under its domination, and even in what is most truly human or *makes the human*. For *trust* is really what finally, once all of the arguments are weighed up, tips our decision radically in one direction or another and leads to a decision ('do I do it with him or not?'): in the same way, it is from this that consent, which is alone able positively to generate a community, proceeds. Trust is really what secures the cohesion and viability of politics, but without being alienating, which distinguishes it from any charismatic effect: it is inherently egalitarian, because it pre-supposes reciprocity, and doesn't arise from the

doubtful prestige of the ascendant. Because it is *resultative*, proceeding from a confirmed past, it is also the only thing that opens a future and makes something possible. But do we know what its tenor, or rather its logic, is, and how not to force the situation to engender it, which would in consequence dismantle it?

The *phenomenon* of trust eludes us because it slips away from our theoretical apparatus; its category is neither moral nor psychological and remains external to the order of virtues and faculties – European philosophy having thought about the faculties with a view to 'knowledge', about virtues with a view to 'action', and about both from that of a self-subject. Yet trust arises neither from understanding nor from the will: it is of the order neither of the perspicacity of the intelligence nor of an 'I want'. While being wholly dependent upon us, it eludes our mastery: there is trust only if there is separation. It arises not so much from the Subject as from the *situation* that is engaged in, not so much from the individual as from the *relation* entered into, not so much from action as from the unfolding of a *process*. In trust, the two partners are equally implicated and co-responsible: trust belongs not to *being*, but to 'between' – this is something to which I will return. It is not attributable exclusively to one of the two partners, and one cannot even discern, when it is anchored or rooted, to which of the two it is due. Effectively, it arises not from a transitive action or from a solitary initiative of a subject but from a silent transformation of the conditions of *co-subjectivity* that have been entered into.

In this respect, trust is radically separated from the 'transparency' – which is related to sincerity – with which it is too often confused. Transparency, which is the great watchword invoked today in political life, as well as in the ethical codes of businesses, is an illusion not so much because it would be impracticable, on account of an inescapable or pernicious opacity between people, as because it is strictly sterile. The pressure of transparency stifles the possibility of the germination and growth of trust. Instead of favouring it, transparency kills it, because it doesn't recognise the other's alterity. In fact, it also needs the obscurity and withdrawal of zones of discretion and silence, along dotted lines, not only so that business might be done but equally so that relations may be formed and prosper. If we are so clumsy in our thinking about trust in Europe, it is because we think only through what the logos loosens, and we do so through an atavistic attention to what is uttered as alone being constitutive of the truth – while trust arises from what is implicit, makes its way into the half-light, increases from its continuity, and has no use for speaking.

It is as vain to utter the vehement 'Trust me!' as it is sententiously to pronounce an 'I trust you … ' The first statement is magical, invoking an undue power; the second is superfluous in itself. This adds nothing, and even, due to its uselessness, undermines the trust acquired and which is of the order of the result: when there is trust, there is no reason for it to be expressed. As for the familiar 'Trust me!', uttered as a petition or injunction, if it is vain – or, rather, if it is stupid – this is because it presupposes a voluntary decision (I urge you to make a choice, I appeal to your reason) which can only be premature and consequently forced. It also lays claim to an act-event (trust must immediately be given) by denying the long period of maturation. And it credits itself with a power of persuasion and authorises a rhetorical efficacy, while trust can only be born from an effect of persistence and endurance, by secretion and propagation. It follows that trust doesn't depend on a causal link, which remains inescapably external to it, and it is not even precisely assignable or imputable, but arises, having been primed, from what occurs independently, through *propensity*, and it prospers without being targeted or concerted. Trust, as an expression of immanence, is a return on an investment that hasn't been calculated.

When it's said in China that we are 'old friends' (*lao pengyou*), it's not that we've had to wait until we are 'old', but that we have come to trust one another over a period of time – a trust which doesn't need to be displayed and isn't subject to doubt: the bond between us is settled and it would not occur to us to doubt it. No decision or will is involved; the benefit is procedural. We have mutually 'rubbed' up against each other over the years (the term is also found in Plato, *tribé* τριβή, in letter VII, but in a marginal way): we have negotiated and clashed but in a non-aggressive way and have persisted and not separated. This has resulted in the unfolding of a reliability with nothing further to prove: the understanding has gradually been sealed in silence and the few words that still arise, in an anecdotal way, are simply a sporadic indicator of this tacit security. I am, however, always a little surprised at the accusation of a lack of sincerity directed at my Chinese friends, as if this might be considered a social virtue. In what way could such a sincerity of the word gain a foothold that wouldn't at the same time be rendered as incongruous as it is arbitrary if we are no longer thinking about morality in terms of an act (in the moment) but in those of (continuous) process and behaviour? To express what one thinks is improper; it impedes social regulation and goes against the efficacy of the conditioning from which morality also arises.

The heroism of *sincerity* isn't vain, but it belongs on another level. The desire to tell the truth is a boldness in which there is no need to hide what is intolerable within it, since it is both asocial and scandalous. We are well aware when we lay claim to teach children the virtue of being sincere that we aren't being sincere with them. This doesn't derive benevolently from an obligation, even an ideal one, or a prescription of morality, but rather from an exultation of the conscience attempting a feat. *To mean to express*, 'to say everything' (already the *parresia* παρρησία of the Greeks), to speak to the greatest extent, as much as one can, without in any way giving in to the capacity to express, to seek here and now to place just the right word in the moment, while dismissing approximation, without being afraid of indecency or what is shameful, is always a snatched victory, one that *other people* would be unable to tolerate. To speak the truth is an intrusion-infringement (of what is tacitly accepted).

The Other is perhaps alone willing to hear it, in intimacy, welcoming this uniqueness – the 'Other' emerging from this admission; or else it is a passion of the intelligence when it is ready to sacrifice everything, and above all this avoidance of the danger that makes it viable and thereby liveable. To 'tell' the 'truth' is dizzying, because it means to pierce this conjunctive tissue (of sociability) that keeps us reassured; to tell the truth is a *challenge* (arising from the cry), because this is where the impossible is confronted. This attempt, on the other hand, is a reward in itself. Perhaps it is done in the hope of being comforted, but without expecting to be applauded: in this confrontation with the limit, the lived and bare existence of the *will* alone decides and allows it, for this attempt to prove itself is all it needs.

V
Tenacity (vs Will)

1 Who would doubt that he possesses within himself a 'will', so much does this capacity define man in his very being and constitute his sovereign spirit? Isn't it what I most initially – most intimately – perceive about myself, and doesn't this mean that this experience must be one that is most universally shared? The will is, furthermore, the only thing within man that has the dimension of infinity, rendering him similar to God, as Descartes proposed. Its purity alone is absolute. For, acting by my will, I no longer feel there is 'any external force' that is 'constraining' me: my own causality takes me out of the causality of things and conditions and reveals my freedom to me. This is our European *credo* and it gives a basis for our *system of the Subject*. 'Credo', I say, for faith is invested in it: a choice hides in our mind, but one so deeply buried that it is taken for evidence, such a basic effect allowing the apparatus of the Subject to consolidate its mastery – at least this is what was long believed. For suspicion about this sovereignty of the will doesn't come only from outside European thought. It emerges in the very heart of its philosophy and today fractures it. But if this base is coming apart, doesn't it mean that everything in our conception of 'ourselves', wavers along with it? Above all, how can we still conceive of action and efficacy, as well as morality?

When anthropology began, carried along by a more or less laicised Christianity, it took the will as an initial, and as such indubitable, term. The Enlightenment philosophers, such as Rousseau or Kant, testify to it. This will was what introduced the first split, giving the self its initial hold over 'itself' – beginning from which everything links up, doing so in such a way as to serve as a key (the only one possible) for the comprehension of the world. The experience of it is assumed to be immediate, the one thing that is unchallengeable, needing nothing to intervene within 'me': 'I want to act and I act. I want to move my body and my body moves' – the assertion seems irrefutable (in Rousseau's *Émile*, 1979: 273). A performativity is at play that comes even before the possibility of a statement. In Kant, as well, the introductory form seeks a true beginning and is intended to be as general as possible, seeking hyperbolically what is most hypothetical in order to reveal more effectively what alone cannot be hypothetical: 'Nothing can possibly be conceived in the world, or even out of it, which can be called good, without qualification, except a good will' (at the beginning of *Fundamental Principles of the Metaphysics of Morals* I, §1–3). In the beginning, therefore, is the 'will', the will 'in itself', in a 'pure' state that alone is absolute.

Yet even if, following the theoretical globalisation instituted by the West more than a century ago, Chinese thought has today translated the term (the notion of *yìzhì* 意志), it can help us go back into the genealogy of the will, to separate us from the *convenience* of its conception. In China, we don't clearly see the distinction between what we do of our 'free will' (*ekôn* ἑκών) or 'against our will', as it was developed in Greece by Aristotle from a reflection which, drawing upon both legal activity and the theatre (Phaedre giving in to her passion 'against her will'), results in this fundamental question: to what extent am I responsible for my acts? It is on this basis that Aristotle unfolded the terminology we still use today, distinguishing a simple 'wish' (*boulesis* βούλησις) from an act committed 'by preference' (*proairesis* προαίρεσις) involving a deliberation and opening onto a judgement, itself assuming the form of an inner imperative. We can go back further still in the evident divergence: since the idea of causality has barely been theorised in China, either at the level of logic or physics, or even, responding to it, that of finality, we won't be amazed that 'will' has barely found theoretical support here to assert itself. It is actually from *causality* that this capacity to choose and decide that has usually defined the will is understood on the Western side. Rousseau considered that we must always 'go back from effects to effects to some will' (1979: 273); I understand this will as an 'efficient cause'. And, for Kant, the will of reasonable beings is 'the faculty to determine their causality through the representation of rules'; although it is of a different order, it is a 'causality of reason', conceived in the mode of natural causality.

What's more, the psychology of the will has developed in the Christian West against the background of a meditation about sin, and above all the will has been apprehended as infinite. *Voluntas* is revealed in its terrible magnitude by the power it offers man to say 'no', to turn from God and 'defect', the *modus defectivus* of Saint Augustine that reveals it through the possibility that is recognised within man to be able to *choose* to do evil, *posse peccare*. Indeed, we have been able to give this idea of the will all of its consistency only by coupling human psychology with a divine psychology which serves it as a model and from which alone the plenitude of man is able to be thought. And so we find this in Rousseau: 'God can because he wills; his will causes his power' (1979: 285); and in Kant: God's will is not only a pure will, it is also a holy will. Yet in Chinese thought, we come upon this realisation: it soon turned away from preoccupation with a personal God and hasn't developed its primitive cosmology into a theology; consequently, it hasn't needed to include personal self-determination of power in the will that would, as such, be absolute. Equally, it has not encountered the experience of sin as a challenge to divinity.

Moreover, when looking at things more closely, we realise that, while having at our disposal no other point of departure than the will, European philosophers are conscious that its 'nature' escapes us. I want to move my body and my body moves, says Rousseau, but I cannot 'conceive' of how 'this is done' – in other words, how the will can 'produce a physical action'. The will cannot shake off the inherent difficulty contained in the dualism separating the empirical and the intelligible, even if this is precisely what is responsible for ensuring the immediate connection between the two. Therefore, just as he makes this an experience that would be undeniable, Rousseau at the same time detects a 'mystery' in the will: the evidence of it spills over into an enigma. In the same way, Kant considers that the freedom in which the will takes such pride is inexplicable, since any explanation would take us back to a determination according to the laws of nature from which our will as reasonable beings makes us independent: such an 'explanation' equals an annihilation. Hence he admits (in the *Metaphysics of Morals*) that we might be roused to a 'suspicion': suppose that the idea of an absolute value of the simple will was merely transcendent and a chimera – and not a pure 'jewel' of morality?

2 It is therefore not difficult to accept that the notion of will has been the product of a cultural history that – coming by way of Greece and Christianity, psychological causality and the infinitisation of the divine – must, on the whole, be particular. But have we made the attempt to *think about* how we could do without it? And what effect has the fact of having progressively cut out and detached this notion of the will in this way had on the rest of our thinking? In Kant and in Rousseau, to confine ourselves to them, this history of the 'will' has succeeded so well that we have forgotten it; in the end, the will is essential right from the start: it *becomes* the first principle and everything else follows. But Nietzsche, after Spinoza, within the very heart of philosophy, already gave us a sense of what a passage via China impels us to discover from the outside. Nietzsche knew how to pin down the 'suspicion' mentioned by Kant in passing. Having brought the notion of will to its apex (the will to power), Nietzsche could at the same time see that what was involved was a thing, one that was not simple, but 'complex', and even 'something that is a unit only as a word' (Nietzsche, 1968, § 19: 215). More precisely, as a philologist (in the best of his works), he suggests that what causes us to believe a thing as complex as the 'will' to be simple is due to the fact that in our languages we have only a single word by which to express it. And philosophers have 'once again' merely exploited and 'impelled to an extreme' this bias of language, which, as such, remains unthought.

This *fold* of the 'will', or rather this rut which hems in Western thought (considered to be 'atavism' by Nietzsche), comes to us first of all in a fact of language – *our* language: from a root which is common to Indo-European languages and enhances a unique and isolated seme of the 'will'. And so we find *boulesthai* in Greek, *velle* in Latin, *wollen* in German, *will* in English, *vouloir* in French and so on. Yet this semanticism of the 'will' is precisely what we don't find when we move on to China. Mencius, who was one of the main Chinese thinkers of antiquity and the first to develop reflections in this area, spoke of 'getting ready', of 'consenting', of 'desiring' – no term predominates. The distinction drawn to think about wisdom is that of 'strength' invested in comparison with 'perspicacity'; the virtue praised in the resolution is 'courage'. One term (the notion of *zhi* 志) has unfortunately been translated within European sinology as 'will', since this is the notion we'd expect, but its semantic field, which is still indeterminate, designates most often in Mencius the resolution taken and to which one holds – what I would call 'tenacity'. This term is clarified only once, and this is to designate what should 'command' the energy breath, *qi* 气, with which our physical being is imbued (II, A, 2). These two functions are then defined by their hierarchical relation alone, the first being to 'maintain firmly', while the second is not to 'do violence'. When the guiding authority 'comes together' (concentrates), Mencius only states that it 'sets vital energy in motion' as it needs to, but when it concentrates, it then sets the other in motion and their hierarchical relation is disturbed. Thus there is no intervention in his analysis of the procedures that Aristotle made clear around the same time: no preferential choice, no deliberation and no decision.

As a matter of fact, we find an *internal* heterotopia in Nietzsche that he clear-sightedly opened up in the very heart of philosophy that we can consider externally in the Chinese heterotopia. Would there be any other *possibility?* (Wouldn't we come across an alternative?) Can this process actually be conceived as internal to the person other than as a relation between opposed forces when we no longer have a unique term like the 'will' at our disposal, or when it is distrusted? The relation with hierarchy is what Nietzsche says is most precisely identified at the heart of this 'complex thing' that is the will. It is a question simply of commanding and obeying, but this relation, eminently simple in itself, operates within a complex collective structure which is that of our body and the diversity of its 'plurality of souls' (see Nietzsche, 1968: § 19: 217). On the basis of this hierarchical relation, what has consequently allowed the 'will' to be organised as a global notion is what Nietzsche called the 'synthetic' concept of the self, and this in fact corresponds with the bias of European philosophy: it is this that reduced this duality of functions – the functions of command and obedience – to the identity of a self-subject (posited as unitary and simple) and, by 'deluding us', it impels us to attribute the execution of the will to the will itself.

The diversity of processes which are then at work at all levels of the person is thereby reduced to a unique procedure at the level of the consciousness of the self. From this point on, we said 'I want' as we said 'I think', and as we did so we made full use of this subject function that Indo-European languages more particularly enhance by their grammar, and we thought we had the immediate certainty of our 'will' as of our 'thought'.

3 It isn't just the notion of the will that is absent in the *Mencius*; actually, more radically, it is the category of the 'will' itself. This can be verified once more at the level of language, in that the expected opposition is systematically lacking in it: instead of speaking of 'power' *or* 'will', Mencius speaks of

'power' *or* 'doing'. A prince wondered whether he was able to deploy those of 'humanity's funds' (*rén* 仁) which, thanks to the Sage he questioned, he finds in himself. If you don't deploy them, Mencius responds, it's because you 'don't' do it and not because you 'can't' do it (I, A, 7). And, so that the distinction between 'power' and 'doing' should be well established, Mencius continues: if you are asked to take a mountain in your arms to cross the North Seas, it is justifiable to say that you 'couldn't' do it; but if you are asked to collect a branch to offer your older brother (to whom you owe respect), it's not true that you couldn't, it's simply that you 'don't' (not being able to keep this opposition as such, considering it illogical, the French translator, Couvreur, feels the need to add: it's due to 'lack of action *or will*'). So this opposition of *power* and *doing*, and not of power and will, structures, from the beginning to the end of the *Mencius*, the whole semantic field relating to behaviour. The sole criterion that Mencius takes into consideration, in comparison with the capacity possessed, is that of its actual implementation. Everyone, he affirms, can become the most perfect Sage (Yao or Shun): to be comparable to him, you simply have to act as he does (VI, B, 2).

Yet could we gradually become familiar with what thereby exempts Mencius from using the category of 'will' (or what leads him to think in this way because he doesn't have it at his disposal), which is that he conceives of behaviour, as we already know, in terms of *propensity*, both of *potential* and of *actualisation*, not in terms of *choice* and *action* ('deliberated' choice – 'willed' action)? There is such a divergence between the archetypes: on the Chinese side, that of the process of maturation, from the germ or seed from which behaviour also arises; on the Greek side, the tradition of representing people 'in their actions', *hôs drôntas*, as Aristotle said, as it comes to us from epic poetry and the theatre, genres with which ancient China was unfamiliar – as for the Bible, it too is a narrative of actors. An initial consequence, one that will easily be grasped, is that, by not passing through the category of the 'will', Mencius doesn't come across the question of evil – or at least not in a frontal way: there isn't (there can't be) for him, unlike Kant, any 'radical' evil. The only alternatives, from his perspective, are to help to deploy the propensity – as such an eminently positive one (that of our fundamental nature) – within us, or to forgo it. One doesn't have to decide it by pondering on it: China hasn't developed the internal monologue. Thus, it hasn't given *choice* centre stage – choice between vice and virtue, God or Satan, good and evil: Hercules hesitating at the crossroads, Adam and Eve afflicted by temptation in the Garden of Eden.

In Chinese representation, which is a continuity of the process that is also behaviour, there is no crossroads that might be abstracted and isolated so as to make it a *limited* and heroic situation at a given moment (the illustrious 'time T'), of a distinct choice. Furthermore, there's no test of temptation which, before the abyss opened by the possibility of nothingness, brings us to the encounter with infinity. These are both tragic and mythic themes, which are of the essence of the tragic and cannot be represented other than in a mythic way, even in Kant. This is why, in spite of the rhetorical effects of parallelism, the moral alternative posed by Mencius is not a real one – it is skewed ahead of time: as he often says, he considers evil to be only a 'non-good', and it has no proper consistency in constituting a principle. On the whole, it could be said that Chinese thought hasn't sought to illuminate what Western thought for its part has found to be unfathomable ('... *das für uns Unergründliche*', as Kant said). Chinese thought is without vertigo – was it appalled by it? In any case, it holds our attention through its coherence, for it has, in contrast, taken care to elucidate, by the attention it has given to processes, how the phenomenon of *propensity*, when it comes to behaviour, could be checked or favoured, inclining towards one side or the other. Instead of asking the fascinating but insoluble (fascinating because insoluble) question of the possibility of will (evil), it offers us a thorough analysis of the effects of conditioning.

We see that Mencius, the thinker of morality, by insisting on the importance of *conditioning*, merely returns to the most common Chinese thought about efficacy and strategy: one shouldn't claim to achieve the desired effect directly, because to do so always implies force and makes the result precarious, and even produces a counter-effect. Instead, we should try in some way to make this effect flow *sponte sua*, as a simple consequence, from arranged conditions. Thus, it isn't necessary to make the people moral by forcing them to correspond with an imposed ideal, and any repressive politics is empty due to its effect of constraint: it will serve only to ensnare the people in the 'net' of punishment. But we must, by intervening ahead of the process of evolution (in other words, one might say, at the level of its 'socio-economic' conditions), ensure that these are sufficient for a morality 'naturally' to result, which education will then support. In any case, this is what unfailingly favoured the entry of Marxism into China, even if this relation of socio-economic conditions with respect to morality isn't conceived in a deterministic way and once again remains of the order of propensity rather than causality.

The moral person retains the possibility of a 'stable' conscience and of being tenacious in his resolution, and to do this in spite of the greatest destitution (I, A, 7). A morality of the training of the person (*xiū shēn* 修身) was thus able to develop in China, but about which we also read in Mencius how very uncertain it ultimately becomes as far as its final justifications are concerned. For what happens if we encounter the opposition of the world, instead of continually being able to embrace it and take advantage of it by conforming to it? What hope would remain in which to trust, or how could one still be firm of resolution, if this adverse condition continues all the way through and isn't allowed to be resolved? We see the question emerge openly when Mencius is placed before his personal failure: he also refrains from confronting it and leaves it uncertain (at the end of I, B). If I have failed in the prince's presence, this isn't due to some schemer jealous of my favour, but to the action of 'heaven'. Period: no more will be said about it – or could be said about it. The invocation of transcendence, made as a last resort, remains evasive since it is without theological support. If Mencius is condemned to be indirect with this negative, it is because he can no more rely on faith in a compensatory Beyond than on an only slightly elaborated system of the Subject.

4 Similarly, if Chinese thought contains no global, metaphysical or religious response to the contradiction between the self and the world from which the vocation of the subject-self emerged in Europe, then the only position that remains open for the self exposed to the opposition of the world will be to 'stand firm', endlessly and without further questioning, without despairing or giving up. In other words, if the (psychological) category of a pure will has assumed little consistency in Chinese thought, the *ethical* capacity not to give up in one's effort and determination, in spite of the resistance encountered, is the only remaining possibility (which is called, in a qualitative way this time, 'to have the will'). But, as this is less a question of the heroic capacity of a moment than of that of persevering over time, without stopping or giving up, without allowing oneself to lose heart, this is a matter of what I would call – in the most literal sense – 'tenacity' (the virtue of *chi* 持). If *tenacity* is the first virtue, it is because it thereby responds to the attention the Chinese give to circulation and continuity, the 'way', *tao*. By calling upon the unfolding of a process whose course demands not to be interrupted, it will need to be placed in opposition to an action-oriented will that is marked by a beginning and an end, as well as by the possibility of a start. At the same time, a conceptual net is beginning to be woven and we see that *tenacity* (from the standpoint of the person) responds to the durative logic of *reliability* (between persons) just as it brings to light, in its dimension of effort and investment, what receptivity, in its capacity to embrace internal coherence in the renewal of things and situations, implied first of all in internal progress, before it could slip into ease and spontaneity.

Thus, rather than arbitrarily (theatrically) isolating what would be a crucial and absolute choice and opening a metaphysical chasm, perhaps we should, in order to think about the effectiveness of behaviour, conceive of two things jointly. First of all, it is through progressive *propensity* that we incline towards what we then solemnly call the 'decision': our choice will then be limited to 'selecting' the best option between possibilities (the notion of *ze* 择). It would then be necessary to establish *tenacity* in order to lead the direction decided upon to its full effect. Chinese thinkers always insist on this total 'holding firm' (*chi* 持); otherwise, the effort would be in vain, it would be equivalent to having done nothing … Confucius (in the *Zhongyong*, XI) says: 'The moral person behaves in accordance with the way; to abandon it half-way is what I could never do!' Or consider the Master's favourite disciple (Yan Hui, ibid., VIII), of whom it is said that, having opted for control in his behaviour, 'as soon as he reached something good', 'He clasped it tightly and hid it in his heart, but without abandoning it.' Or: 'the superior man is active all day, and remains vigilant in the evening' (the third line of the first hexagram of the *Oracle of Change*, Douglas, 1971: 55).

Mencius (II, A, 2) expands on the point that virtuous behaviour is born from a continuous 'accumulation' of uprightness (*ji yi* 集义), and it is obtained neither unexpectedly nor all of a sudden: one has to apply oneself and without thinking about how to attain it directly. One should be preoccupied with it, 'not letting it go', but not believing that it could artificially be 'encouraged to grow'. This can happen only by means of a progressive development and in a 'natural way'. Chinese thought therefore insists on 'non-interruption' and diligence (*wú shǎo jiān duàn* 无少 间 断), since it is only from a definite continuity, reinforced day after day, that the qualification of behaviour can actually occur as a result. This is why the intensity of the internal *investment* will usually be called 'courage', *yǒng* 勇, which means that one never relaxes one's effort, rather than seeing it as the momentary expression of a voluntary decision.

The fact remains that, if the will may appear in this view to be a mythological representation, this myth has its function and therefore its justification. *Imagining* that we might possess a will has its impact in return. This is not because we wouldn't be able to conceive of ourselves as heroic figures without it, but due to the fact that this representation contains an effect in itself – in particular, one that is political. Without its support, could democracy be justified? If we again look to Rousseau, in the absence of consecration, the 'popular will' is its only legitimate basis (and isn't democracy today weakening due to the breaking up of this representation of the will?). Promoted as a unique moment that conceals the diversity of the processes actually involved in it, it constitutes in fact a *common* and convenient referent, giving legitimacy to equal participation between people. I am no longer convinced that the 'will' is the principal and infinite faculty that makes me equal to God, as Descartes wanted, but I note that his conception forms a convergent prism in the heart of the person which, given as a principle, allows a *subject* to be instituted while deploying its initiative. Let's therefore continue to invoke the 'Will', but without deluding ourselves about the evidence for it, the evidence that would deliver experience intuitively, but in a way that is so enigmatic. Let's therefore have recourse to the will, but as a certain way of representing to ourselves our capacity for mobilisation as well as resistance which, rather than approaching the world indirectly, dares to *confront* it, and that even promotes itself through this confrontation.

VI
Obliquity (vs Frontality)

1 China, as we can see in our first concepts, has been particularly at ease with thinking about strategy. This was not so much because it knew continual war at the end of antiquity, in the so-called era of 'Warring States' – when *Arts of War* (Sunzi, Sunbin, fifth–third centuries BCE) flourished – because war, as we are well aware, is everywhere, but because China developed a thought of polarity, in other words of opposed complementaries in interaction (the well-known *yin* and *yang*), which responds to the very essence of war and defines its condition between the adversary and oneself. As in Europe, but so belatedly, war is a phenomenon which 'lives and reacts', as Clausewitz recognised, seeing this precisely as a stumbling block to its theorisation – in other words, when the adversaries are dependent on one another from the beginning, being unable to conceive of one without the other, which also explains how classical European thought, thinking from an autonomous subject, has had great difficulty in considering strategy other than by resorting once again to creating a template (even if here it recognises its failure): the 'war plan' *projected* onto the situation and depending on the will to achieve victory.

What do we read in the *Sunzi* which serves as a basic concept of strategy but doesn't arise from a plan erected in advance? That 'the encounter takes place facing one another', but that 'victory is gained indirectly'. 'Facing' (*zhèng* 正): frontally, openly, in an expected way and giving rise to *confrontation*; 'indirectly' (*qi* 奇): in an oblique and unexpected way, being where and when the adversary doesn't expect it to be, to such an extent that he is helpless. Sunzi concludes that it is always through a 'surplus of indirection' (*yú qi* 余奇) – that's to say that I ultimately prevail over the other by being more indirect than he is. The essence of strategy therefore doesn't consist in aligning a maximum of forces, either on the ground or on paper, any more than in relying on the courage of the troops or the general's genius, but in – 'indirectly' (*qi*) – eluding and outwitting the opposing resistance to such a point that it is forced to give way. I triumph, without striking further, simply due to the fact that the enemy's defence has fallen. Thus, the Chinese strategist defies every established plan, in which his ability to operate would get bogged down and so its reactive capacity would be lost. In contrast, he begins by establishing a diagram of the situation's potential, concentrating on what is 'firm' and where the adversary has 'gaps', because it is when facing them that he will need to be *continuously* resolved, by remaining receptive and without getting bogged down in a restrained position. Or, rather, by knowing how to remain open to their incessant renewal through *receptivity*, he will be able to avoid sinking into a reifying determination that brings about inertia and reduces his energy, which is the worst strategy.

'Frontality'/'Indirectness', these actually increase like two phases, or two states, of the same process (see Sunbin). *Frontality*: each takes a position facing the other and can be located by him; *indirectness*: I lead the other to take a position on the ground and can control him, while – thanks to my reactivity – I remain ahead of any actualised configuration and, through this virtuality, keep myself alert. Against this, the other's inertia leaves him defenceless because he doesn't know what he must respond to. The adversary therefore finds himself destitute and reduced to passivity, simply because he doesn't know *what* to expect or *how* to protect himself. Therefore, far from being one means among others, such an effect of 'surprise' is, in a crucial way, what by baffling (by dumbfounding, disarming and disorienting) brings out the weakness of the opponent and finally allows us to gain the upper hand through what until that point had remained covert and protected. The indirect intervention is what, by outwitting and exposing, gives purchase on what eludes the grasp, and by doing so breaks open the adversary's defence system. At the same time, not knowing how to reach me since he doesn't know where I am – as I keep myself, without a definite position, in this alert state of reactivity – he cannot have a hold over me. From then on, everything that follows is an exploitation of the discountenance produced and has only consequential status.

2 The *direct confrontation* of a pitched battle could be opposed to this, and we know that, around the seventh century BCE, the conduct of war went through profound changes in Greece in this respect: the sort of conflict consisting of skirmishes or ambushes, or single combats between heroes overcome with 'fury', like those celebrated by Homer, came to an end. A new structure was put in place – the phalanx – according to which two bodies of heavily armed and armoured hoplites, arranged in consecutive rows and marching together at the same pace, kept in step by the musicians' auletes [flutes], advanced on one another in a close formation, with no possibility of flight. This face-to-face combat could only result in a heavy and destructive clash, for the only effort these men could make, on both sides, lay in the 'thrust' (*ôthismos* ὠθισμός), so that the front row, which directly endured the enemy charge, found itself supported by the accumulated pressure of the rows behind them. Indeed, the deeper the column and the more tightly packed its rows, the better it could 'press' the adversary and the more force it possessed to strike and gain momentum.

Although this frontal shock might be expected to result in nothing but pure carnage, it actually responded to an easily understood economic principle: cutting down the ravages of a prolonged war that spared neither goods nor families in the 'all or nothing of pitched battle', so gaining, by a brief and direct confrontation between those political bodies constituted as cities, a resolution that would be both as quick as possible and the least subject to doubt. That's why the adversaries engaged in combat according to rules, by making use of the phalange's rigid order, on open ground often chosen by them in the form of a tacit agreement. Inversely, dilatory operations whereby evasion and harassment would alternately wear out the enemy, are disdained since their sinuous nature dilutes this process of rapid and definitive decision obtainable by assault alone. In the same way, any weapons that strike from afar or by surprise, such as arrows or javelins, are disparaged in favour of the lance, the face-to-face weapon par excellence. 'The Greeks', Polybius tells us (1925: XIII, 3), 'considered that it was only hand-to-hand battle at close quarters which was truly decisive and could validly determine a conflict'. In this case, skill in manœuvring loses its value; the only thing that fundamentally matters is courage shown at the crucial moment in order to gain the upper hand. One doesn't even try to weaken the adversary in advance: we learn from Xenophon (1921: VI, 5) that 'Agesilaus decided that no matter what their number it is best to allow the two hostile forces to come together and, in case they wished to fight, to conduct the battle in regular fashion and in the open'.

This model of direct confrontation – in other words, of *frontality* – doesn't mean that the 'Greeks' would have been unaware of the resource of subterfuge, or did not 'show cunning': we know they had a taste for stratagems. Marcel Detienne and Jean-Pierre Vernant (1978) have particularly shown the importance the Greeks placed on *mètis*, that 'cunning intelligence' with which the gods themselves were richly supplied, and which combines 'flair', 'anticipation', 'gambits' and 'various tricks' along with a 'sense of opportunity'. Nevertheless, this isn't the way (that is, by recourse to *mètis*) that the Greeks in the classical period deliberately chose to regulate their armed conflicts. Far more important was the form of intelligence that was shown in the preference for a subterfuge, the *agkulométés* that the Greeks were well aware of and that 'always appeared more or less "implicitly"', Detienne and Vernant tell us – 'immersed in a practice which, even when it was used, at no time showed any concern to make its nature clear or to justify its approach'. Contrary to Chinese obliquity, *mètis* remained in the background of reason and moreover was clearly located only at the level of myth; the term would even vanish during the classical period. Repressed by speculative intelligence, it did not therefore become the object of a theory in Greece.

For if knowing how to create a diversion in order more effectively to attack the adversary can be recommended, taking advantage of his surprise (we find the same advice in Xenophon's *Hellenica* and Frontinus' *Stratagems*), and without neglecting either secret sorties or other cunning means (espionage and disinformation existed in Greece as in China), it was no less the case that this practice of stratagem was always presented, if not as a stopgap, then at least as an expedient: it might be advised, but thinking about war doesn't *start from it*. On the contrary, it even appears that this Greek form of confrontation was all the more central in that it maintained a close link with the organisation of the City; it is actually contemporaneous with the rise of the City. Indeed, there would be a homology of structure between them: due to the uniformity of equipment, the equivalence of positions, even the identity of required conduct, the infantrymen of the phalange were reduced to the similarity of interchangeable elements that corresponded exactly with what they became as citizens in the egalitarian framework of their political life. The phalange therefore – and along with it the logic of a frontal approach – appears to sum up a whole 'choice' of Greek culture as, by erecting opposing positions, it made the *face-to-face* encounter the best means by which to give the conflict shape, so as to settle it.

3 Didn't this face-to-face of phalanges confronting one another on the battlefield in fact find an equivalent in the *face-to-face discourses* around which the City was organised? I specify equivalence and not simply analogy because the structure of *agôn* that constitutes this organisation of armed confrontation is encountered again in the heart of the tribunal, the assembly and the theatre: in the theatrical *agôn*, the *for and against* of the Subject approached is defended in so many verses (is Antigone right to bury her dead brother with the arms he took up against his city?). In fact, whether it is theatrical, judicial or political, the debate was also played out as a weighing-up practised in one sense or another. And it is settled only according to the strength and number of arguments advanced on either side. Similarly, if there is a homology between the order of the phalange and that of the City, this isn't just because the same participants appear on both sides (as citizens–soldiers), but above all from a structural standpoint: in both cases, the decision is won in the same way.

It has to be remembered that for the pitched battle, apart from the cost (the carnage), what makes it economical is that the confrontation of phalanges allows the resolution to be obtained in a manner that would be both as quick and as unequivocal as possible. But the face-to-face alignment of arguments at the heart of antithetical discourses as the Greeks conceived them, whether in the theatre, the tribunal or the assembly, aimed for the same effect. The orators pleaded against one another in a limited time in front of everyone, and this could immediately be settled in all conscience by those who witnessed it: this antagonistic 'thrust' tips in one direction or another and will eventually be decided by a majority vote. This confrontation of discourses is closely linked with the institution of democracy: the question debated will be resolved by a weighing-up of an argued for and against – one has only to think about the importance that today's political life places on televised 'face-to-face' debates. And don't we see democracy slipping when the 'for and against' aren't sufficiently distinguishable? Conversely, this also applies on the Chinese side: without authorising a declared opposition, isn't the democratic 'process' still held in check today due to the fact that its cultural tradition grants a privilege to the *indirect approach* in the management of antagonistic relations?

This face-to-face nature of discourse, just like the vote in which it results, arises from a singular logic whose principle we can perceive: while an isolated discourse is able to bring out an idea, the truth can only be expressed by two opposed discourses being bound as close together as possible through their confrontation. It is accepted that this practice of oratorical debates (the *agôn logôn* ἀγὼν λόγων), as we see it becoming established in the Greece of the fifth century, found its progenitor in Protagoras: 'He was the first to say that there were two opposed discourses concerning everything.' And our conception of *logos* would ensue in large part from this promotion of the confrontation of the word: if an opposing argument always exists to any argument that is already presented, then the art of discourse, which we know goes hand in hand with the arrival of our 'reason', would essentially consist in proposing opposing arguments to those introduced, so making them more convincing.

What this discursive procedure of *confrontation* consists of is well known because it has been abundantly used by orators. Its simplest form is refutation properly speaking, which consists in showing that the adversary's argument is wrong. Compensation also intervenes to annul the opposing argument or, by reversing it, to show that what the opponent believes to be favourable to him is actually either unfavourable (by reversal) or favourable to us (by retaliation). Since the whole art consists in always keeping as close as possible to the opposing arguments, one repeats as far as possible the facts the adversary has put forward through his words and ideas, but arriving at conclusions that are the opposite of those proposed. In this verbal confrontation, the discourse of response must be aligned as strictly as possible with what it is responding to (*logos para logon*), and, in the case of an initial discourse, by anticipation, the orator must be able to envisage the possible arguments that might be used against those he is putting forward. In this way, each of the discourses produces the most condensed argumentation in relation to the other – what Thucydides called *logoi antikatateinantes*: these 'discourses' are 'forcefully extended by one against the other'.

The isonomic principle located in the structure of the phalanx therefore now appears to be just as necessary, since the comparison, and therefore also the decision that follows from it, would be all the more convincing and rapid if the elements to be compared in it were more similar. The rigour of the antilogy would therefore tend towards transforming all of the elements of the argumentation into comparable data, each aligned opposite one another and liable as much for addition as for subtraction – indeed, even being interchangeable with each other. Consequently, confrontation and calculation are the basis of this conflict of words, so much so that it is always through a *surplus* – but here it is the surplus of argument advanced and not concealed obliquity – that one can claim to prevail. Hence we appreciate that a single Greek term, *logizesthai* λογίζεσθαι, means both to 'consider' and to 'calculate'. This is also what philosophy has inherited.

It might even be said that it was born from this organised face-to-face discourse as it extricated itself from the sententiousness of wisdom. Supporting and reversing an argument, proceeding by means of thesis and antithesis, appeared to be the best way of revealing the truth that was being sought. It's true that this construction of antilogy, as we see it become invested in all of the Greek genres in the fifth century – not only in the art of oratory, but even to the extent of how to write history – would subsequently be made more supple. In philosophy, this *antilogy* will become transformed into *dialogue*. All the same, this didn't prevent a certain fold from being taken in thought from the time of the Greeks. This is to think by means of opposing arguments in the most adapted way: we still teach children to philosophise through *thesis* and *antithesis*. And if I am alone when I am thinking with myself, I consider the arguments that could be raised against me in such a way as to test my thought and be able to maintain its truth through this refutation.

4 *Frontally/indirectly*: this would therefore offer an alternative of the most general sort, and it would be as applicable to the military field as to that of thought, for it is also a matter of strategy. (It would even apply in the realm of ethics, meaning to approach the Other face to face rather indirectly, as Face, therefore in a true discourse, as Levinas says, which raises the other into an authentic Other and establishes a relation of equity.) Not, of course, that each of these categories should be confined to one or the other side (Chinese/Western): debates also took place at the court of the prince, as among Chinese thinkers becoming philosophers, and in Europe as well we have known how to proceed by using words obliquely, to express ourselves in roundabout ways and 'turn Chinese'. Nevertheless, Chinese intelligence has been far better at illuminating this *art of the indirect* that had remained in the shadows in Europe, just as its theory of argumentation has remained astonishingly poor. As evidence, we could cite a military expression that has become a proverb: 'kill the horse in order to strike at the knight' – one which is still used in Chinese political life to register an indirect criticism of a chief through his subordinates (the defensive formulation being reversed: 'abandon horses and carriages in order to protect the general'). Another common expression, to which Mao Zedong again had recourse in his reflections on war as conducted by partisans, 'make noise in the east so as to attack in the west', applies still more readily to the order of discourse: on the one side, the whole volume occupied by explicit remarks that are only inserted to create a diversion (for example, the redundant deployment of obvious expressions); on the other side, the insidious nuance which, under this cover, hides the polemical charge and discreetly allows it to run its course. This tactical expression finds its perfect counterpart in this other formula concerned only with the art of verbal attack: 'to point at the chicken in order to abuse the dog' (or: 'to point at the mulberry bush to abuse the cinnamon tree'). My remarks indicate one, but I'm aiming at the other; *the one* is merely the occasion

41

for a detour – as such, it is ostensibly displayed – with a view to reach *the other* more effectively, but in secret.

An equivalent obliquity of the word thus responds to the obliquity recommended by the art of war: in China, the practice of the verbal detour – which leaves more scope for manoeuvre and insidious intrigues that baffle the adversary without having to expose (or explain) oneself – is preferred to the 'propulsion' of confrontation, to that of the face-to-face (or body-to-body) orientation of soldiers or arguments. Evasion and harassment are again in order: instead of openly offering arguments to which the other will be able to respond, sinuous expression allows us to 'evade' any frontal attack that obliges us to justify ourselves. At the same time, it puts us in a position constantly to 'harass' our opponent while keeping him under the threat of allusions as he continues to be under the pressure of what is implied. From the standpoint of verbal confrontation, too, the subtlety of the relation of the indirect opens the path to infinite games of manipulation that don't get bogged down. Just as the strategist operated before the occurrence of things and was far better at dominating the disposition of the adversary, which he has not yet actualised, into disposition on the ground, this verbal strategy profits by always being situated in a purely suggestive – and inchoate – state of expression, for this barely outlined meaning, instead of locking us into a determined position that will then have to be defended, allows us to continue to evolve as we like since we remain master of the game. In this way, the adversary remains hanging on to the initiative of our barely started word, and is reduced to passivity.

This meaning which is only now dawning is far more threatening in that the other doesn't yet know precisely where we are coming from; this merely sketched-out critique is all the more dangerous in that it is never presented openly and therefore offers nothing at which to grasp for refutation. Upon his return from the United States and probably in contrast with the *frankness* (*or bluntness*) he had found there, Liang Shiqiu, a Chinese literati at the beginning of the twentieth century and himself a great translator of Shakespeare, described this art of 'striking from the side and attacking indirectly', which he was so much better able to notice when he was back in China:

> It is stupid to call someone who steals from you a thief in order to reprimand him, or to call someone who robs you a bandit in order to reprimand him. When we want to reprimand someone, we first need to emphasise the art of emptiness and fullness, of the veil and the reflection. It is also advisable to suggest indirectly and to accentuate it indirectly, striking from the side and attacking laterally: having reached the crucial point, a single word is enough to finish it, and as they say you have the other 'on their knees'.

> (see *The Fine Art of Reviling, Ma ren zhi yishu*)

If you directly accuse someone, there's an end to it and there is nothing more to be said: there is nothing 'beyond' your word that can be deployed and might keep it agile. It is dead and inert, because it has been finished and its effect has been defused. The other knows what it is about and can refute you. But if you hint at what you might be thinking …, you lead him into an unfolding of the word that puts the implicit to work and keeps him in suspense, making him anxious and uncomfortable: 'It is only after a period of reflection that he gradually realises that the word was not well intentioned, and then his face, which at first had a smile on it, turns from white to red, then from red to purple, and finally from purple to grey.' The same thing applies in military strategy, so that when you finally attack the adversary frontally, he is already defeated – just as you then barely have to act, so you barely have to speak. The efficacy of *indirectness* results from the process involved as it progressively reassigns the situation and doesn't rely either on the word or on the action.

VII

Indirectness (vs Method)

1 If one notion has prevailed in the European context, it has been the sovereign one of the 'method', which has been used to establish, in the most assured and only way justified, our 'means of operating', the *ars operandi* of the Ancients. Everything has been said about the fashion in which it condenses the power of mastery of 'rationality', as much in respect of action as of knowledge. Rationality is a self-legitimated term, the only one from which there can be no backtracking. But hasn't such sovereignty – which no one would think of suspecting – been acquired in a singular and consequently inventive way with regard to the diversity of cultures as well as the possibilities of thought? *Method* implies that both a goal might ostensibly be assigned ('after' which one sets off: *meta*) and an approach (a 'path': *hodos*) might then be clearly determined so that the goal might be attained. When Plato elaborated the notion of it in order to grasp the ambiguous being of the Sophist that eluded his grasp, he above all promoted the purpose of the model or the 'paradigm' (see *The Sophist*, 218 d), thereby developing its ideal character as abstract, communicable (teachable) and indefinitely extendable – one whose crowning achievement is the 'dialectical method' that would amount to a principle for fixing its conclusions firmly (see *The Republic*, 533 c–d).

What thereby characterises method is that it possesses a formal generality, a 'logical' structure (i.e. one that is *expressible* in *logos*: the 'methodical' and the 'logical' reciprocate one another), such that from the outset it transcends the diversity of situations and can demonstrate its exactitude. But can we forget that for the Greeks themselves this same Greek term – *methodos* μέθοδος – also had its shadowy side, which linked it with *mètis* and formed a diametrical divergence from the self-sufficiency of an absolutised 'reason'? This was a suspect and no longer sovereign side: are we able to neglect this effect of 'heterotopia' – but an *internal heterotopia* this time – which indicates that 'Greece' was also aware of its 'elsewhere', one within itself, external (dissident) to how the later tradition would fix it? For Plutarch, 'method' can also mean (might Plutarch not already be, in his own way, an anti-Plato?) the indirect path, reliant on fraud and artifice, by which one advances under cover and to which we become accomplices. Yet how did we ('we': the European we) finally and sovereignly conceive that such a meaning (according to a strictly inverse mode, one that would be as direct as possible, at once projectable and programmable while also operating in full light – the 'clarity' of reason) would be hidden away? This meant that the idea of going in pursuit of an end (and therefore, first of all, isolating an 'end') would drive its disgraced reverse back into the shadows, with the sinuosity operating secretly and turning on itself in each case.

What did Descartes add to this self-consecration of method? The fact that this notion was systematised at the same time as it was brought into the foreground indicates that it was the expression of an omnipotence of the mind affirming its prerogative in the 'method'. Henceforth, setting off from it alone, and above all isolating this 'alone', to begin not only to think but also to make the world exist, in its operations being dependent only upon itself – this was what the Cartesian *cogito* initially marked out but also provided with a definitive assurance. In it, the initiative declares itself and sets itself to work along with the mastery of the *thinking Subject* – is it possible to go further in this direction? Yet wouldn't this point of departure, if we want to justify a point of departure at any price, be the only one that is reliable? It follows from the generality of method as well as from the power of establishing a design that belongs to it, which will then become guaranteed by mathematics, not only because the mind operates in clarity and distinction but also because it always passes from ideas to things, never having anything to attribute to things other than what we clearly perceive within the idea of them. What's more, these ideas follow an order such that each must be preceded by all of those on which it depends, at the same time as it must precede all of those that depend on it. Yet how far does this option taken by the mind, thereby posing as its *point of departure* and setting itself up as a 'subject', actually extend its pertinence? Even before considering the extension of its field of application, we'll already have to think about the value of the idea of its possible *application*.

Otherwise, in what destitution are we suddenly left as soon as we are no longer able to rely on the concerted support of method? In other words, into what disarray does this plunge us – one that confounds so many centuries of the elaboration of action as well as of 'knowledge'? Aren't we condemned before we start to go groping in the dark, without the clarity that the renowned 'method' projects? Or on what are we able to rely that cannot be 'applied'? Will we have to look to the other pole, that of irrationalism, or to what would be an 'empirical' guesswork, at best to what becomes a 'profession', acquired over the years, but which remains difficult to share, and in any case can never be completely transposed, is prudently confined in its 'pragmatism', tied to 'things', and is not allowed to be codified? In the absence of a rule set out beforehand, we learn to 'sort it out' (the term inevitably slipping into an informal register): an anti-conceptual term par excellence that is so difficult to take forward because of what it avows of renunciation, and since it is expressed so crudely. But 'sorting it out' is understood here in both of its senses: it is about unravelling the threads of the excessively tangled knot in which we find the matter at hand, just as much as it is about getting out of trouble or 'pulling through' as best we can, though we're not sure what we're counting on – in any case, do we even know how to say it?

2 In fact, the poverty of our thought is made apparent when it comes to conceiving of an approach which would be rigorous but might not be *methodical*: an approach with a certain coherence, one that isn't left to chance, but that doesn't pertain to *a priori* prescriptions. We usually ascribe anything we are unable to master by means of causes and principles to chance; we decide that, when faced with anything we cannot submit to *techne*, we have no other recourse than to fall back on *tuche*. Otherwise what play, what margin of manoeuvre, would remain to us between either of them, which would escape just as much from *domination by models* – being too conveniently loosened by abstract subsumption from the diversity of cases – as *from sinking* into obtuse and helpless *submission* as we become too blindly enclosed within the particularity of the case confronted and lack any further perspective? Our thought finds it difficult to think about how to manage things in a concerted but unplanned way, or how to get a hold on the situation and intervene in it without our arbitrariness forcing us to break it open. We already have a presentiment of this, and it is inescapably refractory of what the given situation then inevitably gives way to.

Yet wouldn't this contradiction (of the sovereignty of method *or* pure empiricism) be unblocked precisely by means of *indirect* thinking, thus opening a margin of manoeuvre in what is in-between? When we don't know how to approach something *frontally*, through our reasoning (which in advance dominates, projects and implies), wouldn't our only recourse be to do so in the other way possible – that is, in a way we have defined as *oblique*? Faced with what is instantly resistant to method, this resource discovers along the way, and in its unfolding, an 'indirect' approach that skirts it, by marrying its contours so as to steal or slip into it and become accepted within it. This would occur in such a way that over time this intervention could hardly be considered as such and could be tolerated without giving rise to resistance and a counter-effect. But 'indirectness', as it is ordinarily understood in Europe (that is, in a narrow sense), would risk causing us to lapse once again into the register of what, no longer being intellectual, traditionally arises from the manual and which we fear would be devoted, if not to chance, then at least to an individual gift, to 'something or other' or else to approximation (as we also speak of someone having 'a nose for something' or 'having a natural touch', all such terms being condemned equally to empirical guesswork as to familiarity). This is on the condition that our thinking about the indirect (of how it should be managed when it isn't prescriptible, since access to it is not direct) wouldn't be crushed precisely under our 'theory of knowledge': that it too would not have remained (like the preceding categories, those of receptivity, reliability or tenacity) culturally underdeveloped.

The *indirect* would then be squarely opposed to *method* and reveal an opposed possibility or resource. In the face of a method that science and philosophy have endowed with such prestige, we should learn to think about this *indirectness* which is unassuming and has habitually and negligently been consigned to the acquired knowledge of craftsmen (what in French is called 'biais du gars'). For thinking, too, it is acquired from know-how rather than from learning, and has therefore been condemned as being tacit and implicit. Against what is grasped frontally and therefore in a unique way (the characteristic of the methodological), the indirect implies a multiplicity of aspects, or facets, under which things can be envisaged. This suggests that they can only be discovered as they unfold and that from the start they cannot be arranged and defined: there's no possible projection. What counts most in the indirect is not the plan but the *way of approaching it*: the path to it is *processual* rather than projective. In particular, the 'indirect' is neither theoretical nor practical (one actually doesn't go without the other), but it cannot be detached from the question (which can be shown to be unanalysable) of how to be able to operate: without it being either foreseen or improvised, one is neither prepared nor disarmed by it. It is really a matter of finding a hold, but a hold that would be reconciled to us. Instead of going straight to the target, in the way that a rationally ordered method subsumes the diversity of instances under its generality, indirectness in contrast starts with whatever is individual and singular in each situation as it is presented, so as to enable the choice of a viewing angle (of attack) under (by) which our intervention can succeed, because it is the one that is most opportunely adapted. It is driven by the *disposition* and requires receptivity, and not by the initiative and planning directed by a subject. It is approached *indirectly* in this way because the ground isn't level (and our action isn't remotely controlled), but undermined, or at least not mastered: resistance must be thwarted, or the difficulty must be by-passed.

Since *indirectness* refers to receptivity as its condition, let's look again at the psychoanalyst's art, or profession, or know-how (how should it be described?). In the course of the cure, wouldn't the practitioner of 'evenly suspended attention' equally (consequently), being unable to rely on the impossible method, be an eternal advocate of the indirect? In fact, if it is taken as its exercise ground, and not its field of application, then we see (but without forgetting what, according to Lacan, its 'praxis' still inherited from Cartesian certainty), even in an exemplary way, the sort of resistance psychoanalysis encounters. It comes from the analysand himself, attached as he is to what he has repressed and which constrains him to take detours in order to overcome the obstacle that is all the more difficult to remove because it proceeds from the unconscious and because the patient uses it to protect himself. Freud constantly tells us that, in order to effect the desired modification, 'in the light', we can't rely on the intelligence of the analysand alone, or on his good will. In the conduct of the cure, no method proves to be possible, and it is indirectness that allows us to come to terms with the resistance and overcome the obstacle so that it comes apart at its loosest point. We become an expert in it, prescient and skilled, but without this capacity being directly renewable. We remain in the grip of the singular or, if there really is a genuinely acquired capacity, it must remain supple, so as to preserve its 'incoming' character, and be reconfigured in each case, as he reinvents himself almost completely in learning increasingly more effectively how to locate himself in it, which is something quite different from adjusting or adapting to it.

In fact, Freud frequently repeated that, until one has found an effective indirect way of intervening and breaking down the resistance – in other words, until one has gained a handle on the elusive repression – the interested party will attentively listen to and even applaud any theoretical explanation at all, but will change nothing. This will have a freewheeling effect and will neither 'take root' nor be 'germane' and so is irrelevant. Hence it is not about 'applying' any sort of rule, which would have no hold, for *praxis* here differs from 'practice' (which responds to the theory). Rather, it is a matter of unblocking something that one isn't aware is placing obstacles and that is hidden away, making it all the more difficult to unmask because it appears to be perfectly ingenuous. Consequently, it isn't a methodical effort that is required but one that is primarily *strategic*. This is why *indirectness* is the term required when art and learning, *techné* and *episteme*, are failing. But how is it to be made a concept that finally derives from complicity and the familiar? What I mean is this: can we consider this *indirectness* in a way that would be coherent and concerted and not be just a stop-gap, inclined towards empirical guesswork and losing intelligibility?

3 When it comes to method we shouldn't think, in order to reassure ourselves, that the indirect might be compoundable with it, serving to adapt it, or that it would be, as Sartre once suggested in passing, only a 'slightly more complex method'. What is characteristic of the indirect isn't so much the fact that it draws attention to the particularity of the situation, but that it makes us complicit with it. Instead of advancing an initiative made by the Subject, which is the characteristic of the methodical, it opens a margin for manoeuvre as it reacts to the difficulty encountered, inviting a detour to defuse it. In this, its knowledge is, strictly speaking, 'cunning' – that is, it invites us literally to 'step back', to withdraw (that is, to recuse, from the Latin *recusare*), so as to invest and penetrate more effectively. An ancient Chinese treatise of diplomacy like that of the *Guiguzi*, 'Master of Ghost Valley',[1] corroborating everything we already know about Chinese strategy, moves ahead without expressing reservations or putting on a mask. It brings into the light, in a reasoned way, what the Greeks – without admitting it – recognised as the shadowy and clandestine side of the *méthodos*: it is necessary to 'turn around' the situation like a ball so as to detect the slightest crack in it, for opening this breach will then be shown as a split, a gap, a lack or a ditch, and the adverse element will be easy to resolve. Without this, the intervention will be arbitrary and perilous because it is being forced, and will have little effect. What is most important concerning the Prince isn't so much to know how to plead the cause when in his presence, as to have his ear: because one has learned obligingly to accept all the aspects of his personality, in turn and without ever confronting him, one will no longer even need to speak to him to have a 'way' to approach him and be listened to.

In China, this strategy of the indirect is found operating in a roundabout way in the teaching of wisdom, diverting us from the stake of knowledge and truth. When he sees that the other is holding to his position and enjoying his reasoning, the Master (Confucius) judges it to be a waste of time to try to persuade him or to argue with him: a face-to-face entreaty is as vain as it is laborious. It's better to begin by letting the other go on his way while in some way ensuring that the teaching that the Master would have dispensed – at a loss if it had been framed by a too immediate and frontal refutation – has a chance of reaching his pupil when he has attained a greater maturity and discovered the flaw in his position – this will finally allow him to understand (cf. *Analects*, XVII, 21). 'When we can talk with someone, and don't do so, we are misusing him but when we cannot speak with someone and yet do so, it is our words that are being misused' (ibid., XV, 7). For this reason, Confucius' word is given only in a timely and minimal way, avoiding frontality: all that is necessary when we know that the other's mind is receptive is indirectly to utter a word (about whatever arises), rather than conspicuously and deliberately to give the lesson. This so intrigues the other that, discountenanced and helpless, he finally gives in (about his prejudices) and 'realises' (what the 'way' is).

Therefore, just a few words suffice. The Master doesn't really 'teach'. Rather than squandering his words (which will be uselessly 'spread' by others), he is content to offer a helping hand: a few words are able to produce a jolt so as to aid, or rather encourage, the other to find a way out of the position in which he has bogged himself down. But this given helping hand is also a mode of attack: it is about breaking down his resistance to being awakened (to wisdom). This is precisely why Confucius takes account of the 'environment' – in other words, the place his interlocutor has reached in his development. So he may say one thing to one person and the opposite to another, or even indeed to the same person on another day. This word is strategic: the value of the argument lies in the discountenancing and unblocking that it effects (cf. ibid., IX, 10), by intervening in time, *in situ* – consequently, in its force of impact, and not in its expression. Moreover, if treated as from the perspective of expression, let's recognise that the *Analects* of Confucius are hardly more than platitudes: their value lies simply in the way this oblique strategy unsettles the interlocutor. We learn this from reading the commentators, and the masters of *chan* (*zen*) were the inheritors of it as they systematised the process. The Master's responsibility is confined to indicating, so setting others on the way, tasking them to pursue and fulfil it: 'I introduce one corner to him; if he is unable to find the other three, I don't persist.'

The Master's word, falling at the right moment, characteristically touches a nerve; careful not to show all of his cards, its function is to 'prompt' (*xing* 兴, which is also one of the key words of Chinese reflections on poetry). It is to impel a transformation in the interlocutor which cannot be carried out except within and by the interlocutor himself: the Master resists putting himself in his place. We thus read, in an ancient treatise of pedagogy which the *Rituals* have conserved for us, the Sage's concern to set the other along the way, but by allowing him to discover it for himself: 'He steers him, but doesn't draw him along by force; he urges him to make an effort, but doesn't constrain him; he shows him the way, but doesn't lead him to the end' (*Xueji*, § 13). It isn't – we should be clear about this – that the Master wants to respect the disciple's autonomy and freedom of spirit (as our modern pedagogy might like), but because he knows that the only effective intervention is lateral, by means of oblique stimulation. The process can proceed only from the interlocutor himself – in other words, without the Master being able to precipitate what will unfold, and anything he might do to teach more explicitly could only hinder the course by forcing it, and so be counter-productive. The indirect therefore means that the Master places himself neither completely in front, by claiming to reveal the 'way', nor completely to the side, by acting only to accompany, in equality (doesn't the psychoanalyst also place himself in the indirect?). He knows that he can induce, but not lead; to *influence* is better than to teach. Or that a more direct teaching is possible only if it is preceded by this diffuse, subtle and non-isolatable influence operating tacitly and being extended across time, which alone allows such teaching finally to become audible and actually able to effect a transformation.

Note

1   The *Guiguzi*, 'Master of Ghost Valley', is a treatise from the 'Warring States' period of the Han dynasty by an unknown author [trans.].

VIII

Influence (vs Persuasion)

1 *Influence* is the most successful mode of obliquity – as well as the most difficult to avoid. Indeed, it isn't frontal but its dissemination spreads it in every direction; it operates through every pore and under every angle. It is therefore discreet, not direct: it cannot be confronted because it surrounds us. An influence can't be refuted – or contradicted. Operating upstream, at the level of conditions, it doesn't let its face be shown; diffuse, it doesn't let itself be isolated. This means it is also what we have least hold on. Indeed, it doesn't arise from the category of Being since it is not assignable, nor is it of non-being, since it cannot, even in the long run, be completely evacuated. Consequently, it also doesn't lend itself to being apprehended under the opposition of presence and absence – of 'being before', *prae-esse* – influence is of the order of 'pervasiveness', not of presence. Its distinguishing feature, which makes up its capacity, is to infiltrate and inculcate, penetrating from everywhere without warning, and therefore without its being noticed. This is why European thought, while recognising the phenomenon, has been so ill-at-ease with thinking about it and has hardly developed it as a concept.

We see evidence of the disturbing marginality of influence in our learning in that we have to seek the starting point of its notion not in ontology, the noble and consistent learning of Being, but in astrology, on the suspect verge of superstition. *Influentia* first of all expressed the action attributed to the heavenly bodies affecting people's fates; it was then the action that persons or things can have on other persons and things. Marked by this doubtful origin, the notion of influence consequently gave rise to the same suspicion as what could not fail to be provoked, as far as classical rationalism was concerned, by everything that, in the face of the conquering hold of science imposing its lucidity, became relegated to obscurantism and occultism: that of uncertain causalities, with indeterminate outlines, whose minutiae could not be designated, and which are accordingly judged to lack a stable foundation. Influence, venturing to the indistinct limits of the visible and the invisible, haunting without 'existing', was consigned to the same discredit as the psychology of 'fluids', as Mesmerism shows well. And, conversely, is even 'action', as it is expressed in this definition, still pertinent? 'Action' assumes a subject, but influence is of the order of flux, course, of passing through, and it lacks an isolatable subject. Action operates here and now, in a determined time and place, but influence isn't definable, any more than it is localisable, and it forces us to move beyond the distinction between active and passive. This is why it eludes the categories of philosophy, which leaves it to one side, treating it only marginally and in a makeshift way.

Isn't what keeps us from granting the phenomenon of influence all of its significance, even if we recognise its importance in certain respects, once again, as with receptivity or reliability, that it keeps the autonomy of the Subject in the shade and seems to contradict it? To be 'under the influence' – this 'under' is significant (and pejorative) – is repugnant to our ideal of freedom. What therefore is this *vestige* that influence expresses, which eludes the methodical hold of our intelligence, but whose effects we nevertheless note, or even reckon upon? Psychoanalysis again bears witness to it: as Freud tells us concerning the Rat Man, once the resistances at work have been exposed, its whole art is really about showing them to the patient and encouraging him to abandon them 'thanks to the influence that one man can exercise on another'. For the practice constructed under the hypothesis of the unconscious is really that by which 'we influence the course of conscious processes in the service of an end', *zweckdienlich beeinflüssen*. But what is the *operating phenomenon* that Freud, neither reducing it to suggestion or transfer, invokes here as a last resort, although without illuminating it? This notion of 'influence', deprived as it is of the consistency of the ontological as well as repudiated by the explanatory rationalism of science, will thus need to begin by completely freeing itself from this inhibitive network so as to approach it, and above all to be detached from what I will call, in a most general sense, Western 'ideology' – distanced even from the speculative – as much as it is resistant to the self-constitution of the Subject.

China once more helps us to take apart these theoretical folds that are part of 'us' (of course it has others, the very ones that stare us in the face) – these *folds* in which the notion of influence has remained trapped in Europe and which have prevented it from thinking about the phenomenon to its proper extent, even if we have also been obliged in passing, as Freud was, to mark its place. China has placed influence at the heart of its intelligence. This is due to various factors: Chinese thought doesn't think in terms of 'being' and identification, but of energy flow, of poles and interaction, or rather of 'inter-encouragement' (*xiàng-gǎn* 相感); it thinks in terms of 'modification' and 'continuation' (*biàn-tōng* 变通) and of communicating passages and transition (*jiāo-tōng* 交通); it doesn't recognise the morphological distinction between active and passive modes in its grammar; in its physics, the notions of 'distant echo' and mutual resonance (*gǎn-yīng* 感应) take the place of causality (very early on, China developed a subtle intelligence of magnetic phenomena, which came to the West only much later, and it also understood the phenomenon of the tides); finally, while it recognised the individual as a person, it wasn't preoccupied with constructing an autonomy of the Subject. It considers *influence* to be the general mode announced by all reality – of what we call 'nature' as well as of morality.

2 Yet this opposition can be pushed further still, by ramifying the diver-gences that have been crossed and by re-centring the stake on the word: we'll note that the two verbs to *persuade* and to *influence* are antithetical to one another, arising from distinct logics, even if one (to persuade) can also be infiltrated by the other. 'To persuade' operates through the intermediary of the face-to-face and *frontal* discourse by sticking as closely as possible, and appealing, to reasons, *logoi* – which is the Greek verb par excellence (*peithein*). It is linked precisely to the arrival of the City since it is by per-suasion that the discussion is decided, via a confrontation between the for and against. This applies in the council, the court, the assembly and even in the theatre. It was thus by *persuasion* that the non-culpability and fate of Orestes (so slow to come, between Athena and the choir at the end of the *Eumenides*) were decided in an exemplary way, thereby rationally putting an end to the perpetuation of vengeance at the heart of the *genos*. This was a major stage in Greek consciousness. For, as Plato would later develop it, the alternative in politics is nothing other than between recourse to 'persuasion' or to 'force' and 'violence' (*peithô/bia* πειθώ/βία, *The Republic*, VIII, 548b). Even if, as we well know, persuasion can clandestinely be a sort of deviant manipulation of this ideal, the opposition is nonetheless structuring, today as yesterday, and it is still the principle on which civic life is founded.

Let's also recall that to persuade was the decisive operation in philosophy from the earliest Greek thinkers onwards, the 'path of persuasion' being what 'accompanies the truth', as Parmenides had already said (fr. 2; see also Empedocles, fr. 133). And, as soon as the word is reflected upon, the inter-locutor is no longer the other but becomes the self – so thinking, as Plato defined it, is about 'persuading oneself' (*Theaetetus*, 190c). In fact, what is thinking if not the development of a certain course of reflection producing a self-adhesion by which one is guaranteed through this assent? It's true that to persuade isn't without ambiguity, that classical European thought even enjoyed denouncing, in this art of inveiglement, any seduction that drew upon 'pleasure' rather than 'truth' (Pascal). Nevertheless, it is recog-nised that to persuade can be raised beyond its subjective limit. This means that to persuade suffices to dispel and go beyond mere appearance and then to be objectively based in reason, thereby becoming 'conviction' (the passage from *Überredung* to *Überzeugung* in Kant): henceforth, it is communicable by right to all people and proves the truth of the judgement through the universal agreement of subjects.

What *to influence* and *to persuade* have in common and that justifies their being brought together is that neither can be effected in the moment, and this implies in each case an unfolding: when it comes to persuasion, it is that of discourse; and for influence, it is that of its dissemination – on both sides, this penetration–adoption needs time. But one of them (persuasion) requires a deliberate consent on the part of the interlocutor, even if he is manipulated, and this is the reason persuasion is at the heart of democracy and thinking about freedom, while the other (influencing) is done insensibly and benignly and without the person who is its object being aware of it or having any idea of protecting himself against it. This is why in China importance is placed not on laws but on 'rites': while one voluntarily obeys laws (one has only to remember the prosopopea of Laws in the *Criton*), 'rites' – or what we very clumsily translate as such – are all the more effective as behavioural norms in that they influence behaviour without our realising it. Influence is all the more absorbing – and resonant – in so far as we don't perceive it as it occurs and we are unaware of how it is making its way. While persuasion operates from beginning to end within sight and under the pressure of an adjusted word, to influence, in contrast, doesn't just mean to insinuate: its word also remains diffused – indeed, it is only one aspect of the process of modification and conditioning taking place, or else it doesn't even intervene at all. I find the fact that China has not developed ideas about persuasion is revealing of this divergence (the compound *shuō-fú* 说服, 'to submit by the word', expresses subjection more than conviction even today). On the other hand, it has conceived human relations, like those that weave the world, from the influence they effect.

One fact that speaks for itself and is enough to widen the divergence (which is probably too broad in its effects to generally be noticed) is that China hasn't experienced the appearance of the orator and hasn't developed rhetoric as an art of persuasion like that around which the ancient culture of the West was formed. As expressed in one of its most ancient literary themes (from the *Classic of Poems*, the *Shijing*), it has instead conceived the word to be in the image of the 'wind' and even began thinking about the poetic word according to this manner of discreet influence. Yet what does the 'wind' express if not a far more complete diffusion for being an invasion, but one that isn't sought and is barely discerned? The wind passes imperceptibly and only its effects are felt: 'the grasses yield' under its passage (see *Analects*, XII, 19); in seeping in through the slightest crack, penetrating everywhere in a light and diffuse way (see the hexagram *xun* in the *Oracle of Change*), it spreads indefinitely, and under its orientation the whole surrounding landscape bows. As expressed in one of the most ancient poems, let my song be spread to its recipient by the 'clear wind' and transmit this emotion to him (the songs 'Songgao' and 'Zhengmin' from the *Shijing*). The *wind* also expresses a dissemination between people that is diffused imperceptibly through its prompting. It imparts a direction that is without aim; it impregnates, but without being assigned; it spreads, but without being limited, shaking but without explaining; it modifies a state of mind, but without being onerous.

Yet this virtue of the poetic word, like that of the political word, was understood from very early on in China: it relates to the political word as it favourably influences the people, from the highest to lowest in society, like a mild wind (*fēng-huà* 风化), due to the prince's exemplary qualities. Just as there is nothing that isn't impregnated by his morality, from his family to the end of the world, so the word passes from low to high, from the people to the prince, to rise, like a 'biting wind' (*fēng-cì* 风刺), so that its criticisms have an effect even on power and, through this influence softened by images, encourage him to amend his behaviour. To *instruct* and *influence* (in the image of the wind) are then themselves to be distinguished from one another (*jiào / fěng* 教讽), the commentators add: first of all, the prince must diffuse his beneficial influence, which step by step encourages and conditions in a favourable way, before teaching can begin. In a general way, it is better to use words which infiltrate, bending softly (and, consequently, deeply), through the mood and without force, than words which specifically aim at their object and seek to command (*Analects*, IX, 23).

3 A collection like the *Zhuangzi* delights in evoking such scenes of influence between people. They don't communicate much by speaking, but they stretch over time and this leads to the one who submits (but isn't 'submission' too oppressive and passive a term?) to the influence, modifying their views completely in a way that becomes apparent to them only after the event. Nothing magical, or even strange, intercedes in any case, or even anything that would merit being pointed out, or simply that could be spoken about. There's nothing to report. Nothing is *assignable*. But the relation of proximity developing over the course of days from this shared presence in time, these repeated meetings and from this discreet commerce from which *reliability* is born, results – through ambiance-resonance – in a gradual shift, of both judgement and behaviour, that goes to the point of an inversion. In the beginning, the one who experiences the transformation doesn't even notice the other's quality, even if he is 'so ugly as to induce fear', or possesses neither wealth nor honours: nothing about him may be appealing. Yet you have to stay with him in the long run: the prince even offers him power, but he says neither 'yes' nor 'no' and finally goes away, without giving any explanation…. Who is he? Not a Master, strictly speaking, but a being whose person discreetly infuses. 'Standing up, he doesn't teach; sitting down, he doesn't argue.' 'But one goes there empty and returns full.' 'Isn't there teaching without words?' For 'without anything exactly being actualised', without anything notable occurring in consequence, the mind is nevertheless 'formed' under this influence (the chapter 'Dechongfu').

What is *effectively* being operated in this relation? Time has admittedly passed. Not from the face-to-face, from the 'exchange', as it is too actively praised, but rather from the relation of indirectness as also from silence, but which isn't due to an inability to speak. Neither wanting to speak nor wanting to stay silent: allow things to *pass*. This means in both senses of the term: to let things pass between us and to let time pass. For in this mutually established transformation nothing can be projected or hurried. The trajectory of indirectness provides for a longer course; it tolerates detours and calls for returns. It is less offensive and allows more play: the evolution can come about by itself, by self-deployment, and can actually be beneficent, because nothing remarkable intervenes and nothing in it is forced. But an unfolding is needed and we don't know how long it will take: Zhuangzi recounts that 'on the first day', when we 'evaluate' this man, this Master who isn't a Master, 'we find him inadequate'; 'but (then), after a year has passed, we find that he has more than is needed' (ibid., 'Gengsangchu'). The process should be allowed to occur, the presence to emanate, and the effect to decant.

It seems terribly arbitrary, in its immobile face-to-face relation, to claim to persuade the other standing opposite. For his part, Freud recognised that such discussions with the patient 'are never intended to provoke conviction', 'Überzeugungen hervor zu bringen'; and 'I put these arguments forward only to confirm how ineffectual they are.' The cure also requires slowness and unfolding, for the self-advent can be prompted only obliquely – does anything remarkable take place? By contrast, we can see how much persuasion pertains even better to what we have constructed as reason: how in proceeding through argumentation and intending to carry conviction, it relies on a voluntary assent and addresses itself to my freedom. Yet in the face of the diffusion of influence, there is actually also a force by which the subject was supported in the classical age and this is what makes him a hero of his history. For, while I am so much more profoundly influenced in that this operates without my being aware of it or noticing it, on the other hand, the unshakeable appears when I am *convinced* that I have turned it into a question of truth. My resolution is all the more anchored in that its object is concentrated and my adhesion is reflective and planned. In the name of my conviction, I can *frontally* oppose and denounce: I can risk a *meaning* and assume it.

IX
Coherence (vs Meaning)

1 As coherence is ordinarily understood in the shadow of meaning (*Sinn* and *Zusammenhang* are still synonyms for Freud), I will have to take a knife so as to cut out the pith more delicately still between these two notions, to begin by cutting into their false synonymy, and to do so once again to pit them against one another so as to construct two rival logics between which existence chooses. The logic of Meaning is what we know best as the founding relationship of ontology. This begins with the reciprocal exclusion of contraries, between 'being' and 'non-being', or 'truth' and 'opinion', in Parmenides. It is then articulated through the Platonic theory of the communication of genres as it authorises the operation of predication and so that the dialectician can regulate it. And finally it leads to the institution of the principle of non-contradiction, entailing in its wake that of the excluded middle as the axiom on which all discourse, *logos*, rests, and that anyone who wants to eliminate it still assumes as soon as he speaks. For 'to speak' is 'to state', as Aristotle establishes from the outset, thereby postulating an equivalence from which the logic of *logos* has never left. To 'state' is to 'say something', *legein ti* λέγειν τι: there's always a 'something', no matter how indefinite it might be, which is the singular object of the statement; if it wasn't one, it would be saying 'nothing' and cancelling it out (*Metaphysics, gamma*). So, to 'state something' is, at the same time, to 'mean something', *semainein ti* σημαίνειν τι, which to be a meaning can have only one sense. Anyone who doesn't respect this protocol of the word excludes himself from humanity.

Yet where *coherence* remains subject to the sovereign monopoly of Meaning (that is to be understood from the start as a consistency internal to the order of discourse, ensuring the legitimacy of its semantic function), I'd prefer to think about it according to its actual virtue, and to do this, freeing it from this subjection, by bringing out its pertinence in step with what this term itself states: *co-haere*, says the Latin – 'hold together'; 'co-herence' is what makes things *hold together*. 'The world', Cicero would say, 'is so coherent', being an integral part of it in such a well-adapted way – *ita apte cohaeret* – 'that it cannot in any way be taken apart'. Or, expressed negatively – and this even applies to the word – 'its discourse barely holds up' as it forms a coherent whole with itself, *vix cohaerebat oratio*. This is already a way of thinking about a coherence that might be that of the word and not of what is spoken (according to which to say is necessarily to say 'something' that would mean something, because it has a single sense). And therefore to pose the possibility of a word that actually 'speaks', but without saying 'something', *ti* (that is, something about 'a' thing), by discriminating and isolating without necessarily aiming to 'signify'; indeed, that allows its statement to *hold together*, to be 'coherent', even though what its words signify are contraries that exclude one another from the standpoint of meaning.

Heraclitus was the first in the West along this path to preclude ahead of time the development of the ontology that rested on the exclusion of contraries. By opening contraries up to one another without mediation, associating them opposite one another without even co-ordinating them, he explicitly took it upon himself to allow the fundamental coherence of things to come forth in his words in a way that ordinary discourse, that of signification, as disjunctive as it is, only occults (an occultation that metaphysical discourse only ratifies): 'God is day night, winter summer, war peace, satiety hunger', he pronounced (fr. 67). 'Day night', and not 'day and night'. It isn't by taking hold of the day, or winter, on one side, and the night, or summer, on the other side, that it would be possible to grasp this unity by interdependency, *relating them together* and forming *co-herence*, that Heraclitus has chosen to name 'God'. 'Day-night': they must be kept correlated, not be spelled out distributively one after the other as the 'many' do who haven't 'awoken', not realising this indissociability, and conceiving of peace without war or summer without winter. Day-night, winter-summer, war-peace, satiety-hunger: strictly (selectively) speaking, there's no 'meaning' in them, but a coherence of opposites is maintained in an active state at the level of the word.

Strictly speaking, this intimate conjunction of opposites cannot 'claim to be' since it is not 'something', 'a' something (this and not that), but it goes precisely against any isolation and de-correlation of opposites, which is what all discourse that respects the principle of non-contradiction, on which Aristotle founded the possibility of 'signifying', invariably brings into focus. In contrast, the word of Heraclitus is constantly signalling towards a con-joint of the world in various indirect ways. The contraries support and reveal each other mutually–contrastively: sickness puts health to the test, as injustice does for justice. They go together, as do 'mortals' and 'immortals', collapsing into one another in the same way as 'hot' and 'cold', or the 'living' and the 'dead'. While one pulls upon the saw, the other presses forward, and the one doesn't go without the other; the movement is one beneath these opposing actions, and this goes against the unilaterality in which language ordinarily maintains us, and therefore goes against its native partiality. Indeed, as Heraclitus says, it is a matter of 'what is opposed co-operating', *to antixoun sumpheron* (fr. 8); it isn't just an opposition.

Yet, to grasp precisely this 'co-operation' of the other, coming from the other, giving access to coherence, there is born what I would call the 'com-prehension' of Heraclitus (with the intention of opposing him to the Parmenidian disjunction of 'being'/'non-being', from which Aristotle drew the principle of non-contradiction). To understand, 'com-prendre', is literally 'to take with' (*cum*; cf. in Greek *suniemi*, a word privileged by

Heraclitus), and therefore it works inversely to separate and exclude: I 'com-prehend' by taking both on each occasion and necessarily keep them indissociable. So war with peace or winter with summer, since one is only understood through its other at the same time as it contradicts it. I therefore won't let my word focus on one to the detriment of the other, snared by their apparently obvious opposition, and consequently arbitrarily to break the continuous 'flow' of things (the memorable 'everything flows'). This is precisely what the 'many' subject themselves to, since they 'don't understand how what is exists through what is opposed to it; an adjustment occurs when actions move in contrary senses, as in those of the bow and the lyre'.

Heraclitus consequently doesn't signify, but 'indicates' (*semainein* in its original meaning): *indication* (towards that omnipresent inseparability of what is opposed) thereby being opposed to *signification* (by specification of the content of each of the words). In the same way, *coherence* is opposed to *meaning*: the fundamental link in the differentiating demarcation, or *com-prehension* to *disjunction*. But this com-prehension of co-herence is inevitably destined to be rejected by the semantic function when it is no longer understood. Similarly, while Heraclitus, in following the path of non-disjunction, and consequently of de-exclusion, thereby widened the divergence from the logic of meaning, he has still been read and judged from the perspective of meaning, which has meant that this choice of meaning, definitively settled by Aristotle, has subsequently dominated European culture, allowing 'logic' alone to subsist. This is why Heraclitus is called the 'obscure', *skoteinos*, as we find his words unintelligible. Hence also that, under the reign established by a determinant-discriminating statement that became integrally semantic, this other vocation of the word, once it was abandoned by philosophy and even repressed under the all-powerful apparatus of *logos*, would make a claim to divergence in Europe by taking refuge in the anti-discursivity of what is usually called 'poetry'. From Heraclitus to René Char, the poetic word embodies this resistance with astonishing obstinacy.

2 By posing (imposing) the fact that the word necessarily expresses a 'something' (*ti*), however indefinite it might be, and consequently something that is about 'one' thing, Aristotle's *logos* indeed already assumes that this *one* would be individualisable, isolatable and detachable, as a unity in its own right, and that it thereby sets us off towards its determination. At the same time, this assumes that the object of what is said could be an entity, one that therefore possesses an id-entity, which will be recognised and *identified* by the discourse. In setting out as a rule, and from the perspective of *logos*, the fact that 'the word means something and means only one thing', so that the meaning might have (or be) a unity, Aristotle established the word's vocation as being to express the stable unity of things, therefore to speak in terms of 'being', and he instituted it 'onto'-logically. Yet it is on this unity of 'being' establishing the identity of the meaning of

words – to which Aristotle would give a new name, 'essence', *ousia* οὐσία – that Europe would come to establish the condition of possibility of its learning as it fixed this *essence* by 'definition'. This is so culturally inscribed and so universal that the perspective of coherence seems to me so crucial precisely because of the bifurcation it opens up in relation to it. In short, it (right away) takes us away from this essentialist perspective of knowledge and introduces another description of things.

In partially drawing its modernity from this, we cannot forget how much difficulty it has since given philosophy in emerging from the essentialist standpoint, whose limit it recognised without being able to establish a new point of departure. Phenomenology itself struggled with it and was therefore most often condemned to endless arrangements that never lifted it up beyond this initial perspective, established as it was above all by (European) language and its grammar. Yet the interest in thinking through a *principle of coherence* is that the unitary it contains is not the supposed unity of meaning and, behind this, of essence, but that of a 'holding together' that operates *from the very fact of the internal relation*, without there being any need for the support of Being and 'sub-stance'. It thereby alone provides what I would consequently call, adversatively – respecting this purely associative *cum* ('with') – '*con*-sistency'. It's the fact of creating a relation alone that then, by its own virtue, makes its force of correlation 'relate', and it does so in a com-prehensible way, one that is therefore able to establish a rival rationality of signification. There is no further need for the invocation and imagination of the base and of the 'sub' ('sub'-stance), of the 'behind' or the beyond (of meta-physics), of support and foundation. Relationality possesses enough effectivity in itself to secure an intelligibility of what is existent. *Con-sistency* would therefore be opposed to *essence*, as coherence is to meaning, or comprehension to separation.

3 From what I have already proposed about Chinese thought, it may be considered a thought of *coherence* rather than *meaning*: it examines the con-sistency of things rather than enquiring into their essence and definition. From its parataxical structure and very lightly regulated grammatical construction, the characteristic of the Chinese language was already to privilege what is stated by correlation (what is called, in an inadequate way, 'Chinese parallelism'), instead of engaging in the singularisation of discursive meaning, in which the Chinese formulation is poetic as a principle. In contemporary language, *duì* 对, which means 'precisely' or 'exact', still expresses what is 'coupled' and 'paired'. We shall understand such a logic of *correlation* better by divergence from that of *composition*, even by making it its rival. The logic of meaning, as European thought-language for its part has developed it, is, inversely, *constitutive*. It unfolds by composition in the principal or subordinate clause, in the sentence, and goes to the point of discourse from the smallest unity of meaning that is the word, which itself arises from alphabetical composition (while Chinese writing is ideographic,

and because it has remained so). We find constitutive logic at the start of European physics as well: bodies are composed of atoms, by way of prime elements, *stoicheia* στοιχεῖα, as words are composed of letters, something Lucretius had already noted (whereas, as with the Chinese 'five agents', the world may be understood from correlated factors, *wǔ xíng* 五行). The same thing goes in painting (see Alberti), whose language was inspired in Europe by a compositional form of geometry (which Chinese knowledge has not developed very much): from the point to the line, to the surface element, to the body, and finally to 'history', as a complete deployment of meaning, analogous to what discourse is for rhetoric. Yet Chinese pictorial language is essentially *correlating*: one feature calls upon another through opposition–compensation (the 'full' calls upon the 'empty', the 'dense' calls upon the 'thin', what lies 'at rest' calls upon what has been 'raised up'), and when a 'mountain' is painted, 'water' accompanies it to give the landscape con-sistency.

Chinese thought-language does open a divergence that contrasts in respect to the European 'tradition', in that it has not conceived of any unitary and isolated term thereby able to be hypostasised. It has no more considered the atom to be a prime element than it has regarded 'God' to be an isolated creator: it has thought about 'Heaven' but in correlation with Earth, not apart from it. If the virtue of Heaven lies in its 'initiatory' capacity in the ancient *Oracle of Change*, it is because the Earth, at the same time and correlatively, applies its 'receiving' virtue. The *Tao* itself isn't a monist term since it is only the regulated alternation of one and other, of *yin* and *yang* (一阴一阳之谓道). Thus, proceeding by means of divinatory figures through a combination of strokes from the *Oracle* that treats everything in terms at once of odd and even (of Heaven and Earth, masculine and femi-nine (*yang* and *yin*, etc.) – in other words, from opposed complementaries forming a polarity, each time showing a *co-herence* appropriate to a situa-tion), it secures *con-sistency* and consequently its capacity for evolution by propensity. This is revealed by the relation of two types of stroke in such a way that the person consulting it could, without understanding the mean-ing issued by the oracle or awaiting some Revelation in an *expression* coming from God, insert himself advisedly into the correlation of factors at play so that his conduct conforms with it.

What is interesting about the notion that will serve to express Chinese 'reason' (the term *lǐ* 理) is that it is not just theoretical and speculative but implies an 'operative art' in itself. Far from referring to the expression as well as to the construction of an argument, as Aristotelian *logos* does, the written form of this term corresponds with the veining of jade. In order to be able to carve it, the lapidary needs to follow its conformation with his chisel: 'As hard as jade is, it is enough to find an intrinsic reason (*lǐ*) in its layers in order to have no problem in turning it into a piece. This is what is called reasoning, *lǐ*' (Duan Yucai commenting on the *Shuowen*[1]). This *ars operandi* will therefore elucidate the internal coherence within the lineaments of the slightest situation encountered. The situation owes its consistency to this and it is best to adapt one's conduct to it in a *comprehensive way*. For what is the veining of jade that favours the splitting if not the unobtrusive vein, or internal fibre, by which this materiality is gradually organised in a correlative way and so structures itself? A veining of the stone, or a branching of the branch, or a texture of the leaf or the skin: in each case, the lines of separation are so many lines of force or of life whose twin network reveals a consistency in which these 'branching out networks' form 'reason' (*tiáo-lǐ* 条理).

Therefore, far from claiming ideally to erect an order from a preset plan, or an optimum calculated and projected as an imperative, the Chinese thinker reveals an internal arrangement proceeding by coherence and making opposites 'hold together'. He does this by following only those various fissures and lineaments according to which the compactness of things is allowed to be penetrated: hence he *co-operates* (with the process of things) rather than *constructs* (by composition). Hence, too, that this consistency and coherence of the concrete, each time so fragile and singular and such that it appears in the slightest phenomenal event, is actually connected on a larger scale to the coherence of the course of things. So it holds together the whole world, and this is what is called *Heaven* or *Tao*. 'The *lǐ* ["reason", 理] is the configurational motif (*wén* 文) of the advent of things and the *Tao* is that by which all things occur. This is why it is said that: "The *Tao* is what makes things happen through the *lǐ*"' (Han Fei,[2] ch. XX). There are therefore not two levels of 'being' between these two stages (those of the perceptible, 'configuring', manifestation, and its latent Ground), one of which, as ontology would have it, would be deficient in relation to the other, or of which this Other would be theologically presented as its external Cause or Creator. But it is a question of a before and an after of the same Process that continually – that is, without any metaphysical break – goes back to its 'source' (*yuán* 源): any advent of existence is configured according to its veining or the internal fibre as it is formed by correlation, to which it owes its coherence, allowing us to communicate directly through it with the great Regulation of the world.

4 Consequently, coherence is erected as an initial choice of thought from this *distinguo* of *meaning*, entailing along with it the means of conceiving existence and therefore of living and acting. At least let it be clearly understood that this is not a matter on either side of naïvely resultative 'visions of the world', but rather of having opted early on, according to whatever intellectual tool was decided upon, and, as we keep our eyes wide open, following the particular vein and measuring its incidence. The groove of Meaning, as it sinks ever deeper or becomes an end in itself (allowing itself to be hollowed out by the religious: is this a hypertrophy?), leads to the development of the question of an astonished 'Why?'. This notably poses the question of Evil, therefore calling for the appearance of a Subject that is responsible for the choices it makes and what these choices promote.

Reliant upon a discriminating and disjunctive logic, the perspective fluctu-ates between the eloquent and the dramatic. Either a greater hidden Mean-ing is to be revealed or else the world becomes absurd. For, once this touting of the question of Meaning has been launched, it has no reason to stop: the only way out lies with itself. Or do we discreetly close again the door through which it rushed, and tiptoe away?

In contrast, the groove or vein of coherence leads to an examination of *how* things come to appear but, without having to be limited to the realm of science alone, such a 'how' of the operative relation extinguishes rather than imagines resolving the unfathomable (insatiable) question of the end as well as of the origin. Following this thread, the fracture of 'evil' is closed up and becomes the 'negative', cooperating with the good and being justi-fied as its condition of possibility – this was already the old, everlastingly repeated discourse of the *Theodicy*. It doesn't lead to the emergence and promotion of a Subject that, due to its autonomy, breaks into the texture of an infinite sequence. Instead, its 'comprehensive' logic is one of *integra-tion* at the heart of the great process that makes the world – that there is a 'world'. While the aim of Meaning is dehiscent and dismantling, and soon turns life into an enigma, making it difficult to disengage it from the thought of salvation, the thinking of coherence leads us into the economy of things or, as the Greeks named it, their 'syntax', *sun-taxis*. It is no longer necessary to have recourse to an explanatory Narrative (in order to respond to the enigma) or to mount a *muthos*: it is enough simply to *describe* things, by descending into the fine vein of their union.

Wouldn't 'harmony' *ultimately* be the catchword of coherence? But this might be too lazy, and we might say, along with Heraclitus (fr. 54), that a harmony is more powerful for not being apparent: we aren't neces-sarily reduced to the contentment of a self-satisfied ideology of the 'wisdom' of nations and its serenity in order to develop thinking about coherence. We are rather steered in the opposite direction. At a time (the present) when the great Narratives are dead, or rather abandoned, where the eloquence of Meaning (the illustrious 'meaning of life') has become weary or is simply exhausted, where the (religious) play of the 'Mystery, or else the absurd' no longer has a hold, this vein of comprehensive coher-ence will still give us plenty of work to do. Besides, isn't this what contemporary art tries to explore and exploit in breaking with rhetoric through its minimalism, a minimalism that is as ethical as it is aesthetic? For we have long since ceased to believe in the Message and we no longer inscribe it with a 'meaning', but we can still effect coherence here, mean-ing that a 'work' of art can still exist – in other words, its con-sistency can be made to *work*, and above all in that an internal tension is promoted in it through its negativity. Since Mallarmé, at least, we no longer read a poem from a passion for its meaning and determination alone, but for what it 'holds together', in a non-'logical' way – and even by challenging the *logos* – and in how it 'operates'. And above all what holds together signifiers which concur and are revealed *in connivence* (Mallarmé's 'abolished trinket of sonorous futility …'), therefore other than though the skylight of a signified tasked with imparting 'knowledge'. From coherence, connivance is tacit understanding, which doesn't need to be divulged.

Notes

1   The *Shuowen Jiezi* is a Chinese character dictionary compiled by Xu Shen during the Han Dynasty. An annotated version published in 1815 by the Duan Yucai (1735–1815) is one of the great works of Chinese philology [trans.].
2   Han Fei (*c.* 280–233 BCE), a philosopher of the Han period [trans.].

X

Connivence (vs Knowledge)

1 When confronted with knowledge and its hegemony over European culture, what should its other (which it has concealed and not thought about) be called? I'll choose to name this other relation to the world that knowledge has tended to hide away, but which it has nevertheless been unable to abolish, *connivence*. And when confronted with this established world of knowledge, I also need to recall 'coherence'. Developing as speculative learning, in other words as learning for the sake of learning, knowledge would be detached, *via* science, from needing to be adapted to the world from which it is born. Taking itself as an end, it would also be cut off from what is vital, henceforth conferring on us this strictly correlative task: that of returning to the relation that has been buried by reason and which, consequently operating in the shadows, still keeps us in a tacit understanding with things – but in an 'understanding' we don't think about. 'Understanding' therefore remains implicit, *predating* the relational work to which reason itself is devoted, and which could only be illuminated by being led to take a step back, to revisit its history and explore what has been separated from it. This means not what it has heroically fought against (obscurantism in the face of the Enlightenment), but what in its legitimate and powerful struggle to establish itself it has needed to leave out – and which henceforth becomes *part of our non-knowledge*, and therefore eludes our understanding. If we know that the contrary of *knowledge* is ignorance, what contradicts it is *connivence* which institutes parity with it at the same time as it turns its back on it. *Connivere* is the Latin term: to agree 'whilst closing one's eyes'.

Knowledge isolates a 'nature' and situates it as an 'object', organising its progression in a methodical way, elaborating the tools of abstraction and constructing mediations, making spaces indifferent and projecting an equal and planned time. It develops a reasoned discourse that promotes the conditions of science as well as those of politics. But is this *all* there is to know? Doesn't *to live* assume a mode of intelligence or, to express it better, of 'understanding', which, being woven with the passing of time, and even without our thinking about it, without our thinking about thinking about it, grips us with its adhesive effect – instead of a distancing and *enlightening* through thought? Isn't knowledge simply the enlightened face of what is only made possible by its connivent other side, against which it leans, only for it to become forgotten? This connivence is a shadowy learning, which remains integrated in its surroundings, doesn't cut itself off from a landscape, doesn't extract itself from a conditioning and doesn't separate theory from practice or detach a 'self' from the world: it *predates* every possible exposition, coming before any explanation – and, above all, it doesn't question.

Connivence is that learning which hasn't broken its attachment. The child on the mother's breast or in her lap practically still has only this form of learning. Then, with schooling, with the equalising settling down and distribution of learning in disciplines, objects stand out and are isolated, plans are distributed that must be linked by reason: connivent learning is covered over once the knowing subject conquers its autonomy. It is also this connivent learning, which is excessively complex when it is considered from the outside, that anthropologists discover in cultures that are said to have remained 'primitive'. In other words, they have been separated from it: it is a learning where meaning and intelligence aren't dissociated, in which comprehension occurs through acts and discovery is made through each limb, where prudence is supreme and vigilance is its path of acquisition, where humans remain actively involved in their environment and find partners everywhere around them with whom to silently converse: with the mountains and the waters; with the dead; with animals, the spirits and the plants. Connivence comes to them from what is lived in unison: with the elements, with the ages and with the seasons.

2 Is this connivence nothing more than a vestige, about which we perhaps remain secretly nostalgic, but that we have definitively consigned to its past – a lost paradise of our own childhood as of that of humanity? Or doesn't it still weave a ground of understanding within us as between us in a subterranean, but active, way, in silence, predating the work of knowledge and ready to reappear? Don't two lovers experience this reappearance together? – Or isn't this reappearance what allows them to *live* as lovers? Isn't this hidden resource what they rediscover together and that they uphold as they withdraw from the commerce in knowledge and its bustle? And so they may spend a whole day speaking together without really saying anything, in any case *nothing* that would be worthy of interest or from which an object could be made, that could be retained as a statement. Saying 'nothings' which do nothing but speak of their connivence: 'Have you seen?', 'do you know that...' Beneath the banality of the exchange, they revive an assent together as they breathe: the entire day is this blinking of eyes – what Rousseau called 'amorous prattle'. Indeed, that we are able to speak without saying anything can be understood in two opposed senses: either it is vain and the word is hollow, or it is, so to speak, 'full': they have no need of a 'something' to express, as Aristotle would like, since they speak only in order to forge the *intimacy* between them. In this regime of connivence, one can equally well be silent as speak and either one amounts to the same thing: to be silent is not dumbness, not even being reserved; it doesn't embarrass or weigh on them. And to speak, even to say nothing, isn't to be talkative.

I even wonder if the whole of social life (in the family, in groups and even in business) isn't based on a lot more connivence than is suspected: words that teach nothing and don't even aim at anything, but which maintain a relation of adherence, folding the sphere of exchange into its 'surroundings' and allowing understanding to filter through – all the more so in that they don't 'communicate' a message and don't provide information. To survive in society, haven't I had to learn what I had never been told, or that was never expressed to me, which may even go against what I had so often been told, and all that I've been taught, in a connivent way through discreet registering and at the level of experience? Whatever the effort involved in grasping knowledge, doesn't it always remain something more fundamental, something that, eluding expression, can only be shared silently? Indeed, aren't we all placed in a connivence inherent to being human, as *living* beings? This has never been completely formulated, in spite of the millennia of literature, in every language as in every country, but it means that we tacitly understand our condition, palliating its want of 'sufficient reason', and therefore predating any externalisation through the word, of any explanation and possible clarification.

Isn't poetry in its entirety, when it corresponds with its vocation and unless it is nothing but discourse in verse, a connivent way of speaking reconnecting us with the immanence of what is vital and that favours a whole play of internal understandings and adherences (of images, rhymes and assonances)? Or let's say that in poetry, as it deploys such an echo chamber, the word withdraws in connivence. Rather than fitting into a discursive progress, it tries to give voice to this *implicit* which is that of a more *fundamental* nature, which cannot ordinarily emerge through the word – knowledge has no hold over it. In short, poetry reverses the relation and encourages humans to retrace their steps. Where knowledge would be what breaks with connivence, the poetic word detaches itself from the discourse of knowledge and returns to something originary and 'primitive'. In fact, don't we need to change *ethos* in order to operate within ourselves a discreet but profound mutation of the mind (something like a conversion), and *again become connivent* – as one speaks of becoming a child again – if we are to read a poem? Isn't the naivety of the poetic – a *naivety* that is more than serious, in the profound sense of romanticism – of this order?

3 A 'landscape' occurs when my knowing capacity is upset – or overturned – into *connivence*, when the relation of objectification, and above all of observation, that I maintain with the world is propelled into understanding and tacit communication. From knowing that I am in a relation with the 'land' (the knowledge of geography), I once more become connivent in a landscape. Not, strictly speaking – as has been said and repeated in Europe as if in compensation for the rationalism of knowledge – that I 'personify' elements of the landscape, or 'project' myself onto it, that I lend my subjectivity to things or animate the inanimate, common romanticism and gossipy romanticism (all of which are operations over which the subject still wants mastery and which are only facilitations). But, in fact, this transmutation takes place: when the land becomes landscape, what I grasp in it is no longer

alien but signals to me, 'speaks to me' or 'touches me', as is more familiarly said (but will we be able to emerge from this familiarity?). In other words, as the Chinese literati-painters have magnificently expressed it, when perceptive becomes affective at the same time, or when I perceive from within as well as from outside of myself, hence a dimension of infinity or mind then emanates from the physicality of things and emerges from it, with which my mind 'accords' (móu 谋, as the Chinese say strategically). The land becomes landscape – we know, or rather 'we know well', but Chinese thought-language has shown itself to be particularly endowed to express when something relational is established – when, as this 'corner of the land' establishes itself in this way in partnership, the bringing into tension that promotes it enters into me and causes me to share it. This means there's a 'landscape' when a relation is established (re-establishes itself) with this 'land', which takes me back upstream – finds its source on this side – of the one that is established by discursive reason; that the *place* suddenly becomes a 'link'; and that this 'corner of the land' from then on 'becomes world': that I link myself to it as to *what creates a world*.

If I find the experience of landscape revelatory, it is because it reveals my more fundamental involvement in the world, cancelling my ordinary relation (when I see nothing but 'land'), of which I would otherwise not be aware. Actually, I'd not even suspect it. But by suspending my function as a knowing subject, which constitutes me both intellectually and socially, at the same time I disentangle, in and through the landscape, what concealed this more elementary linkage. In this respect let's recognise that the dictionary in Europe still gives a rather short definition for 'landscape' (in the French *Robert*, 'part of a land which nature presents to an observer'). Wedged as it remains in knowledge's set purpose (the primacy of visual perception – the part–whole relation – the subject–object relation), it is unable to take account of this mutation that momentarily folds the opposition of self and world together, or disinters a more fundamental connivence between them, of whatever must come from the 'landscape'. At the same time, there is no amalgamating conversion, no compensatory slippage, into the ecstatic or the mystical, as extolled by so much bad lyricism in Europe. I don't lapse into any irrationalism (it's a question of being *before* reason and not polemically rejecting it) – on which the celebrated 'communion' or symbiosis with nature, coming in reparation for discursive reason, at the very least leaves an equivocation in the air.

Chinese thought-language in its plays of correlations has indeed very effectively been able to describe, through the landscape and the connivence I discover in it, how I can join together my relations with the world at a more elementary level. There's no need for a 'beautiful' landscape – a road sign, a 'panorama', or a postcard indicating a 'viewing point' actually contributes the least to connivence.

But in accordance with whatever 'understanding' is secreted, distilled and accumulated between 'us', between this landscape and myself, through an unwinding occurring again over the long term, due to the fact of return-ing to it or inhabiting it and thinking about it when absent (one also becomes an 'old friend' of the landscape), I find myself more anchored, *enté*, in my relation with the world. One encounter, one evening, on this detour from the path, is enough for this landscape, which has nothing extraordi-nary about it, to remain forever after with me in my thoughts so that a concordance beyond my own concordance could be scaled though it. A subject-self would therefore not be what is projecting itself onto the land-scape by making it the confidant of its emotion (what I just stigmatised as the banal posture of bad romanticism), but it would be the landscape which, by making itself conspicuous, brings me into its tensional field, res-onating with its variation (the landscape is like a *bow* 'which plays on my soul', as Stendhal said); it brings the reappearance – from beneath the mind as it asserts its autonomy (the insular knowing and wanting subject) – of my more original belonging in the world, a world that emerges from its indif-ference and to which my vitality is connected.

In actual fact, we live in the alternation of these two registers – or, more accurately, two regimes – even if it's the discursive aspect that, by intellec-tual penchant, (European) philosophy has most illuminated: I become discursant when I study or speak in public; I once more become connivent when I withdraw into an intimate relation or I am walking (which is just what 'wandering' is). When I set out on holiday, go for a walk, 'revitalise' myself, go into the forest, I retrocede, return to concordance and latent learning (in relation to the trees, the meadows, the mountain) and become connivent again, learning what I was. I press one key or the other on my internal keyboard, constantly moving the cursor from one pole to the other. For we live by discreetly moving from one to the other and in the agility to progress (assert) knowing or else retro-cede connivence, regressing from our autarkical self. Yet, for the knowing Subject, the ideal is to establish a design. But how, one step farther on, should one name the other side of this, another side that remains in the shadow, which confers and increases capac-ity, but does so in silence, without our even having any regard for this continuing process, until finally we notice its result?

XI

Maturation (vs Modelisation)

1 I'd place 'maturation' among those unfortunate terms that apparently evoke the capacity for conduct only between the lines, through lack or as an expedient, and for which it is difficult at first sight to see how they could be raised to the dignity of a concept. It is a notion as modest as the indirect, receptivity or connivence, but one about which it is even more difficult to see how it could constitute a strategy. For maturation expresses internal development in nature working towards its result: it is the silent transformation of seeds, tissues or cells that cannot very easily be hastened – or, in any case, that can't be controlled: *what is never commanded*. It therefore expresses what arises from processes due to their own rhythm. It isn't governed externally and so eludes the grasp of the will. We don't 'make' something ripen, and the expression is inexact: we can only favour the conditions rendering maturation possible. In this respect, maturation is diametrically opposed to our capacity to construct an imperative and project it onto the situation by claiming the initiative: from the time of the Greeks, this is what we have conceived as the power of *modelisation*.

The 'model form', *eidos* εἶος, is in fact the Greek concept par excellence. Isn't it even philosophically the first one? In any case, it is what Plato relied upon to lift philosophy out of the obscure regime of experience and opinion and to construct his thought by conquering abstraction: the model-form is what the mind 'sees' of its own activity and makes things 'exist' in their truth and beyond appearances. Moral virtues are regulated on its basis to save them from empiricism and its routine; it is what the philosopher king founds his conception of political regimes and the ideal City upon, or on which the demiurge constructs the plan of the world, and this is done 'all for the better'. We know how much Aristotle distrusted any abandonment of the perceptible (the Platonic theory of ideas leading to leaving 'things themselves' behind), but he nevertheless maintained this charter of the *model form* determining what the thing itself 'is' by constituting both its legitimate cause (the 'final' cause) and its internal programme of development. Otherwise, if it did not have a basis in modelisation, it would mean, in the absence of causality, that everything real is just the result of blind chance and would be unable to justify its 'essence' – that by which it established its definition.

Yet in Europe we are so used to the practice of modelisation that we no longer see what is inventive in it: how strong a hold it has on the world, especially on what we call 'nature', and how it has been the object of classical, mechanistic and causalist physics, whose learning, via technology, has, over a few centuries, completely changed life on our planet. Since the time of the Greeks, this model has certainly been provided by mathematics, a model of the model. The inspired idea symbolised by the name Galileo, an idea as fertile as it is crazy, is that God has written the 'great book' of the world in characters which are ' triangles, circles and other forms' – in other words, in the designing language of geometry (in Galileo's *Assayer*). This was an unheard of stroke of audacity since we are well aware that these bodies that are eternally moving in a straight line and with a uniform movement in an infinite empty space, as Galileo conceived them, and that would lead to the formulation of the law of inertia, are never able physically to exist and that such a void is never encountered. And yet it is there, according to the famous formula of the philosopher Alexandre Koyré, 'to account for reality by the impossible'. Even so, we well know that the laws of motion can successfully be demonstrated in their universality as they govern physical bodies in this modelisation plan.

The bold step Galileo took in eliciting the value of this theoretical possibility of modelisation, which Plato had opened up by promoting a plan of essences – of which Archimedes was the great initiator in physics, and whose subsequent yield in this realm has proven to be unlimited (Galileo classed himself as a *philosophus platonicus*) – assumes that this ideal explanation of a phenomenal world would be completely purified and raised to the absolute which alone forms its truth. Released from the conditions of the world, even if conversely then submitting to them for verification (by experimentation), such modelisation is alone in furnishing an effective hold, and does so due to its exteriority unveiling *a priori* a necessity, allowing an account to be given of the physical facts occurring in this world, always in a particular way, and to use them to its advantage. In practice, this means that concrete phenomena and movements don't have any satisfactory explanation except in relation to an abstraction that also defines their perfection, even if this is never completely realised. But the question then arises of knowing how far this mastery obtained by modelisation can be extended, or what the sphere involved is. Can it be assumed that what has worked so well in the universe of physics has the same value, or the same success, when we move out of the realm of knowledge into that of the management of situations concerning human behaviour and strategy?

We don't, in principle, doubt this infinite extension. The general puts together a war plan instigating operations; the economist traces a growth curve describing the best future evolution; the politician draws up an electoral programme setting out how the campaign is to be conducted. In each case, it is a matter of constructing an imperative that is projected onto the situation to which one has to submit, just like wax impressed by the seal. The model defines the end sought, according to the old Greek coupling of *eidos-télos*, εἶδος –τέλος, and the means that will lead to it are determined from this stated aim: the more direct the means are, the more effective the plan will be judged to be. Clausewitz thus thought that the 'model', or absolute, war is what is prepared in a room, which the 'real' war, conducted *later* on the ground, will do what it can to approach. He is forced to recognise that a slippage is nonetheless inevitable from what he called the 'friction' that emanates from 'circumstances'. Or, rather, Clausewitz will finally see the essence of war or what formed its concept here – but which, concerning strategy, also constitutes its failure: as soon as it is engaged in, war always deviates from its projected model. This is always so: the essence of war is that it never takes place in the terrain that has ideally been prepared for it. Hence, Clausewitz ultimately distrusted the possibility of real strategy and would stop thinking about it, resigning himself to doing no more than 'cultivating' his general.

2 I find it remarkable that the *Arts of War* in ancient China, which I've already mentioned, aren't formed in terms of modelisation and *application*, and therefore in view of a means to an end, but from condition to consequence, and accordingly in terms of *process* and *maturation*. We already know that the good general isn't the person who draws up a plan in advance, but someone who detects the elements that favour him and, from an 'evaluation' of conditions encountered (the ancient meaning of *ji* 计), directs the deployment of their *situational potential*. But this 'directing' is too active and interventionist. Let's rather say that he supports the development of these favourable conditions as he exploits what constitutes the propitious 'terrain' (the notion of 形 'xíng'), or, as the *Laozi* says, that he aids what appears naturally. The art of strategy is therefore about making the hoped-for result come about from the implied situational development: strictly speaking, there's no specific 'goal' to aim at but an advantage to be 'harvested' (to be 'reaped': the character *li* 利, depicting the ear of grain and the scythe to cut it). This is why he does not operate or 'act' until conditions are ripe, and, when he does act, he will not actually be 'acting' – the familiar theme of 'non-acting', *wú wéi* 无为, which doesn't at all imply renunciation or passivity: success comes when a ripe fruit is ready to fall. This doesn't so much entail patience (a quality that remains too moral and psychological and is again linked to the subject-self) as the capacity to let the situation itself produce its effects from the 'bait', or the seed, that has been sown there, and whose development one accompanies as it *evolves of itself*. I wait for the situation to reach the point at which it is mature before intervening – consequently, I hardly intervene. For instance, from what I was once told, Marshall Giap waited for two months before deciding upon the assault that would result in the fall of Dien Bien Phu in Vietnam, saying that 'It's not yet ripe … '.

A land of agriculturists and not of breeders of livestock (who were only to be found on the borders), China has constantly thought about a phenomenon that is as strange as it is familiar: the ripening of a plant. We don't see the cob of corn growing, a phenomenon that is both universal and continuous, but one day we notice that it is ripe and it is time for it to be cut. A peasant, Mencius tells us (II, A, 2), must refrain from 'tugging at the shoots' in order to obtain growth: in other words, he must avoid 'directly' seeking an effect. That would mean he would be straining the process and soon cause the plant to wither: taking such an active role and importing and imposing his plan, he has unknowingly produced a counter-effect. But should he then do the opposite and stay passively on the edges of the field and watch it grow? I'm waiting for it to grow ... What should he 'do'? What any peasant knows: at intervals, 'hoc' and weed around the base of the shoot and promote its growth from one day to the next. He should neither put pressure on the shoots (by taking an active part) nor watch it growing (passivity), neither force the process nor leave it alone. It requires nothing inspired or heroic ('there is nothing to praise about the great general') but what is *modest* and discreet, and just *carries* the effect along. The shoot can (and must) be primed, stimulated and assisted, but *as it progresses* it forms itself in its own way.

This is so for any maturation, including what alludes to inner life, which Mencius also tells us follows its own course just as water does. In fact, water advances only proportionately – let's clearly understand this principle which expresses a lot while seemingly saying nothing: 'Water won't go any farther if it hasn't filled in the hollows in its course' (VII, A, 24). Yet 'to penetrate' by means of the mind and to 'com-prehend' are just as much of the order of maturation: accumulation and the passing through occur step by step and so produce a *self-deployment* that is beyond our control. It is impossible to dispense with any of the stages, to straddle the landmarks or induce comprehension. Conversely, whenever it fills up a hollow it has encountered, water naturally overflows so that it can advance. It continues to progress imperturbably, borne along by its own movement. The same thing goes for the mind: from what our own efforts have started to clarify, the light acquired is propagated and spreads progressively and 'communicates' thoroughly, going from one thought to another and from one mind to the next without our being aware of it, *sponte sua*, as it makes connections that branch out from it. This continues until one day we finally harvest the fruit, like a narrowly acquired victory, as we suddenly realise that we 'have an idea', have 'discovered': a *eureka* moment.

3 We then realise that it is arbitrary to speak of 'dead time', or rather that this expression is inconsistent and unreflective. What Clausewitz most hated in war was the time when one doesn't act and therefore when nothing apparently happens. Dead time would simply be a loss of time that unleashes the sequence of actions and engagements. Yet a dead time is, on the contrary, a period in which the process involved continues to develop discreetly, in which the seed ripens before emerging: this 'dead' time is living time. That is how ramifications are imperceptibly woven, as displacements silently take place and consequently modifications are secretly produced. And this occurs before the situation has started to tip over and its result become more harshly apparent – this last period is just the prominent result of it. Or, in inner life, it is when one does nothing, doesn't think but

73

muses or relaxes, that ideas begin to ripen and expand. It is then that they fecundate, experimenting, connecting, and making their way imperceptibly before declaring themselves to thought.

Because they are arbitrary, wouldn't the demands of modelisation therefore be vain compared with this silent development of what is *effective*? These demands won't disappear, but perhaps they aren't where we think they are: their effectiveness would have been moved to another level. We construct an imperative – and this also applies in society, in the City, as in every enterprise – because this ideality projected before us makes an advance, with everything that is adventurous about this 'making': this project determines a progress as it takes off – no doubt excessively, but with an abuse that is propulsive – from the immanence of the process. Let's say that we form models in order to *mobilise*. A model, as Plato had already said, contains its relevance in itself, in its theoretical form, and not in the fact that it can be implemented: I trace a map of the ideal city because this ideality furnishes a foothold – or, better, a springboard – that promotes *the* political, which is essentially the construction of a project, to be distinguished from 'politics' (which is only management of the balance of power) – and therefore, from the outset, isn't concerned with whether such a city could ever exist. We are well aware of how an electoral programme is even enacted not to be applied but to stimulate thought, debate and choice, so as to arouse desire and give the project of progress a shape – in short to create democracy, even if it is fantastical. This is why the Greek thing of modelisation goes hand in hand with the invention of the political and of the City. Yet we know that China has traditionally lacked democracy. This is not just because it hasn't conceived of the institution, but above all because, attentive to discreet maturations, it hasn't promoted modelisation which, as a principle, is devised in unison and in public. This is what, as it formalises aspiration, creates the civic community.

A good strategist (a 'great man'), knowing how to fold together these two opposed resources, will do both: he models in order to mobilise minds and wills, because he knows that freely invoked human potential is a force that drives history, but this also makes the situation ripen discreetly (or allows it to) so that – or in such a way that – this modelling would be able to promote itself without having to be forced to the point of the Revolution also bringing about a reaction, a 'Restoration' which will henceforth permanently threaten it, or that then gives itself the justification to pursue any means at all in order to impose itself, with a view to what is the 'right' End that has been announced. In fact, this construction of an imperative contains the risk that, without the implication of a compensatory realism on its reverse side or in its shadow, it will go even as far as cynicism in the guise of idealism – this is evidently what politics suffers from in contemporary democracies, including on what is called the 'left'. There's no shame in leaving something to mature. It also commends the ethical intelligence which is that of implied processes leading to their results: trust in the silent transformation of maturation therefore has nothing in common with ordinary pragmatism, to which politicians are too often resigned and which rightly earns them criticism. Indeed, because it is not steered, history will only be able to grope its way forwards as long as we cannot strategically reconcile the production of the model, which promotes the ideal, and the procedural progression of what is real. Hence, it will be by fits and starts and therefore will go from one disappointment to another, its course taking no notice of *regulation*, and so it will become far too violently forced.

XII

Regulation (vs Revelation)

1 As the most conspicuous of divergences extending into history, between Chinese culture and those of the Mediterranean basin (the 'three monotheisms'), China is assumed to have known neither the Word nor Revelation. 'God' never made himself known there. A few elementary traces emerged from the River, on the back of a dragon or tortoise, *Hetu* or *Luoshu*, linking proto-writing to the groundless Ground of the advent of the world (*shén lǐ* 神 理), of which they are the first representation (as *wén* 文; cf. *Wenxin diaolong*, ch. 1),[1] but they aren't such as to constitute a Message. 'Heaven doesn't speak', Confucius said (*Analects*, XVII, 19) – however, 'the seasons follow their course, all existents prosper': 'what need would Heaven have for speaking?' In its image, the Sage would also like 'not to speak'; he'd like to avoid having his teaching being constituted – and fixed – in what is expressed, that might be 'propagated' and debated, that might be in need of proof or that lays claim to the truth. Such a word, in being imposed, would be an imposition; it would inevitably be an *add-on*. It would also present an obstacle to coherence proceeding through immanence, *sponte sua*, such as the way that the regulated course of the seasons, the endless engendering of beings, is constantly being realised under our gaze. Any insistence in this respect would be to interfere with it; any stress given to it would already be a *deviation*.

In the beginning that constitutes Genesis, God causes the world to emerge due to his creation, detaching it from the *confusion* of the formless: he instigates an order by separating the elements day by day. This advent is a rupture, proceeding from a pure Will infected by no influence, which enters into no interaction and already signals towards the story of Salvation. Yet the first lines of the *Oracle of Change*, whose antiquity and centrality at the heart of Chinese culture are comparable to Genesis, relate no such History or set any Narrative in motion. No Meaning is projected onto it, but a first formula is advanced that accounts for the *coherence* at work and whose linking up of the seasons illustrates it (beginning, *yuán* 元; springing up [*essor*], *hēng* 亨; profit (harvest), *lì* 利; rectitude, *zhēn* 贞). These four words suffice simply by their succession, with each continuing the previous one, in expressing a course that is not separated from its 'way'. Hence, this logic of *regulation* will submerge the expectation of a Revelation and render it superfluous, since it is a circular formula. This is because 'rectitude', which means that the course of things doesn't deviate, allows this course to renew itself and experience a fresh surge [*essor*] – this is what will represent the notion of Heaven tending to assimilate itself to Nature apprehended in its infinite renewal. Order isn't introduced from without, nor does it express a progress: it is internal to the unfolding and promotes it in the process of the world, which continues without wearing itself out.

In China, 'Heaven' becomes this first term that is the foundation not of a Faith but of our confidence in such a *continuum* from which the reality–viability of things comes – the 'way', *tao*, expressing both at the same time, or, rather, both having the same meaning. Prevailing over the earlier notion of Shangdi – a 'Lord on High' who was prayed to, who was feared, to whom sacrifices were made and who reigns over the human world (and does so even so far as to marginalise this notion during this late period of antiquity) – 'Heaven' comes to name this groundless Ground of the Process of the world which, by the internal alternation that governs it and forms its 'coherence' (*tiān lǐ* 天理), is called upon to perpetuate itself *from itself*. It is therefore not, as in Genesis, that a first beginning opens time and forms an Event, but that every beginning, at every moment, is a discreet priming that will amplify itself and establish its path. In the same way, there is no final end – no Apocalypse is announced, but as much as such a course is *regulated*, then any end is at the same time the bearer of a new beginning, and this course is just a continuous transition. There is therefore no causality to assume or finality to project (in Greek: *aitia-télos* αἰτία -τέλος), but an *operativity* is constantly at work (as *yòng* 用) from the polarity which thereby takes shape and becomes *physicality* (as *tǐ* 体). This reveals 'Heaven' and 'Earth' which, by coupling, form the matrix of this system of which *yin* and *yang* are the factors.

2 This notion of *regulation* will therefore have to be extracted from its usage, which in Europe has continued to be local. This use has either been technical (the regulation of traffic), physiological (as a homeostatic condition, for example in the thermal regulation of an organism) or economic (the regulation of markets). It will need to be elevated from this local usage to a conceptual level, even the most general one – even one that, faced with Revelation, will also actually come to mean the absolute. In fact, the *coherence* of such an operation envelops us universally at every level, within as well as outside of us, and indeed it is all we ever experiment with – if we don't, this 'real' becomes no longer 'viable' and withers away. Yet it dispenses with having to question the origin, to pose the Beginning and the End, disregarding the insolent 'why': an equilibrium is maintained throughout the heart of change, which confers its 'constancy' (*cháng* 常) and consequently its permanence to the unfolding. An order isn't established in advance, nor is it introduced from Elsewhere: there's neither an enigma to penetrate nor a mystery to be examined, no explaining or unveiling to be done. Bringing this immanence into the light, *elucidating* what comes 'from oneself in this way', will suffice. A reciprocity is then 'encouraged' between opposed factors forming a polarity whose interaction, by maintaining a 'harmonious' relation across its variation, is sufficient to allow the collaboration at work

to be grasped in its 'inexhaustible' ground (*wú qióng* 无穷) – hence there's no need for 'revelation'.

Hence, too, being maintained *in process*, regulated as it is, constitutes the only requirement and takes the place of an ideal. The whole of reality 'is' only in progress, ceaselessly balancing itself and compensating for itself, from which its renewal arises ('one time *yin* – one time *yang* [alternatively *yin* and *yang*], such is the way … ', *Oracle of Change*, 'Xici', A, 5). This is why, when everything is taken into consideration, the only requirement that matters for the ground is not to deviate from its internal coherence so as to stay in transformation: not to stop – or become blocked – in any position. And this is valid for the course of behaviour as much as for that of the process of things, providing the basis for morality as for what we call first philosophy or cosmology – the one only 'prolongs' the other (*jì* 继, ibid.). On reading the *Analects* of Confucius, we are at first surprised to find no fixed rules (prescribing action) any more than definition (fixing essences) in them. Yet, not only does the *rule* respond to action as *regulation* does to transformation (and Chinese thought hasn't isolated an 'act' with a beginning and an end), but the two are above all diametrically opposed in terms of their principle. A *rule* prescribes in advance; by starting from 'method', it projects a norm as it is authorised by a more general necessity that overflows any specific case in point. Thus, the characteristic of the rule is that it should be 'applied' – in which it relates to modelling. *Regulation*, on the other hand, arises from an internal appropriateness that constantly depends on the situation and always varies as it is transformed: it therefore doesn't allow itself to be reduced to the identical – in other words, to be 'identified' and *codified*. The proliferation of 'rites', *lǐ* 礼 in China, acts as a counterbalance as compartmental norms 'channel' behaviour – in other words, regulate it like a water course that is always threatening to overflow. And they are far more effective in that they operate without our knowledge and so are more profoundly assimilated.

   This explains why the Confucian topic avoids generality, of prescription as well as abstraction, and does no more than show the way. The Master is content to *remark* and *indicate* in relation to each interlocutor according to the moment in which he is in his course and the stage he has reached: he doesn't set out lessons, but on each occasion shows an excess or a defect that leads to a deviation from the way and hinders the disciple in his progress. For he must effect a continuous progress until he rises to the state of pure processuality such that the self-regulation of his behaviour embraces the inexhaustible renewal of the Ground of things, that harmony with the world as well as with oneself that serves as auto-nomy (Confucius: at seventy years of age, I am following my desire without deviating from the norm). If even his dearest disciple, Yan Hui, was discountenanced (*Analects*, IX, 10) and sighed that 'I see it before me and suddenly it is behind me', if he wanted to infer a rule or, so to say, erect a model, but finally realises that he will have to renounce it (that this 'that', *zhi*, he wants to achieve isn't codifiable), it is because this is a question of such a delicate 'balancing', commentators would say: that it cannot be determined, and that this is why the Master's purpose in itself is 'subtle' and indexed and cannot be fixed (*wēi yán* 微言). Yet, just as it constantly varies, as its continual adaptation requires, this equilibrium that cannot be named (standardised) is also the only one that allows behaviour to maintain its steadfastness through the evolution taking place, and this 'steadfastness' is consequently understood as moral steadfastness, in the sense of an unshakeable *tenacity*.

The only rule of wisdom, in short, is to be without a fixed rule – that's why there is *regulation* but no 'rule' – and this is how the integrity of its receptivity is maintained (*Analects*, XIV, 41). This is so even if the Sage's receptivity, seen from outside, is judged as opportunism (XIV, 34); and if others find nothing to praise in him (IX, 2; VIII, 19) – indeed, would have nothing to say about him (VII, 18) – this means that the Sage is without character or quality. For only what is sufficiently stabilised to be determined can be named. Other Sages are classed by categories that oppose them to one another: according to whether they remain attached to their integrity or they display tolerance, whether they withdraw in disgust from the world or come to terms with it. Confucius is aware of opposing them all precisely because he is without a definite position and that he 'can' equally be one or the other, evolving from one to the other, depending on the situation as it occurs (XVIII, 8). According to the terms of the alternative that will be posed to all Chinese literati, he is as equally disposed to 'take on a task' as to 'abandon it', and remains open to any opportunity: when it comes to wisdom, he is the 'moment', as Mencius would appropriately say about him (V, B, 1). That is why his personality is without hindrance, his mind is without dogmatism and he is indefinable.

I shall, therefore, now translate the central notion of Chinese thought, itself expressing 'centrality' (the notion of *zhōng* 中), as 'regulation', maintaining its evolution through non-deviation and producing an unhindered unfolding, conceived as it is for any use and applicable on any occasion (the complementary notion of *yōng* 庸; see the *Zhongyong*, having become one of the classics of the literati). This is regulation 'in ordinary usage', as it evolves from one extreme to the other, without partiality and not rejecting any possibility, not becoming bogged down on any side, and not, as it has been translated, as the 'middle way' or the 'golden mean' – thus determining a fixed and ideal point between excess and default and defining it as a particular quality and type, as is the case with Aristotle's 'mean amount' ('liberality' thereby being a determined golden mean between avarice and prodigality, and so on). For we already know that 'by attaching oneself to the centre' we are also making it a position, and therefore an exclusion, and so 'despoiling the way', by promoting one possibility but missing a hundred others (*Mencius*, VII, A, 26). This means refraining from evolving from one end to the other and from experiencing, through the amplitude of behaviour, the plenitude that is both 'viable' and 'liveable'. While the well-intentioned person still makes an effort, the Sage is someone who reaches it spontaneously – *cóng zóng zhōng dào* 从容中道 – in which it merges with the Regulation of Heaven, as it governs the process of the world: a capacity that becomes immanent, but passes unperceived, while constantly being at work. Or, rather, it will be unperceived because it is constantly at work. In this respect, it is opposed to the Annunciation of the Revelation, effectively rupturing it.

3 It's easy to illustrate this. Chinese medicine is obviously a medicine of *regulation*, and this is so in the most general way. To those who still doubt that cultures can carve out inventive divergences between one another, each opening up another possible approach (to health in this case), the opposition between the two medicines of the Chinese and the Europeans provides a testimony that is not at all speculative, for it is directly confirmed in the practice and management of cases. In the same way, if we believe – or fear – that any cultural diversity, due to globalisation, is doomed to disappear, the contrary can be shown by attesting how strongly these two medicines are called upon to deploy their *resources* in parallel: still today, or perhaps even more tomorrow than today, we choose to go to the (European) surgeon or the (Chinese) acupuncturist – or we can cross from one to the other (without mixing them up), so as to take advantage of both modes of efficacy.

Western medicine manifestly arises from modelling. The Greeks thought about *defining* health so much that they were able to distinguish, when it came to living itself, between ideal and actual health, or between absolute and relative health, the latter of which alone authorises a latitude between health as it is conceived (paradigmatically) by philosophers and that which is studied (practically) by doctors and 'physicians'. Moreover, Western medicine trusts in the imperious and definite action of its effects – just listen to our vocabulary: you are 'operated' upon, which is an 'intervention'. Yet we know that Chinese medicine doesn't aim so much to cure the sick person as to maintain health. Again, it is a matter of strategically intervening beforehand, at the level of conditions, therefore of having as little 'intervention' as possible, since this is at a stage at which deregulation has hardly started and so is easily rectified, and to do this through treatment which is itself also an unfolding that allows for time and so 'operates' gently. There is nothing more foolish than saying, as one often hears, once more giving in to the prestige of the event: 'I've fallen sick!' In fact, one never 'falls' sick. But a tiny deviation (outside of the regulated path of health) has been set in motion which, if we aren't careful, if we don't remain vigilant, will continue to make its way until it assumes an infinite development, one day breaking out and being (officially) diagnosed as 'sickness'.

4 At the historical level and in political management, regulation will be conceived in opposition to Revolution – don't Revelation and Revolution

moreover maintain a secret link: the same belief in a rupture in time, an analogous expectation of the Event that will change everything? As Revolution is noisy, emphatic and spectacular, so regulation is silent, discreet and accomplished without announcing itself. Revolution is a radicalisation – a hypertrophy? – both of *modelling* and of *action*: its 'practice' responds to its 'theory'; an imperative is projected, which one then strives to fit to the facts by means of the forced entry we all recognise. This is what history latches on to. But regulation passes imperceptibly because, by constantly maintaining equilibrium between the factors that are in tension, it cannot be detached from the continuous course of things – nor is it constituted as a programme and this means it cannot be 'applied'. While Revolution is set in train by a goal (the ideal of a better society), exciting consciences and splitting the supporters of the Future and of the Past into two camps, regulation is an unfinalised process; it doesn't even suggest that it constitutes Progress, and introduces rupture still less, for not being seen in operation. In being processual, it isn't even 'consensual', since one is caught up in it without having chosen it: it cannot be constituted as an object *about* which we have to make a decision.

We can see how opposed the two are and how they follow on from one another in the history of China over the course of the twentieth century. Following the break instituted by imperialist Europe, China first borrowed the revolutionary (Marxist-Leninist) model from it, which it applied scrupulously and dogmatically as a truth, but Mao owed his success to the fact that he then inflected it so that it could be adapted. In fact, a logic of regulation was already secretly substituted, as happened each time that the gulf that had become hollowed out between the model and the reality became too glaring and showed that the course being followed was no longer 'viable' (China being a land of peasants and having proletarian masses only in Shanghai). The Great Leap Forward and the Cultural Revolution, a 'total' revolution, then went vociferously back to the logic of a great Forcing that, of itself, would bring forth its compensating reversal. A regime of regulation has since then prevailed, promoted by Deng Xiaoping in a non-modelled way when he undertook the silent transformation of China, going from socialism to hyper-capitalism and the bulimia of enrichment without a rupture and without an event: power liberalises but also periodically suppresses, sometimes accelerates and sometimes slows down, blows sometimes hot and sometimes cold, a hand 'opens' and then 'closes again' (*fàng-shǒu* 放守). According to the Chinese language, the 'Events of Tian'an Men' (in 1989) would not even be an 'event', in terms of what this suggests of rupture and uprising (which the Latin expresses so well: *e-venit*), but an embarrassing 'affair' (*shì-jiàn* 事件) calling for its rectification. Deng Xiaoping, the 'little helmsman', refrained from theorising: to cross the river, he contented himself with proposing, it's enough to put your foot on one stone and then on the next. And, in this very radical transformation that China has today experienced, power is essentially *vigilant* – rather than being erected from a plan – with respect to threatening deregulations, and is concerned instead with extinguishing any advent of fracture or conflagration. But will China, as it gains hegemony, becoming a world power and having to assume its responsibilities in the history of the world, continue to be content to regulate and not to have to pay the heavy price or run the risk of a modelling in its responsibility, which it would need to invent?

There will therefore be two modes in the management of things to think about. As with *action* and *transformation*, one of them ostensibly promotes itself between a beginning and an end, while the other discreetly distils itself through an unfolding, so that 'regulating' and 'regularising' erect an antinomy. We will therefore have to learn to discern both, and to do so at the most elementary level, as it is commonly seen before us. Traffic can be regulated in a normative way, with marked-out passageways and red lights, a highway code and 'rules' to be respected. This involves prohibition and permission: we stop, or go on – it is entirely predicated on a regulation. But anyone with just a little experience of traffic in a Far Eastern megapolis (a recent memory of Hanoi) realises that there is a completely different possibility in the art of managing the flow. There are neither traffic lights nor any other form of signalling at the crossroads. No one stops among the vast mass of cycles, scooters and vehicles of all sorts that constantly block the road in crossing, but everyone continues to advance, more and more vigilantly: each of them, as they sound their horns, anticipates what he is passing but also allows others to pass, constantly avoiding them but without letting himself be carried off course, both giving way and progressing. In this mobile compression in continuous adaptation, an outlet opens in proportion to this massive crush that never ceases flowing: a redistribution emerges from it at each instant, due to an uninterrupted operating of possibilities, without crashes – or almost – each one following their own path.

I wonder if this doesn't today represent, insidiously but universally, a paradigm shift: from the model of Revelation–revolution, from the rule and its application, to the unmodelled model of regulation; if this isn't a case of a silent transformation of the ideology of the world swinging from the political (modelling and applying) into what has become – and not only in relation to nature – an *adaptation* to the environment, an 'ecological' adaptation if you like, allowing processes, as they self-regulate, to maintain their 'viability'. It's true that this swing is kept in the shadows and has never been presented as an event in the history of thought, much less as an alternative giving the possibility of choosing. Thus, we notice it in the very evolution of these concepts and the slippage from one to the other. Even with a thinker as innovative as Freud, we see the term 'regulation', *Regulierung*, begin to make its way in relation to the 'mobile quantity' operating within the psychic apparatus, as well as in investment displacements ('automatic' displacements he calls them, but is this the correct term?): since it is really a matter of avoiding a blockage or a jamming, those that lead to traumatic 'fixation' and once again making 'viable'. But, here as elsewhere, it doesn't seem to me that this notion, as it enters indirectly, would ever be justified or ostensibly take sides against the reign of the cause and the act, which is still so present in Freud. Yet if 'to regularise' really comes from 'to regulate', the Latin *regulare*, it turns against it and seditiously reverses logic, by making the 'silent transformation' embarked upon – of which the subsequent event is only a result – understood.

Note

1   The *Wenxin diaolong* 'The Mind of Literature and Carving Dragons', a literary critique written by Liang-period scholar Liu Xie 劉勰 (d. 522) [trans.].

XIII

Silent Transformation (vs Resonant Event)

1 I'll call *silent transformation* a transformation which occurs without a sound, therefore about which we don't say anything. It is silent in these two senses: it operates without warning and it wouldn't occur to anyone to speak about it. Its imperceptibility isn't of the order of the invisible since, on the contrary, it happens in a patent way, before our eyes, spreading gradually. Nevertheless, for two linked reasons, it isn't conspicuous: because it is both universal and continuous, it is never sufficiently differentiated on one point or another, or from one moment to the next, to introduce a rupture that might hold our attention. It is never, so to speak, sufficiently differentiated for anyone to notice it. As it concerns every part of it, and as it takes place over a long period, nothing is sufficiently detached from it as to cause it to emerge. Or, when it finally does emerge, it is understood and spoken about only by way of its results.

This is what makes this transformation 'silent' and not invisible: it isn't isolatable or locatable, and is mingled in with its unfolding. We note that sight is the sense of the discontinuous and the local: the eyelids open and close, like a curtain that is raised and lowered, but hearing is the sense of the continuous. We say we 'turn a deaf ear', but we can't do it: we no longer listen, but we still hear. In the same way, we necessarily look to one side or the other, at one aspect or another, always in a partial and specific way – but we hear comprehensively: while sight, being projected outside, momentarily falls on one point or another, hearing is the funnel, or cornet, that constantly amasses from all sides. So such a transformation will be called silent because, arising from the *auditory*, as the sense of what is ambient and regular, it nevertheless tends to escape our attention. In contrast to the privilege the Greeks accorded to sight, including to the 'eye of the soul', when our eyes no longer see, it is therefore our *hearing* (for it is also a 'hearing' of the mind) that will need to be developed, that one must learn to train, in order to enter *universal* and *continuous* perception processes. The truth is that the course of things continues by night as in broad daylight (Baudelaire): 'Listen, my dear, listen to the sweet Night on the march.'

The articulation to consider will therefore be that which links this silent unfolding with what I would call, by opposition, its *resounding emergence*. I'd even say that the more silent the transformation is in its course, the more resonant is its result and the more sound it makes when it erupts; what we didn't perceive as it developed then comes back to us a lot more violently and full in the face. Or, expressed in a contrary way: the event is all the more resonant for the transformation that led to it being discreet, and that it progressed without warning. This occurs to such a point that one starts to wonder, shaking this myth, whether an 'event' actually exists in isolation – in other words, dissociated from time and effecting a rupture with it (*e-venit*)? Detaching itself in a singular moment, don't we take what the advent has produced so silently that it has escaped us (having done so 'by night', if I can now dare to use this adverbial phrase) for a sudden appearance?

Yet isn't everything in what we call 'reality' (the term we think is the most neutral, but which is so laden and lacking in subtlety – that is, perhaps, opaque) a *silent transformation*? In nature, we can't perceive rivers as they hollow out their beds, or the winds as they wear down the summits, since their actions are so diffuse and continuous, but it is nevertheless they that have, little by little, designed the relief that we have in front of us and that forms the landscape. Or let's take global warming. It involves so many diverse and interrelated factors, and it does so over the course of time; it is a phenomenon of such universality that we don't see the earth warming up – but we notice after the event that the glaciers have melted and that schools of fish have migrated farther north, or have gone deeper into the sea. Or let's take History: revolutions are much more resonant and make so much noise because we don't know how to hear the slow, global and continuous transformations that make progressive inflections and simultaneous evolutions, of which they are the shattering outlet.

2 We don't perceive our children growing up, or perceive ourselves growing old. Because *everything* within us ages and because it does so ceaselessly, we don't perceive ourselves *ageing*. This has meant that in Europe we have made it an age, a state, a being ('old age'), while finding ourselves at a loss about how to mark its effective beginning: when did I start to age? Yet we learn that cellular death has made its mark even before we have been born: the process is too continuous for us to be able to give it a date and, as it affects everything within us, we can never specify or separate any 'place' for it within us. 'Everything': not only our hair as it turns grey, but also the brightness of our looks, the timbre of our voice, the complexion of our face and the texture of our skin … And the bearing and actions and appearance … And thought and sleep … *Everything*: there will be no end to expressing this 'everything'. And as 'everything' is transformed, which we will never be able to inventory or enumerate to the end, as 'everything' within us ages and then nothing is sufficiently detached from it or separated so as to be noticed – or only anecdotally (the proverbial first white hair that women in their thirties discover when seeing themselves in their mirror). Then, one day, we come across a photo from our youth and exclaim: 'Oh how old I've become!' A 'resonant' event, even if we hold it *in petto* and keep it to ourselves: suddenly this observation rises up, as a result, in a way that we barely recognise ourselves. And then, suddenly doubting our own identity, we will even wonder: is this still 'me', still the same 'subject'?

We experience a loving separation as an event: lovers one day quarrel violently. They suddenly loudly accuse one another, precisely as 'subjects', 'you' and 'me', and they do so without any further consideration or attention to what, *in the situation*, is silently – insidiously – transformed: to how a fracture has become a fissure – a gash – a lack – a breach, and finally a trench – the *gap* – to such a point that, today, they've reached the moment that they contemplate the damage and record the result. A silence, a hesitation, a 'nothing' or, let's say, a 'nuance', something that has so far been considered anecdotal and, at most, simply an 'incident' has made its way silently or softly carved out its niche, thereby gradually contaminating and infesting everything, until this morning they discovered that they have actually reached a point at which they have become strangers to one another. Possibilities are imperceptibly retracted, intimacy is broken down by night, something unsaid has congealed, a wall of indifference has hardened as the hours or days have gone by, without their knowing how it happened or having noticed it. And, of course, with no bad 'will'.

Then one fine day, this wall that has silently been accumulated between them stands definitively before them, impassable and staring them straight in the face. To what extent are they, due to their own choices, themselves responsible for it as *subjects* of initiative and as they will then inevitably and clumsily accuse one another? Isn't it rather a general evolution that has gradually undermined their relationship, and has over the course of time become all the more dangerous in that it escaped them, that they did not hear its progress and therefore hadn't found sufficient reason – or basis – to discuss it? This discreet power implicated in the silent transformation is such that it ends, without our being aware of it, in what is finally resolutely confirmed as a complete reversal: we have gone from love to indifference, without having even noticed the fact. If the result now surprises us so much, retrospectively, in comparison with the past state, this staunch power is even greater since it nonetheless appears to us to have happened naturally, as a result of the situation and as carried along by the unfolding of things. And, as disconcerting as this may be, it almost seems intrinsic. In other words, what one would once have believed impossible, or could not even have imagined, has finally resulted from this silent unfolding that we are finally unable to control or oppose, or only in thinking about how astonishing it is.

3 The Chinese (Wang Fuzhi) speak of 'submerged displacement(s) – silent transformation(s)', 潛移 默化, to account for this imperceptible soundless pathway, about which we never think of speaking, but whose result is finally imposed. The first lesson to be drawn will therefore be that of the vigilance to be exercised, as previously in respect of health, to listen to this *discreet* modification. Chinese thought trains us for this because we know that it discerns a transformation in every state and a propensity in every situation, because in this way it has not so much aspired to divide the world in two, between physics and metaphysics, as to grasp the play of

influences and incidences that all the factors of the world exert correlatively together, weaving this world into its renewal. Thus, it learns to discern the inclination which, from the minimal and from the *local*, gradually ends in the *universal*, or goes from the tiny to the infinite (see *Zhongyong*, 23). It similarly makes us attentive to the detection of the slightest indications of a transformation which fundamentally escapes us ('Heaven'), at the same time as it is 'natural'. Rather than clinging to the (Platonic) opposition between the visible and the intelligible forming two levels of Being, it is inclined to examine the transition bearing on *emergence*, when the phenomenon is barely emerging from imperceptibility to the state of the 'subtle' (*wēi* 微), of the sketched, and is still only just dawning in the heart of what is perceptible. From the state of the settled and loud manifestation, it thereby teaches us to go back to its 'source' (*yuán* 源), to the time of the 'beginning' (the notion of *ji* in the *Oracle of Change*), when we begin – with difficulty – to understand the evolution to come, but that can already be predicted by following its features.

Chinese thought thus helps us to grasp more closely the processivity implied in the silent transformation, or what I earlier called by the familiar expression that it is henceforth necessary to assign to thought: 'to make one's way'. How, on the one hand, we articulate the long period during which the silent transformation remains unnoticed and, on the other hand, the suddenness of its resonant emergence, which constitutes an 'event', is still to be clarified. We are prepared to think of it as a rupture; in any event, we perceive a discontinuity from one to the other. For we don't see the ear of grain put forth, then suddenly one morning we notice that it is ripe and ready to be harvested; or we don't see the progress being made during an apprenticeship, then suddenly we take account of it and 'realise', one day, we have 'arrived'. Between the patience of the waiting and the gush of the result, the present – the median – escapes. 'As if by a leap', Mencius says laconically (VII, A, 41): it's precisely because progressivity is silent that only *after the event*, in surprise, do we take account of the advantage in which it ends, when the results are already apparent. But this consequent gushing forth, operating 'as if' by a bound, only apparently introduces a discontinuity.

4 Our reading of History will be able to benefit from this. When Braudel denounced factual history, as it is learned in school, formed of dates, actions and great subjects, of kings who ascend to the throne or who die, who make war or conclude treaties – in short, what he called the 'resonant event' – he was obliged at the same time to recognise, under this feverish staccato, what he couldn't call anything but the 'longue durée', the 'slow' duration or even the 'quasi immobility' of History – but for a historian wasn't this latter the expression of a limit? For example (*his* example), a universal and continuous mutation from 'feudalism' to 'capitalism' occurred in Europe over four centuries, from the fourteenth to the end of the eighteenth, that was as much economic, financial and social as it was political and ideological. It was

consequently one without heroes or events, and even without precise places (it occurred in Antwerp as well as in Genoa), during which time it effected its great project without dates or names that are remembered. What was this transition if not a 'silent transformation'?

Yet in retrospect this concept of *silent transformation* should also be envisaged as prospective, or descriptively let's consider it not as prescriptive but nevertheless *in loco* of the impossible method or the faltering model. If there is a 'benefit' (*li* 利) to be drawn from *silent transformations*, it is that they are more effective than *explosive actions*, those that are talked about and are sensational but which, being localised and momentary as well as dependent on the project of a subject, remain always more or less in the realm of (theatrical) representation and miracle (the *deus ex machina* of History). At the same time, isn't it inevitable that this benefit, being recognised only *after the event*, as a delayed action – if it is, indeed, recognised at all – should not be attributed to our ability (as great politicians know perfectly well)? For, carried along by the situation we have inferred, it then appears to result 'naturally' and could not attract attention, still less recompense. Great merit, which belongs to whoever has known how to set up these transformations (although by allowing them to follow their own course), is not seen. It mingles with its success, and this is why it has actually succeeded, assimilated by the situation and not by the forcing which is immediately noticed, but will infallibly produce resistance and counter-effect.

Thus, we prescribe psychiatric 'acts', as they are understood in medical circles, because they have a marked beginning and end, have been decided and justified by a responsible agent, so we can add and record them and consequently pay for them. But are these the most effective methods? What is a 'cure' in psychoanalysis if not precisely a silent transformation that makes its way slowly and silently to the point of once again restoring viability to psychic life? But can we recognise a silent transformation when it is eminently diffuse, avoids appropriation and is not assignable – will we be able to claim it? We can see that the question isn't simply theoretical. If, for the (real) great general, 'there's nothing to praise', as the *Sunzi* says, since he was so well aware of how to bring the victory to fruition in a silent way that it is thought to be 'easy' (and so it doesn't occur to us to thank him for it), this is found again equally in any management process, and therefore just as much in politics. So we prefer to announce measures and grand gestures, to which merit is attached ahead of time, rather than to initiate discreet modifications which, as they make their way by night, could actually reverse the tendency (for instance, today, in regard to unemployment and to the initiation of social mutations): when will we then make the 'silent transformation' into a strategic concept that illuminates 'maturation' and its power to proceed?

Our conception of effectiveness in Europe is linked, as it enhances the value of the act, to the purely descriptive and therefore to what is spectacular and heroic: for us it always comes, directly or indirectly, from the epic, the more so in a media regime whose function is to make resonant, fixated as it is on audience ratings, instead of being attached to what is discreet. Through abundantly commented upon 'sound bites', or incessantly repeated surveys, time is given no time, but 'an event' (which can be spoken about) needs to be created at any price, and its democratic life is perverted. And even though silent transformations create the reality of our society, when have you had the opportunity to give your opinion about them and vote? So we hardly know how to rely upon these covertly instituted transformations, which make their way in silence and then present their yield which, discreetly set in train, has a hold over the course of things because they are carried away by it, absorbed as they are by the situation, proceeding without being trumpeted, and even without becoming localised, in an 'evasive' way, as one might say, that cannot be defined. It's therefore necessary to give this *evasiveness* a status, because it is not definable and not locatable, because it is what brings us most radically out of the thought of Being from which it initially arises: in the will to mark a place for each 'thing' and to *assign* it.

XIV

Evasive (vs Assignable)

1 If there is a Greek choice, anchored in ontology, or what I'd call a 'ground of understanding', at whose heart the Greeks have thought, it is to consider that the more determined something is, the more it 'exists', that de-termination creates 'being'. This 'term' forming a limit, *peras* πέρας, as it marks borders, saves us from the inconsistency of the unlimited, the *apeiron* ἄπειρον (in the *Philebus*). Hence the undefined is, at once and in the same sense, whatever has no limit or end and is vague, indecisive and uncertain and therefore constitutes a dilution of being. For it is between a marked beginning and end, *arché–télos*, separating itself out into singular being, that everything assumes consistency, which is constituted as a presence–essence, an *ousia*. The characteristic of Greek thought is therefore to *assign*: to confer on each thing its own theoretical place, marked as 'in itself', which constitutes its prerogative, where it retains its pertinence and which forms its 'property'. This means that it can be an 'itself' in relation to self, 'in itself as to itself' (*hauto kath'hauto*), detaching itself from the rest of being and which, by its quality, is sufficiently stable and circumscribed. And, as far as the Greeks are concerned, even if an exhalation or a current of air or spume is volatile or subtle, the phenomenon still possesses a 'nature' and therefore a fixed specificity. For, as difficult as it may be to locate and concretely define, in whatever relation, environment or sphere it immerses itself, there is nevertheless still a 'that' which possesses its unity, conferring it with a basis as an entity.

Let's say that the Greeks made this *fixation* (in all senses of the word): it is only to the extent of this *assignment* which at the same time limits and attributes, and thereby allows predication, that rigorous knowledge becomes possible, as knowledge of *identity*. The *logos* itself, reason-discourse, is legitimated only as a segment that is determined by its beginning and end, between what should first be set up, in 'principle' (even if it might be axiomatic, from which one couldn't progress), and what must be set up as its end, at once its aim and its impediment, which cannot be exceeded, and without which this discourse is 'empty'. Aristotle said that it is necessary to 'remain' between the two and to 'pause' there, *ananchè stênai* – the formula, by its insistence, equals a symptom (of Greek anguish faced with what is *without borders*?). Hence, to know would first of all be to determine; in this, 'to think' and 'to exist' are logically considered co-extensive with one another and to overlap, according to the great statement made by Parmenides. Or, if anything unassignable remains at the heart of Greek thought, isn't it still appropriate to assign it? In this place that is not a place but a universal receptacle, the 'third genre' is situated between the intelligible model and its copy within what is perceptible, in this first 'this' – a genre that is formless because it is indeterminate, but due to this very fact it allows each 'thing', as it stands out, to be this or that by determining itself and affirming its quality (*khôra* in the *Timaeus*). Or else this unassignable refers, on the other side, to some frenzy, *mania* or divine pneuma, or it serves some Good 'beyond' essence itself, transcendent of any apprehension. The zone of pertinence is fixed between the two, founded on the identitarian definition of both 'Being' and 'knowledge'. As long as there is 'being', there is a possible assignment: 'Ideas' themselves have their own 'place', the *topos tôn eidôn* τόπος τῶν εἴδων, that 'Over there' standing out in the celestial distance of the 'plain' of truth.

Yet it is necessary for us to think about another mode of 'reality', or rather of effectivity, against the grain, on the reverse side of our intellectual habitus sedimented into demands: no longer 'being', but *evanescent* – avoiding the demarcated prehension, but operating indefinitely due to this. Or, to express it by a variant and through various indirect means, in a way that its expression (its thought) can be made supple: influencing–dissipating (itself), overrunning–vanishing, contiguous and pervasive at once. It will be necessary to go by progressive slippages to make a place in our language and open a register in it: no longer what is assignable, but what I'll call in opposition the 'evasive'. Indeed, if 'evasive' presently has a negative connotation in French or English, confronted as it is with the prevalent demand of the determination (an evasive response is, as we know, a response that avoids, sidesteps and doesn't assume), it will consequently also be necessary to learn to reverse this choice so as to perceive what it causes us to miss in our own experience, a choice which is not only theoretical but equally, as Nietzsche said, that of our morality of knowledge. The evasive is what is non-confinable and which, because of this, has the capacity not to be limited, but to remain expansive: it is a hollowing-out/evasiveness of a 'self' and is therefore freed from the fraught consistency of this self ('self as self') that is demarcatable–appropriable. If the characteristic of thought about Being is to assign, leaving the thought of Being will therefore mean thinking about how the unassignable quality of what is evasive can be *productive*.

2 In fact, alongside what other possibility that we *live*, but don't *think about*, does the thought of Being lead us to pass by? It is in any case, in referring to Chinese thought, what it constantly makes us think about, but which is no longer precisely a 'what': a mode that is no longer of Being, but of the *tao* – which is not ontological, but 'Taoist'. The fact that Chinese thought has not conceived 'Being' therefore also means that its resource is at ease with grasping the ungraspable of this non-determinant and making a place for it, but a place which is no 'place' – or, rather, so as to make it the undifferentiated ground of things. In this light, we no longer think about essence–presence, when defining identity as an entity, but think between

'there is' / 'there isn't', 有 无 之 间. We no longer enquire about truth, but harness what lies at the source of any effectiveness; not to demarcate and define, but to 'probe' what, continuing to communicate by its evasiveness, cannot be reduced in any respect or quality and which, by differentiating, stiffens and narrows, loses its 'capacity' (the notion of *de* 德). The *tao*, says the *Laozi* (§ 14), is the virtue of the unassignable being maintained ahead of the determination which is at the same time a negation: 'too fine to be seen, too subtle to be discerned, too delicate to be touched', this *delicacy* consequently doesn't let itself be marked.

Hence, what it has by right is not to have anything by right and not to be characterised from any perspective: 'high, not to be light; low, not to be dark' (ibid.). In the same way, 'continuum', which has neither beginning nor end, can be neither defined nor named: 'welcoming him, we don't see his head; following him, we can't see his back'. This is why it can only be characterised as 'hazy', 'vague' or 'undetermined', *hū huǎng* 惚恍.

This indeterminability is what makes it possible not to be limited or tangled up in anything, but to *proceed* continuously: this is where we find the 'way', the *tao*, which is never hindered, of *viability*. Yet, if this eludes assigning perception, it isn't because it is of another order, or from another world, than that of the perceptible, that, detaching itself from the phenomenal, pertains to intelligible ontology. It does indeed possess a 'configuration', it is said, but one that is 'without a particular configuration' that would restrict it, 无状之状, which is why it lends itself to every possible configuration. Or it has, or rather is, its 'phenomenality' (otherwise it would lapse into the metaphysical), but this phenomenality is 'without determined content', 无物之象, which is why this prior determination is what allows the most diverse determinations to be deployed. Its evasiveness means that, not allowing itself to be actualised, it maintains itself in the fertility of the virtual and doesn't reify itself or get bogged down. This indeterminability is thus the condition of its inextinguishability; or its 'hollowing-out', that of its endless 'functioning'. By this very fact, the evasive, in constant evasion of an 'itself', doesn't allow itself to run dry due to the restriction of any sort of 'self', and what is tenuous about its emergence preserves it in its ground or its reserve: 'to look at it doesn't mean you see it; to listen to it doesn't mean you hear it, but nor does the fact that you have made it work mean you have controlled it' (*Laozi*, § 35). Staying distant from the determination, at the same time it overflows all limitation and its *withdrawal* forms its *resource*.

Let us now evoke it in a perceptible way, or, rather, more precisely, *on the verge* of the perceptible: in the state of the *barely* perceptible, of the imperceptible-perceptible – in other words, a perception that is neither fixed nor fragmented. This evasiveness cannot be confined and its functioning capacity is all the greater for the fact that [it] remains diffuse and impalpable and cannot be defined, as is testified by the wind, *fēng* 风 – one of the most ancient motifs of Chinese thought and poetry, which we have already encountered in relation to *influence*. We feel the breath of the wind everywhere around us, but we don't perceive it in itself; it broadcasts indefinitely along its course, but the only thing we notice about it is its result. People feel the morality emanating from the personality of the Sage, but this is due to discreet impregnation and it occurs in an unknown way, through an indefinable impulse – but this is more effective than any command which, being abstract, can only constrain. The wind, which seeps in through the slightest opening, steals into the slightest crack, is of the order of the *phenomenal*, but it remains imponderable, inconsistent, and is all the more *animating*. It is the propagating modality par excellence, the continuous course or current that passes thoroughly through – that establishes contacts and spreads. If we remember that 'Wind(s)' constitute the most ancient poetic rubric in China, we then suddenly realise how it had been attentive from early on to what has sustained so little interest in the West: a significant and pervasive diffusion that is all the more prominent and invasive for its not being discerned, and that is more operative because it cannot be confined. As such, this concept of the *wind* undoes (dissolves) any ontological thinking about self-consistency or the literal, the isolatable and the watertight, of essence and the assignable, by its own means and due to what it inscribes as a passing through and an opening through the tangible.

Similarly, this theme of the 'wind', as a power of endless dissemination and animation whose propagation is both insidious and diffuse, has given thinking in China what the ontological register of assignment (which is, at once, of determination and attribution) has allowed Europe to approach only in a feeble way: the 'appearance' (of a face) or the 'atmosphere' (of a place, a moment or an epoch) and everything that, being all around, is at the same time *evasive*. Chinese thought has composed a rich fan of notions from it, all of them in configuration with the wind. 'Wind-teaching' (*feng-jiao*) expresses the moral atmosphere of a land: not the education strictly given to it, but the manners that universally result from it, through a slow distillation that occurs over time. 'Wind-attitude' (or wind-'bearing', or 'manners', or 'behaviour': *feng-zi, feng-yi, feng-du, feng-cao*) expresses the particular atmosphere a person emanates: not some character trait or other that as such is separable–analysable but as what runs through a whole personality and also expresses it. In a similar way, they speak of 'wind-mind' (*feng-shen*), 'wind-feeling' (*feng-qing*), 'wind-resonance' (*feng-yun*), 'wind-colour' (*feng-cai*), 'wind-flavour' (*feng-wei*) and so on. In one or another way, the inassignability connoted by the wind makes it the privileged theme for speaking about this *pervasive–evanescent*: what doesn't get reduced (but this 'what', as it is objectifying, is always too much) to an individuated and stabilised essence or quality, but *emanates* from it indefinitely.

3 How else should a landscape be considered if it isn't like this diffuse power of emanation and impregnation? Chinese thought also expresses it by coupling it with the wind ('wind-light', *fēng-jǐng* 风景). For, if 'land' names what is localisable and which is consequently physically identifiable and

determinable, there is on the other hand a landscape that, from the moment the phenomenality of things is re-opened, through a tension between its elements, manages to extract itself from its physicality and unfold, thereby freeing itself from the limitation of the perceptible, and widens, emanating as an *aura* from its tangible form: this is deployed in 'spirit', but without for all that abandoning its texture, its singular framework of 'mountains' and 'waters', *shān-shuǐ* 山水, as the Chinese says. We'll then speak of the 'spirit' of a landscape, as when we speak of the spirit of a wine or a perfume: that is, when the 'physical' and the 'spirit' are no longer considered to be two isolatable entities, but when, from the perceptible, something is 'exhaled', 'decanted' and 'quintessenced' – hidden away by the triumph of our dualisms as they have been, these old words will have to be taken out of the shadows so that they may serve to express this *emanence* and *evasivity*. Just as the 'flavour beyond flavour' – the 'blandness' – which, because it is no longer fixed and determined, is rich with an infinite unfolding and should be preferred, so should the 'landscape beyond the landscape', *jǐng wài jǐng* 景外景, be celebrated as it is freed from the latter and decanted from it. Nevertheless, it is not of another world, since it is not alien to what is perceptible (Sikong Tu): 'The blue fields [under] the warm sun: from beautiful [buried] jade is born a mist. We can contemplate [it], but [it] cannot be directly placed before us.'

One would gladly oppose these haloed summits of mists that rise up from the valleys, in the land of monsoons, and whose forms blend indistinctly into an *aura*, to the summits actively outlined by the dry light of the Greek skies. The Chinese literati (Qian Wenshi) would prefer to paint the evening than the noonday sun which causes the contour of things to stand out sharply. In the evening, forms retract into the half-light and begin to come apart so that 'the landscape is lost in confusion: emergent-imergent, between the there is and there is not'. But, despite this, we cannot pause at what would risk becoming only an inverse picturesqueness. For this 'blending' (of forms) contains nothing anecdotal: 'what is rooted in physical actualisation blends the spiritual [into it]', said one of the first Chinese theoreticians of painting (Wang Wei, in the fifth century). *To blend* (*róng* 容: at the same time to liquefy, mix in and amalgamate): in itself expressing the interpenetration that makes indivisible and indecisive as what is solid becomes fluent, this is the term, par excellence, that doesn't separate and presents an obstacle to dualism; it is as distant as could be from 'cutting', the Platonic *temnein*. Indeed, as soon as it ceases to be perceived as 'Being', the landscape also proceeds from the flow of energy or respiration which, as they become concentrated, form the concretion of what we call 'bodies'; but, emanating, they also unfold within the dimension of 'mind'. By giving us access to the *freeing* of this physicality which opens up and is already fading away, the Chinese painter-literati even values such an evasiveness of the landscape as the only possible 'revelation': liberating a 'beyond', but without abandoning the perceptible and the immediate (as in the first rhetorician of landscape, Zong Bing, in the fifth century).

This first notion of Chinese thought expressing the reality of the world being condensed into a landscape – or, rather (this term being far too substantialist), expressing what is effective – has the form of a cloud in primitive writing, and is then conceived (written: *qì* 气) as the steam rising from rice as it is being cooked. In the transition between the visible and the invisible, it just as equally expresses the concentration of what we call 'matter' as the expansion of what we call 'mind': at the same time, all individuation of beings and things physically proceeds from this, and what they retain of the fluent that inhabits them, animates and allows their surge. Consequently, this doesn't mean in terms of 'being' but of passing through and ambience, or of the exhaling–infiltrating – of the evanescent–invasive. But we should learn to think about this modality in other than ontological terms in order to illuminate the *capacity* of the evasive: not of being, but of the *vague*; not of knowledge, but of *influence*; not of a predicate rule, of law and codification, but of *incidence* and *induction*. Chinese thought has especially approached this as the poetic mode par excellence – what I'll call the elusive–effective or the inconsistent–encouragement – of this prompting that especially harnesses the vague, in such a way that it engages the poem at its beginning and allows this poem to surge (the notion of *xìng* 兴). Both fragile and pervasive, the formula here isn't once more paradoxical but precisely infers the prevalence of fragility. For, 'when we close our hand above it, [it] has already escaped' (from the same poet, Sikong Tu, in the ninth century). This suddenly, in a flash, places us close to Mallarmé (in 'Crisis of Poetry'), but precisely at the price of what poetic or theoretical revolution or 'crisis' in Europe, emerging from the ontological and from where our modernity comes 'beyond the confines of a fistful of dust or of all other reality ... the volatile scattering which we call the Spirit' (Mallarmé, 1956: 40).

When Lacan indicates 'the function of limbo' (1979: 30), or the 'split' by which what is appearing is at the same time disappearing, giving this 'seizure' a 'vanishing aspect', and he repeats what Freud said about the primary process (that what happens in it, being as inaccessible to contradiction as it is to both temporal and spatial location, is at the same time 'indestructible' and, among all realities, what is the most 'unsubstantial' (desire)), we are still confirmed in these terms. Here, therefore, is what led Lacan to recognise the evasiveness of this effective. So he concludes: 'therefore the unconscious ontically is the evasive' (in *Four Fundamental Concepts of Psychoanalysis*, III). 'Its status of being', he repeats, 'is so evasive' and 'so unsubstantial'. But why was it necessary to require this 'status' (of being), as Lacan does here, to want to situate it on the 'ontic plane', as he repeatedly said, as if these were the only ways of approaching what is without borders, or to take hold of something ungraspable, by discarding it? Or why else do we still need to think that what is therefore 'so fragile' would belong to the 'pre-ontological' realm, not therefore emerging from that category, and that he consequently needed to refer it to the 'ethical' level (forming what alternative with it?), as Lacan then proceeds to do?

This makes me wonder if it wouldn't be worth taking a further step in deconstruction, whether in 'metaphysical' or 'psychological' terms, and getting rid of this 'status' as well as this 'plan'. These representations may be convenient, but they are still a burden, due to what they confer and situate, and they place an obstacle against our grasping what we want to grasp here, which is not a 'what' – this 'what', in being made an object, is unable to be expressed in our (European) language unless it makes itself poetic. In other words, by taking language apart, undoing it – at least when ours is the language in question – from what, in spite of itself, it constantly assumes and conveys about all of the things it touches in the forming of Being, like Midas in the forming of gold. And it does this, even when language claims to be free from it, simply by assigning. Therefore, it needs to be undone from what it constantly articulates and *constitutes* as such, in spite of what one wants to designate as 'unsubstantial', and therefore that makes this *effective–evasive* fail just as fundamentally when it is at work in the world as in what we call psychic life. In such a way, we might finally be able to make the *evasive* a literal modality in its own right, in the shadow of no other, to which the *allusive* will respond, as also occurs in psychoanalysis, in terms of the capacity to evoke through the word.

XV

Allusive (vs Allegorical)

1 This makes it necessary for us to return to what in Europe is sealed like a piece of evidence, that which justifies meaning on the basis of the determination of Being: that to 'speak' necessarily means 'to say something', as Aristotle initially presents it, and that to say something 'means something' (*legein ti* λέγειν τι, *semainein ti* σημαίνειν τι). What Aristotle thereby presents, laying the foundation stones of European reason but without allowing the slightest choice to appear, is that our word is justified only if it gives itself an object (*ti tí*), as indefinite as it might be, but already giving it a unity as an entity. The word would otherwise be empty: it would be about 'nothing' (*ouden* οὐδέν) and 'say' nothing, and so it would itself 'be' nothing. The word thus has as its vocation to express what things 'are', to fix their essence–presence (as *ousia* οὐσία), specifying it from difference to difference, and to link language unfailingly to Being. The principle of non-contradiction, posed as the first axiom of reason, is itself simply the consequence of this 'onto-logical' pact. This means that anyone who'd like to refute it still has to submit to it as soon as he 'says something', since this already assumes it in fact. To fail to respect this is to smash the legitimacy of the word and straightaway exclude oneself from humanity.

Yet if there is no longer a 'what' (that the word expresses), serving it as both support and object and inscribing it in Being, or if, emerging from the ontological regime, one wants to evoke the effectiveness indefinably at work, but which precisely is not a possible 'what' (I will have to correct it each time), the effectiveness which constantly runs 'through', without being fragmented or sedimented (the convenient word is 'pervasive'), the word, conversely, will not be expressed *by name*. In other words, the *allusivity* of the word will respond to the *evasiveness* of the 'without-ground' and 'without-form', without consistency (*hu mo wu xing*, Zhuangzi, ch. 33), in continuous modification and without constancy (*bian hua wu chang*). Allusivity doesn't 'express' something, 'a' something, but *indefinitely lets it through*. The *tao* isn't 'expressed', since it is not isolatable-objectifiable, but everything can allude to it by constantly referring to it. Zhuangzi formalised this by putting the word out of kilter with the reference: 'Where there is no reference, there is reference, and where there is reference, there is no reference.' The reference isn't targeted, adapted or accurately defined, but it is significant, and it is pervasive as it emanates from all sides. The *Laozi* calls this 'speaking without speaking' (*yan wu yan*): 'to speak', but without making it a 'statement'. As there is no object to speak about, it cannot be expressed by name, but can be understood indefinitely. To claim to grasp a 'that', but which is not a possible 'that', in an isolated and 'emphasised' way, is of course to miss [it]. There is no defined place [where] it is located, [where] it is *assigned*. On the other hand, everything we say is impregnated by it. This is why the word expressing this non-object object is 'barely' spoken (*Laozi*, § 23) and can only point in the right direction, in an indexical way, 'with empty and distant remarks', 'expressions without end or border' (*Zhuangzi*, ch. 33). And it is not 'well seasoned', being allowed neither to emerge nor to be detached, but is 'bland'.

In the typology of the words he erects (in chapter 27, 'Yu yan', which can serve as a point of entry into his work), Zhuangzi prioritises the word *receptive* which, without seeking to express anything, constantly allows a passing through. Alongside 'fixed' or transposed words (*yu yan*) (which are figurative words expressed indirectly by a third person and that cannot be suspected of partiality, because they are mediated and not tied to the person who is stating them, as also are words 'of importance' (*zhong yan*), which are words of authority pronounced by the Ancients, but about which one has a right to wonder if they aren't outdated), 'willed' words (*zhí yán*) are in the image of that antique vase that yields when it is full and becomes firm again when it is empty, words that renew themselves from one day to the next, without fixity, but which alone, by constantly discharging and flowing out, are capable of evoking *by effusion*. They are 'free of any intention' as well as staying 'attached to any position': by coming as they do, without anything to fix or restrain them, because they aren't governed either by the 'near at hand' perspective – one that is already rather stubborn – of whoever would claim to be their author, or by the order added by the rigidity of language and logic, they are also disposed, by their evasivity, says Zhuangzi, to go 'to the end', each time, of the 'portion' of what 'thereby comes from oneself', endlessly, in its continuous process (*jin qi ziran zhi fen*). In other words, they alone can espouse immanence in each of its gushings and inexhaustibility. These words are constantly allusive because, not aiming at anything and not linking or imposing anything – this 'nothing' in which Aristotle considered that the word would inevitably become undone – they continue in their hollows to harness and gather together.

In Chinese poetry (poetic formulation is predominant in China), a good poem doesn't express any proven sentiment (which often accounts for the apparent divergence between the poem and its title). But everything lets it filter through. Everything within it is *allusive*, indirectly evoking what, spoken by name, would immediately become circumscribed and dried up. It doesn't speak of the melancholy of an abandoned woman (or an exiled official), but of how the grass in front of her door has grown (now that no one is coming to visit her), or how her waist has become slack (she hasn't the strength to eat). Or when a temple was depicted in Chinese painting, the literati's brush was careful not to trace its architecture, with its walls and pinnacles. This was because painting it as an object would from the outset limit the atmosphere, in fact the effectiveness, which emanates from it, but without being able to assign anything to it in particular. So the artist always sketches 'mountains' and 'waters' – tensions that animate the landscape – with the discreet figure of a monk 'cutting wood' or 'carrying water' on the path that zigzags down the hillside, or in the shadow of a luxuriant valley, and barely standing out. This is an indication that a temple is close by, which it would be worthless to claim to depict and describe in an 'appropriate' way – that is, by implying its 'distinctive quality'. This half-perceived silhouette, on the other hand, sends us indefinitely back to it, into the very heart of the most everyday work, referring to it without referring to it, without fixing [it] as a 'something' in a significant and determined way which would result in it losing its significance.

The same poet who evoked the evasiveness of the land hazily opening out onto a landscape expressed this with a poetic word: 'Not to express by name a single word / is to reach winds and waves completely' (Sikong Tu, in the ninth century, in his poem 'Hanxu'). It isn't necessary to claim to express through 'sticking to' (an object, *zhù* 著), and the atmosphere of the evasive, in its mobility and permeability (in the fashion of the 'wind'), is sporadically–universally apprehended. Thematically, 'the word doesn't approach the self' is what is said in its wake, but it is 'as if the pain was unbearable', even though it isn't spoken about. It emanates 'like distilled alcohol'; contracts or condenses 'like the flower when autumn returns'. It 'unfolds into infinity like evanescent dust', is 'volatile like the froth of waves'. It evolves according to the ungraspable 'immersing–emerging in concert' (*yǔ zhī chén fú* 与之沉浮). 'According to', Mallarmé likewise said – something I shall return to – finally promoting, in Europe, these new terms; still 'ventured', he said, but rebelling against the 'veiling' of 'volatile dispersion', that 'which has only to do nothing' – in other words, against that veiling operated by the description of what would be 'something': evocation, allusion, suggestion. Or let's recall Braque, taking away the object: 'to write is not to describe', 'to paint is not to depict'.

2 To understand the significance of the *allusive*, we need to grasp the word by what is expressed by the Latin term *ad-ludere*, which literally means to come to 'play' around or 'in proximity'. This is as dolphins approach and play near a boat – *accedunt atque adludunt* – or as the sea, as the ordinarily so unpoetic Cicero said poetically, 'approaches' by 'playing' with the shore: *litoribus adludit*. 'To make an allusion' thus maintains the idea that the word that arises further away will evolve all the more freely 'nearby'. In our ancient rhetoric, therefore, allusion already consisted in how the expression makes the relation be felt more intimately because it is distanced from what one intended to say, since it does so without being imposed. It begins with a divergence (opened by what was 'said') in order to reach better, through the going beyond that it calls upon, what was summoned in what was beyond the word, but nevertheless wasn't

abstract, because it was retained in what wasn't said. This makes allusion the other of allegory. Allegory means something 'other' than what is verbally expressed – 'aliud verbis, aliud sensu ostendit', Quintilian said – because, while saying one thing, it wants something else in order to be understood analogically: it is projected onto another level, one that is ideal rather than concrete. The Greeks had thus already begun to 'allegorise' Homer when they judged his narrative to be morally unacceptable: the battles which the gods physically indulged in are no longer scandalous as soon as they are understood to represent the one that the dispositions of the soul or the natural elements indulge in. As the *allegorical* and the *allusive* set up the word in its two dimensions (those of the represented *or* the implicit), they are really the two privileged modalities of what is indirect. They form an alternative to one another, even if one also discerns 'allusive allegories', which is when the allegorical puts itself at the service of the allusive, and enters its 'play'. There will, therefore, be a general advantage to be acquired from this cleavage in order to see how the word surreptitiously splits. And, as we re-open our old treatises of rhetoric, we may be able to locate this opposition in their classifications, even if they don't increase our understanding of it. They are figures of *fiction* or *reflection*: according to the definition given of it, allegory, which heads the figures of 'fiction', presents a thinking that is *under the image* of another thinking likely to render it more 'perceptible' and 'striking' – while allusion, which belongs to figures of 'reflection', as Fontanier elegantly said, calls upon the thought that is stated and to 'reflect' on what is not stated so as to *awaken* the idea. This is therefore done not to render the intelligible more striking in a sensible guise, but to overflow from the spoken in quest of that to which it only relates in an indexical way.

In consequence of this, the great opposition dramatically exposed by the Romantics between the *allegorical* and the *symbolic* will subsequently be revealed as just a subdivision of the first case in arising from the same comprehensive logic and orientation of thought. This is because the symbolic and the allegorical equally lead us from one level to the other: from the imager to the imaged or, expressed differently, from the concrete to the abstract or from the particular to the general. In allegory, the signifying aspect is admittedly immediately crossed with a view to reaching the signified, while in the symbolic it retains its own value and opacity. While allegory, which is completely transitive and functional, is entirely dissolved in its signification, the symbolic signifies only secondarily or, as the Romantics said, it 'is', at the same time as it signifies, and it signals towards what cannot be spoken. In both instances, it remains the case that the indirect supports it on a relation of *resemblance* – in the case of the symbolic, it's true, going all the way to participation. In contrast, we discern that the *allusive* implies on the other hand a relation of *reference*, or rather of *widened* reference – of reference without referring – in which what is being referred to has to be sought out.

The *allegorical* exists in a double sense and asks to be interpreted; the *allusive* puts us at a distance and wants to be approached. The distancing it effects is an appeal to closer identification – it is measured by its *indicative power*. What ultimately separates them is that the allegorical, as well as the symbolic, implies a *division in two* – between imager and imaged (matter and idea), between the beneficial lucidity that the sun spreads from the height of what is perceptible, as Plato constructed it, and what is spread by the idea of the Good, 'beyond essence', from the summit of what is intelligible. The allegorical is consequently the privileged form of the metaphysic which, according to this Platonic gesture, cut being in two and conceived one part (the concrete) as the image that has seeped out of the other, *eidôlon* εἴδωλον, towards the 'Being' which our mind must rise to by abandoning the perceptible. Just as it arises from a relation of reference and not of resemblance, that encourages contemplation, which is not of the 'other' (of an other order: the *allos* ἄλλος of the 'allegorical') but of the *un-said*, the allusive arises from a logic of *detour* and not of a *dividing into two* (we 'introduce thought into it only with a certain detour', as Fontanier rightly said[1]). As it assumes neither a shift in levels, as between literal and figurative meaning, nor the relation of the image to what it is an image of, but goes from the explicit to the implicit, it contains no 'veil' (of the perceptible) to be lifted (in order to grasp the idea), as in the allegorical, but an immediacy (of speaking) should be outlined so as to seek its further reference, thereby providing a means by which to 'approach' what is actually at 'stake' without being determined.

3 This makes it necessary for the allusive to overflow its figure or 'trope' – which is too scholastically–sectorially limited to morality, the mythological and what is historical – in order to confer it with its full measure and set it in *tension*, sucking in the word, which, through the *detour*, offers *access*. German Romanticism, confronted with the domination of the symbolic, started furtively to do this by opening the *Anspielung* so as to speak (and read) the reference to 'Infinity', freeing it from any object. As Friedrich Schlegel said: 'Any work of art is an allusion to infinity'; or, more clearly, to exclude the temptation of metaphysical rupture that cast the absolute into a beyond: 'The flash of the finite and the allusion to the infinite flow into one another' ('der Schein des Endlichen und die Anspielung aufs Unendliche fliessen ineinander'). Yet isn't this allusive resource or potentiality to be deployed, in a more general way, as the vocation of the word as it responds to the evasiveness of [what] cannot be either enclosed or fixed, either defined or determined? The modern work, whether pictorial or literary, will readily be conceived as a continuous allusion to what cannot be made present: Lyotard says that 'allusion' is perhaps an indispensable turn of expression to evoke this *un-presentable*. But is 'turn of expression' sufficient? What does this turn – a 'deturn' – mean?

Chinese art as well as thought can inform us much better in this respect: not having developed an ontology that bases the word in Being and therefore not having promoted any presence that would isolate and define,

Chinese thought knows no other possibilities than those of detour and interweaving. If, regarding the *tao*, 'what can be named is not the constant *tao*' (an opening formula of the Laozi), it is in contrast recognised, and in a more informed and most banal way, that every word – the slightest word – can be allusive of the *tao*. Like the most familiar actions, such as 'cutting wood' or 'carrying water', any statement that comes to mind, no matter how crude, terse, incongruous or even weird it might appear, reflects the 'way'. The *chan* (*zen* in Japanese) has even made its pedagogy of 'awakening' from this: in signalling from a distance, in an anecdotal and fortuitous, unwonted and even absurd way, this allusiveness 'points' even far more pertinently *towards* – and it does so at each instant – by being purely incidental, without affectation or abstraction.

I shall call such a resource of the word 'allusive value', or *allusivity*. Let us note how China has only slightly developed the allegorical (a few untypical poems in the *Shijing* apart) because it has very rarely been concerned with dividing the world into two and hasn't widened the gap between Being and the phenomenal, and so the symbolic, rather than being deployed as an exploratory form of the ineffable, readily turns to cliché and emblematic function, the values of which are encoded (as we already see in Qu Yuan[2]). On the other hand, it has exploited this allusive capacity that begins by only 'barely' expressing in a hazy outline, and it has done so in a very intentional way. The brush is said to be held 'at an angle' (*ce bi*). One doesn't paint the clear 'sunlight', as in Plato, so as to evoke, on another level that resembles it, the transcendence of the Idea (the perceptible and the intelligible being in a relation at once of 'separation' and 'kinship', *chorismos* χωρισμός and *suggeneia* συγγένεια). But, according to the Chinese formulation, which relates as much to the word as to painting, one paints 'the clouds [so as to] evoke the moon' (*hong yun tuo yue*). For the clouds and the moon really belong to the same landscape, the same order of reality, and aren't separated from one another. But the clouds (that one paints), immersing the brilliance of the moon, make its *aura* appear: they aren't painted for their own sake, but to make it emerge *alongside* and through the ambience. The 'moon' cannot be painted, as the literati admit (see Jin Shengtan[3]) but, when the clouds are so finely executed, under the moistening of the brush, that too much heaviness or lightness is avoided, that not the slightest trace of opacity remains, it's the moon that we then see appear nearby, playing with them and attracting our attention as it stands out in this halo. And from everywhere, impregnating the whole landscape, its luminosity even becomes all that we see.

Only *allusivity* will be able to capture this *evasivity* – as is proven once again by what psychoanalysis brings out as it locates a crisis within European discourse. Let's recall that, even before Lacan, Freud had brought attention to the status of the elusive, and he gave the analysand only one rule to be followed in the course of the cure. This was to express everything that 'comes into his head', even if he finds it disagreeable, even if it seems unimportant, not relevant to the subject, or is simply weird (Freud, 1979: 40,

'The Rat Man'). We gain a better understanding of the possibilities of allusion, or the allusive capacity, to which he has recourse, when confronted with the evasiveness of the unconscious. In particular, we have a better understanding of how this single rule for embarking upon the cure follows without warning the opposite path to that which is fundamental to European reason, at least since the time of Aristotle: whoever speaks must necessarily say something, 'a' something, otherwise the word would be in vain. The psychoanalyst tells his patient to do the opposite, to 'speak, and even to say as much as you want', to 'recount' *what you like*, but in particular 'don't try to say anything!…' This is because the analysand himself can 'say' nothing about what he has repressed. But his word, whatever he utters, constantly 'plays' with and approaches it – and indefinitely lets it through, as Freud himself says, 'in the form of an allusion', 'nach Art einer Anspielung'.

Once a desire is unable to be directly expressed, it can in fact no longer be stated at the indexical stage of the symptom except in a deflected way: when a conflict of ambivalence cannot be resolved regarding the same person, this desire will be circumvented – *Umgang* – onto a substitutive object (from the father to the horse for little Hans). The whole language of the symptom is therefore, from the way in which Freud describes it, a prudent and strategic means of diverging from the object of censured desire so as constantly to be able to linger and 'play' around it nearby, in proximity: *ad-lusio*. And to do this (in a far freer way, so that it eludes control) means that the symptom is ostensibly separated from the outset – in other words, it is sheltered from such vigilance through this very distance. Rendering himself receptive to allowing this elusive repressed through (to be heard), the analysand's word allows us all the better to perceive what (but which, having become an unconscious form, can no longer be located as a 'what') it is constantly, and even inescapably, making an 'allusion' to. Indeed, when the principle of non-contradiction founded on the 'say something' is lifted, it reveals from this unconscious its original *ambiguity*.

Notes

1   Pierre 'Émile' Fontanier (1765–1844), a grammarian noted for the teaching of rhetoric, author of *Manuel classique pour l'étude des tropes, ou Élément de la science des mots* (1821) and *Des figures autres que tropes* (1827) [trans.].
2   Qu Yuan (*c.* 339–278 BCE), one of China's greatest poets and the first to be known by name [trans.].
3   Jin Shengtan (*c.* 1608–61), an important literary critic renowned for his commentaries on two popular literary works: *The Water Margin* and *The Story of the West Wing* [trans.].

XVI

Ambiguous (vs Equivocal)

1 We wouldn't be able to put an end to suspicion by continually slicing between the terms of language in order to open up the divergence between them and cause them to reflect by offering them an opposing perspective. Wouldn't some cracks already be hidden beneath the most adjacent meanings and lead towards their opposition? Evidence of this is that the equivocal and the ambiguous are considered to be synonyms and are ordinarily glossed in similar terms without any further thought being given to it. Yet I think it would be interesting to turn these synonyms into antonyms so as precisely to dissolve what is equivocal. There is 'equi-vocation' when I maintain two meanings 'equally' in my 'words', which should be distinguished from one another in order to avoid misunderstandings and prevent any confusion that is detrimental to thought. The 'ambiguous' designates exactly the opposite phenomenon: below the separations instituted by language, it reveals a fundamental inseparability which the distinction of our terms tends to mask. The equivocal therefore names a tainted usage from which the word must be purged by dissociations made in the heart of the same term, while the ambiguous on the contrary names an actual indissociability (in Being, the 'real', or what I'd prefer to call more resolutely the *effective*) that our linguistic boundaries have concealed and caused us not to see. This is why I'd risk summing up what thinking means by turning them back to back. To think is to do both at the same time, and even by doing one we are also doing the other: to *expel the equivocal* is at the same time to *explore the ambiguous*.

I found myself particularly constrained to mark this opposition when I wanted to separate love from intimacy: love is 'equivocal', intimacy is 'ambiguous'. Love is equivocal in that it says both one thing and another, and that these actually have little to do with one another. It expresses both the Greek *eros* which, even being raised to the divine absolute, is nevertheless always an experience of aspiration and conquest, and one riveted to lack, born of deprivation and aiming at satisfaction. It also expresses the Christian *agape*, God's love sending his Son to die on the cross in order to save humans: a love which is not a matter of a lack but of a gift, which is given without any return, without calculation and having no aim. It is a love that isn't born from a void or any defect, but from plenitude and its effusion. Yet our term 'love' maintains a misunderstanding between the two in containing both of them indiscriminately and without separating them. Indeed, it even prevails due to such confusion: love has had to use its strength to establish its mythology in the West and become the banal and voluble theme (the 'raucous' theme) that we all recognise because of the way it plays between these levels or on these two charts. In fact, this equivocation is what Wittgenstein called a 'false' word, *ein filches Wort*, a word about which in the end we don't know what it expresses when it is used, which must interminably be addressed when speaking about it.

The fact that a possible double meaning does exist which is not cut short, *Zweideutigkeit*, is really, in a general way, what promotes and prolongs the play of how the word is used in ordinary exchange: each person receives the same term in his own way, according to the sense that suits him, but that he wants to believe the other shares. This means that the misunderstanding engendered revives the conversation of itself, and it does so in order to escape the illusion that, not being denounced, cannot be exceeded, and in consequence is continually deferred. Thus, as it turns into chatter, the discourse prospers in these muddied waters, whereas it isn't limited when the equivocal is evacuated by being demarcated. The fact that the equivocal is not lifted or cut short is what continually maintains the word in expectation of 'novelty' – 'Neugier', as Heidegger says – and, because of this, it is continually carried forwards and inclined to flow out, and this sustains our interest in it (it persists in the *Betrieb*) without encountering the strict inspection of what is effective (2010, § 37). And, in the end, it is even taken for what is effective: this equivocal constantly nourishes the curiosity and 'gives idle talk the semblance of having everything decided in it' (Heidegger, 2010: 219). Yet it isn't just a matter of 'Love', in its verbose discourse, maintaining its prestige through this equivocation. I believe that the secret strategy of it will also be verified notably in the way in which the media discourse in today's world, by maintaining this suspension of the equivocal, continually deferring its result, expertly preserves its ratings.

On the other hand, the fact that the intimate is *ambiguous* means that, in order to think about the intimate, we'll have to dissolve the oppositions instituted by language, to abandon these convenient separations: refusing the dualism and keeping with the transition of the two, the intimate brings us back us to the point of non-separation of what has too easily been dissociated. For it considers that only this in-demarcation is real – or, let us say, is effective. The intimate is ambiguous because it doesn't have to know, and doesn't even cause us to imagine, the classical dichotomies of 'body' and 'soul', or the 'sensual' and the 'spiritual', or the 'physical' and the 'metaphysical'. A sexual 'penetration', as it might be called when it opens onto the intimate, of itself raises these dissociations and undoes them. It carves out an infinite in the very heart of the perceptible. From the heart of this penetrating momentary focusing of bodies, it provokes an incredible overflowing that gives us an intimation of eternity. It is at once indissolubly 'physical' and 'metaphysical', 'carnal' (the most carnal) and revealing of the 'beyond' – such oppositions become fallacious and cancel themselves out. In this inside – 'the most inside' – that it opens (*intimus*), 'possession' is revealed at the same time to be in the highest sense a sharing; or let's say that the self causes the Other's frontier to fall, but in order to disown itself. Something more fundamental suddenly appears – vertigo – which allows these exclusions to fall.

Because the *equivocal* maintains the misunderstanding in the word, I therefore have to work towards reducing this harmful equivocity, and to do so in order to attain a rigorous univocity. This should be done in such a way that a word, a statement, might now have just one meaning, which is the condition of the word's lucidity as it is of thought and, therefore, of their rightful comprehension. But *equally*, in an inverse sense, because instituted language leads us to fragment and artificially diffract in our words what is fundamentally one and isn't separable – in other words, the *ambiguous* – we have to learn to go back to what predates such separations (which are nothing but conveniences of linguistic representation) in order that the unitary, undifferentiated and indissociable grounds that are concealed from us by these words are made – or rather *allowed* – to appear. The question that consequently arises for us and which takes the form of an alternative when we approach these darker and more dangerous zones of thought is, in each case, to ask ourselves, as we remain vigilant, whether this is an equivocation that is imputable to my word or to my thought as I negligently confuse what should be distinguished, *or* whether it is an ambiguity that must not be concealed because in the end it precisely signals what, beyond established distinctions, in the indentation that suddenly opens up – even though it is not yet distinguishable or distributable in plans or entities – is effectivity itself, and which, as such, is still to be *explored*. This is what we should hasten to consider before it inevitably becomes dislocated by our categorical oppositions as, returning to orders, they all too soon gain the upper hand.

2 To think is therefore to remain on the alert, vigilant on both sides: to be attentive to *eradicating the equivocal*, but, at the same time and in parallel, to ensure that *the ambiguous isn't hidden*. Yet hasn't philosophy in its history successively devoted itself to these two tasks, between which, going from one to the other, what constitutes its modernity has been played out? In its Greek invention and promotion of the *logos*, it has above all defined the *reduction of the equivocal* as its condition of possibility. Aristotle, as the first teacher of philosophy, magisterially gave the lesson that classical teaching has retained – of extolling clear and distinct ideas as the first rule of its method. When Spinoza spoke of God, 'or moreover nature', *Deus sive natura*, he didn't open the door to the equivocal but, on the contrary, founded his thought on this supreme univocity, an unequalled feat: that 'God' and 'nature' designate only one and the same thing, or that these terms that are so often opposed might actually have the same meaning. *Then* this would perhaps constitute the modernity of European thought before all else: not to be reassured by a carefully univocal speaking (or thinking) when confronted with what would perhaps be found to be an unfathomed ambiguity. An ambiguity or 'duplicity' of Being, before being covered up,

or hidden, by the clarification of language – or rather wouldn't it more radically be by the ambiguity of 'living'? – the question would suddenly be displaced. Nietzsche said that this was what was 'perhaps' so dangerous; modern thought, since Nietzsche, has dared to confront it.

Against the Sophists and what he denounced as their dangerous paralogisms that consist in using different meanings of the same word in the course of the same reasoning, Aristotle established the first, and even unique, task, by which good speaking means good thinking: since the characteristic of the word is to say 'something', 'a' something (*ti* τί), therefore something about an 'a', this task is to make sure, when we speak, of the univocity of our words. The multiple meanings of the same word should be distinguished from one another, failing which it may happen that the person asking the question and the person who is replying 'aren't directing their thought to the same thing'. Such is therefore the condition of a rigorous *dialogue*, with others as well as with oneself, which therefore diverges from how the ordinary play of 'conversation', which is neither broken off nor replete, is formed. For, if the 'multiple signifieds' of the same word are within the order of things – things being infinite, while there are a limited number of words – on the other hand, the fact that the same word might signify in 'multiple ways' (*pollachôs* πολλαχῶς) runs a risk against which we need to protect ourselves by the definition–distinction of each of the meanings. 'For not to mean one thing is to mean nothing at all.' This unity of meaning is itself founded on an identity of essence, or 'logic' on the onto-logical, and 'Being' is its surety. It is because words are so many determinations of Being that we are justified in banishing their equivocalness or what Aristotle called their 'homonymy'.

This rule of a singular meaning securing the legitimacy of both the word and thought, and founded in Being, would indeed put an effective end to any difficulty if it wasn't itself precisely threatened by this word 'being', by this smallest of words, but one which is contained within all of our words, as has been noted (by Heidegger) when considering its 'historical' importance in the West, and on which this logical edifice of univocity is perched. We cannot fail to note that, since 'being' is itself expressed 'in multiple ways' ('homonymically'), not only does it mean different things (because it is general and things are singular), but also it signifies them differently. There is indeed the equivocalness of this term 'to be' when I say he is a man, or he is a particular height, or he is white, or he is taller, or he is here, or he is sitting down, or he is wearing shoes, or he is loved, or simply that he 'exists'. As Greek thought was founded on Being, Aristotle could not in fact encounter a greater danger: suppose that the first tool is also revealed to be the weakest one at the same time as it acts as the surety of thought? Suppose it should be discovered to be the one that is most lacking in the univocity of which he wanted it to be the basis?

Aristotle's greatest theoretical effort, or let's call it his feat, may have been to emerge from the rhapsody and confusion in which the validity of the verb 'to be' places us, as much as to secure the base of Being as to guarantee the rigorous use of the word, of the *logos* – the very one on which the possibility of what we in Europe have called science is founded. If common language is equivocal in its imprecision, in that of 'science', on the other hand, each term must always be used in the same sense (as Galileo, among many others, would reiterate, making it a condition of scientific rigour) and be explicitly defined. It is therefore by dispersing this primary equivocalness, by distinguishing, distributing and cataloguing the various meanings of 'to be', as 'modes' or 'forms' of predication, *schemata tes categorias*, that we will be able to gain knowledge of Being and, through it, of science. This requires distinguishing and separating the point of view of essence (of 'quiddity') from the quantity or the quality or the relation or the place or the time or the disposition or the having or acting or to suffer in Being. Through this table of categories, the multiple meanings of 'to be' are beneficially distributed and the Aristotelian logic of categories would have succeeded – by means of a supreme challenge and effort – in expelling the equivocalness that most intimately threatened the *logos*.

But, while we are in this way thoroughly attached to the idea of evacuating all equivocalness in the use of the verb 'to be' through this categorisation that legitimates predication, isn't it an *ambiguity* of *Being itself* (a more radical, and even gaping, one) that would appear beneath it? Would we have succeeded only in knocking the problem of logic off balance into the ontological and, in doing so, have done no more than postpone and so aggravate it? Aristotle seems to have resolved the question by ensuring that, if being is spoken about in multiple ways, it is relative to 'something of one', *pros hen* πρὸς ἕν, to a 'certain unique nature' posed in principle (*Metaphysics*, gamma, 1003b). But if this unique principle is the 'essence', *ousia*, how can it also be represented among the other categories, even if it is the first to be posed among them? Or else how can this founding 'one' be accessed, or at least a community of reference be founded, if I cannot even begin to extricate the concept from it? Here Aristotle encountered a difficulty that, expelled from the use of words and their faulty equivocalness, as Pierre Aubenque remarks, reflected an ambiguity of Being that threatened the very possibility of the ontology he wanted to establish. He thus paused before this greatest danger. He was content prudently to fold the thought of Being into this supposed and defined unity as 'essence', defining the very object of philosophy by it as the 'science of Being as being', instead of daring to confront this ambiguity.

3 Such a renunciation has marked philosophy in its advance [*essor*], or perhaps, more accurately, it found its development in what this renunciation has conceded to the logic of *logos*. Plato had already known the dizziness of the ambiguity of Being, but prudently – ingeniously – he turned away from it. After Parmenides, the 'father', had performed the initial separation, by distinguishing between the paths of 'Being' and 'non-being', Plato, setting off in quest of the Sophist's vanishing nature, was left to produce the great earthquake at the very heart of Greek thought that still affects us. This was

to dare to undertake 'parricide' and to recognise that 'non-being exists, to a certain degree, and that being, in its turn, in some way, doesn't exist' (*The Sophist*, 241d) is the most 'audacious' statement. In any case, what is most troubling is that, instead of being and non-being being completely cut off from one another, one *is* in a certain way *also the other*. Under the marked opposition of terms, to be exceeded, a more fundamental inseparability appeared: wouldn't Being, no longer being sufficiently distinguished from its opposite, be revealed as literally ambiguous? But, faced with this greater danger, because it destroyed the possibility of a knowledge of Being and therefore of the truth, Plato was already introducing the inventory and distribution of genres from which Aristotle's categories would be born: 'being' will be just one genre among others, in which all others would participate, insofar as they 'exist'. Hence 'non-being' is no longer the contrary of 'being', but its 'other' being able to interfere with it, and the genres can communicate with one another, in a manner determined by the dialectician, like the letters of the alphabet that match and mingle according to the rules enacted by the grammarian.

Plato had therefore overcome the danger of ambiguity by thinking about *mixture* and 'interlacing' (*meixis* μεῖξις, *sumploké* συμπλοκή). In a mixture, each of the things that are opposed preserves its essence, holding onto its own characteristics; while being associated with another, it still distinguishes itself from it. The Platonic solution of mingling or of the 'crasis', which will remain that of classical thought and form its psychological delights, allows the two opposites to co-exist without abandoning their respective *en-soi* and therefore their status as knowable 'being', with an ontological vocation. When I drink after feeling thirsty, says Plato (*Gorgias*, 496e), I experience at once discomfort (of being thirsty) and pleasure (of quenching the thirst). There is indeed a contradiction (in the heart of a subject) in this, but pleasure and pain aren't called into question in their essence and definition. There is something *mixed*, and this can even be the equal participation of both, producing what Spinoza called a wavering of the soul, 'fluctuatio animi', between these two contrary affects, but each of the contraries is still a contrary. One is *with* the other, but is equally *also the other*: each is maintained in relation to the other in its identity, and the 'analysis' – destined for the future we know of – will be able to separate them.

Whether it is their very opposition that comes apart, or whether the separation effected by our words ceases to be pertinent and falls away so as to bring into view one that is more fundamental and to be explored – since it is no longer distinguishable and therefore identifiable according to the dissociations established by our concepts, but on the contrary escapes them – the ambiguity that arises when the frontier between one and the other is erased is completely different. I've already wondered if this isn't the case with, for example, the sentimental response formed in the core of a landscape and revealing one (arising from it) that is more originating:

this sentimental response is no longer distinguishable–identifable as 'joy' *or* 'pain', or even as both finely interlaced at the same time, but arises from what *predated* this separation which cracks it in an arbitrary way. It isn't therefore that I experience joy and pain at the same time – in a contradictory way – but that this distinction between affects can say nothing about it, or even already misses this actual sentimental response, as a more radical capacity to be affected. This sentimental, more fundamental, response (born from my more elementary involvement in the world, which is what causes the landscape to emerge) can no more be dissociated from the perceptual than it can be dissociated into various affects which we will then be able to consider 'blended'.

The dialectic promoted by Plato is therefore a powerful logical machinery destined to *bring ambiguity to an end*. Just as each genre communicates neither indiscriminately with all others nor with any one of them, but only – in a rigorous way, which needs to be described – with some of them, Plato concludes in the same way that anything can be legitimately said about anything else, instead of being caught up in a sterile tautology (and the possibility that a discourse would be delegitimated), but without this being just anything at all (and thereby losing the possibility of truth). The same thing goes for the Hegelian dialectic, at the other end of the history of philosophy, when it is conceived as a system – not simply as a condition of possibility of discourse and *predication*, as in Plato, but as that of *becoming*, as the truth at once of being and nothingness and consequently as the unity of both, from which History will be understood (*Logic*, § 41). So that the one might be 'the other as well', it will then be conceived in what the one *passes into its other*, instead of keeping within itself. Indeed, as soon as 'one' and the 'other' are distinguished, instead of each of them falling back on each side, obstructed in their development, they never cease in their self-surpassing to exchange their determinations and fall back into their opposite. This is where the *movement* comes from which, through this internal work of negation, promotes the substance, no longer being imprisoned in its properties, as a Subject out of kilter with itself and drawn towards 'becoming'. This movement, departing from the fixity of essences, allows us to think about the 'fluidity' of the process of the world or of life constantly passing into its other. But this 'identity of identity and non-identity' doesn't emerge from the concept of identity to the point at which it expires.

Ambiguity can therefore only be approached by coming out of the dialectic and onto its reverse side. This is a dialectic which makes sharp contrasts, opposes and mediates – that sets in opposition in order to mediate. It believes it can begin by inscribing a separation in order then to traverse it and find its course (according to the *dia* of the 'dia-lectic'), whether one of the discourse or of becoming, which begins by determining the 'one' and the 'other', so as then to displace and go beyond these terms and even to free itself from them. To think about ambiguity is the contrary of this. It means not knowing where to begin to pass beyond distinction and refuse the convenience of *making contrasts* in order to be able to make a start. It means not setting up a separation in order then to have to surmount it and open a future in discourse (in Plato) or History (in Hegel), but to withdraw to what predates any possible separation, because it is suspected of an arbitrariness which is no longer recoverable, no matter how much effort is made to integrate the 'other' and reconfigure the presumed identity. Nietzsche rightly saw this lifting of the separation that opens onto ambiguity as the only possible way out of ontology, as a metaphysical enterprise, whose first act was to dissociate contraries and so consolidate language in its exclusions. This allows it then to set itself to work between them as much as the ambiguity wants, a marking that is initially done to reassure and confirm faith in morality as much as in knowledge once they go together as a pair.

4 Even if he still remains dependent on metaphors of 'knotting' and 'entanglement' resulting from the atavistic representation of the mixture, Nietzsche effectively envisaged a 'relatedness', and even an 'identity of essences', between contraries (*wesensgleich*) whose inseparability alone can give an account of the delicate, but continual, transition as much between conduct as between things (see *Beyond Good and Evil*, I, 2). Moreover, in the register of psychoanalysis, if the ambivalence still maintains a distinction of oppositions co-existing in the same subject oscillating between them, it is the unconscious that has the task of revealing the undemarcability of what the register of the conscious presents as opposed. 'The very relation of the sharpest contrast between "mother" and "prostitute"' is what 'in the conscious, is found split into a pair of opposites [that] often occurs in the unconscious as a unity' (Freud, 1977: 237). In the same way, we appreciate that 'the objects to which men give most preference', 'their ideals', proceed from 'the same perceptions and experiences as the objects which they most abhor, and that they were originally only distinguished from one another through slight modifications' (Freud, 1984: 150). In the interpretation of dream, the same 'blossoming branch' represents sexual innocence as we love to imagine it, but also its contrary.

It is therefore fascinating to consider how European philosophy, turning in the most incisive way against its ontological enterprise founded on dualist contrast (the Platonic *temnein* τεμνεῖν) through the hard-fought attack of suspicion (whether Nietzchean or Freudian), has finally emerged from this *fundamental undemarcability* ahead of any demarcation. Only Heraclitus, whom for this reason we call the 'obscure', had perceived it ('God is day night, war peace ... '), but his teaching, buried by Aristotle, has since been lost. This meant that so much effort and theoretical over-elaboration had later to be done in order to restore this 'grounds without ground' which 'holds in reserve, in its undecided shadow and vigil, the opposites and differends that the process of discrimination will come to carve out' (and that, in 'Plato's Pharmacy', Derrida wrongly – it seems to me – still calls

111

'ambivalence' rather than *ambiguity*, or else confuses both of them). Fascinating, I say, and even all the stranger because this more original unde-marcability is what Chinese thinking, as it passed over Being and therefore ontological determination, constantly brings to thought. Not as an enigma, a dizziness, or even just as a truth, but by way of evidence, or rather as the ground of unspeakable evidence, ground or source of every process, of things as of thought, but that we should ceaselessly bring to the surface from beneath the oppositions and demarcations of language.

This ground that is undifferentiated from all differences, this *ground* of *de-exclusion*, is what Chinese thought most commonly calls *tao*, the way of viability which, through its ground of inactualisation (the *wú* 无 which is not nothingness), connects all differences which, in unfolding so as to 'return' to it, are constantly being temporarily brought into light and made current. The *tao* is what 'brings oppositions into communication as one', *dào tōng wéi yī* 道通为一, as the *Zhuangzi* ('On the Equivalence of Things and Discourses') says most succinctly. This means that 'supreme knowledge' is that in which, one degree below, there isn't yet a marked-out frontier. One degree below means where there isn't as yet any disjunction. For 'it is when disjunctions are brought to light that the *tao* is lost', and 'preferences happen with the loss of the *tao*'. And so, against any demand for clarity and distinction, the *tao* cannot be described except by words like 'hazy', 'vague' and 'indistinct' – and saying that it is *evasive*. It is also why it will in consequence be necessary to gain access to a word that is 'barely expressed', *xī yán* 稀言, restraining oneself from determina-tion, remaining on the verge of enunciation and *allusive*, in order to approach this fundamental indistinction. And, once again, this is also why the *tao* is said to be 'tasteless', *dàn hū qí wú wèi* 淡乎其无味 (*Laozi*, 35). It is *bland* because it isn't split into opposing flavours; in not being 'pro-nounced', it is not so much the blandness of the neutral, a description that remains negative, as one which – on the threshold of determination, and thus which predates the demarcation – is maintained in an undefined *between* of savouration.

The consequence is that thinking will no longer be trapped by extrem-ities, extremities that detach and focus, and we will no longer be fascinated by the slicing up of opposites. We will no longer have to distinguish and distinguish again in the hope, going from difference to difference, of attaining the ultimate essence and definition. We will no longer constantly have to separate, and also then to surmount these separations and pene-trate, as we follow the angle of the *logos*, into an unending sequence of determination-surpassing (the dialectical exhaustion that can only be concluded with the arbitrary decree of an absolute Knowledge). Inversely, this won't entail abandoning the word, taking refuge in the ineffable by definitively accusing language of concealing under its fallacious distinc-tions an original unity that, like any paradise, is already lost (the complacency of mystical comfort). But thinking will evolve *between* the two and maintain a tension within this double requirement: at the same

time as being attentive to expunging the equivocal from its word by req-
uisite distinctions, it will reveal more effectively what, predating it, is
effectively – fundamentally – ambiguous and can't be dissociated. Between
the distinctions to be made by my word and those to be unmade in language, the thought-word, keeping itself working, in activity, won't allow
itself to be caught in the trap either of words or of silence. It will neither
be the plaything of words which disfigure what is thinkable nor give in to
the silence that no longer thinks.

XVII

Between (vs Beyond)

1 If ambiguity is what cannot be defined (not because opposites co-exist in it as in a 'mixture' but because they aren't sufficiently differentiated for it to be possible to detach one from the other), it becomes possible to say that ambiguity is the 'between' of their non-separation, or that the place of ambiguity lies in the in-between. *Between* 'joy' and 'sadness': the most original and all the more profound affect, like that aroused by the landscape, cannot be split between these two contrary feelings. Not because one is mingled in the other, or because it oscillates between them both, but because it doesn't yet give rise to their *distinguo*. Yet at the same time it is to recognise that in itself this place of the *between* is a non-place, that it is conceived only through what is other than the self, which is what constitutes this between, and has no *en-soi*. It is therefore without its own determination, possessing nothing that properly belongs to it and having no essence or 'property': it therefore *evasively* eludes the grip of ontology. Strictly speaking, the between does not 'exist'. How could we say 'something' about it, to speak of it other than negatively?

This is why the Greeks, with their eyes fixed on contraries, *antikeimena* (which, in terms of 'being', are the only things that are determined, the only things that are defined by marked features), have not recognised the capacity of the 'between', as inconsistent as it appears, and in consequence they didn't think about it. They envisaged it only in terms of *whatever it is between* and that is the only thing to be described. They have similarly thought in terms of presence *or* absence, or either empty or full, lack or satisfaction, one of which terms forms an alternative to the other and contradicts it – but they neglected what is in-between them, or the *median* that eludes characterisation. But what ethical consequence follows from this, which is marked by the tragic in advance as it squeezes *living* into this dilemma? Either, says Socrates (in *Gorgias*, 492), life is to be regarded as a cask with a hole in it, that is constantly leaking and which we are forever condemned to refill in order to make good this lack that is impossible to fill: we then live under the constant pressure of desire, without ever being able to satisfy it. Or else we know how to stop up this hole of desire and the cask will be full without our having to pour anything into it: we will finally be living in peace and liberated, satisfied and without any further needs. In this latter state, which is that of a perfect rest, we are no longer living, Callicles then rebels – lacking the desire that arouses and thrills us would be to reduce us to the state of a 'stone', having no further aspiration. But in the other state, retorts Socrates, as we are still pouring without ever being able to retain anything, never being satisfied, we would then only be living the derisory life of a 'plover', the bird that evacuates what it has only just absorbed ...

Strangely, but as the logical consequence of ontology, the Greeks thought only in terms of these contraries: either emptying out or fulfilment. But they didn't consider what is *between* desire and satiety. They didn't deploy median time – time to *live* – between the glaring hollows of the one and the satiated fullness of the other. They considered our existences, and the patristic that follows in their wake, in this cruelly tightening vice of a desire that, once fulfilled, becomes repugnant: either the desire that causes our suffering as a result of its lack, or the satisfaction that wearies us and results in disappointment. Hence the difficulty of finding a way out of this contradiction, one that Pascal would consider our 'condition', according to which either we would continue to desire and therefore always to suffer, or else our desires would be satisfied and yet we would be left bored. Or, as Augustine had previously said: 'if I say that you will not be satisfied, that means that you will be hungry; if I say that you will be satisfied, I fear your loathing'. Thus, being unable to conceive of a way out of this dilemma, not knowing how to emerge from this vicious circle in which we either lack or lack because we no longer have a lack, the Greeks, or at least 'Platonism', have been unable to envisage consistency in this life. And they have needed to postpone 'life' into 'another' life. But does thought about paradise itself escape from this aporia?

In other words, I have difficulty in still believing that Plato, the fine and proud aristocrat, would have postponed thought to the 'Over there', *ekei*, so dividing the world into two and fleeing this one, due to asceticism and renunciation, because his desire had become corrupt, as Nietzscheanism insisted. It was rather for want of the necessary tools. Since he did not discover anything to engage with in an effective way in thinking about the *between*, he was only able to depend on the mixing or the 'mixture' that muddled up identities in a confused way that had to be unravelled – and this was something from which we need to 'rescue' ourselves. Haunted and fascinated by Extremities, which alone can be detached and possess characteristics able to be distinguished, and from which differences can be formed that can therefore be constituted as essences giving rise to a definition, the Greeks therefore needed to neglect what happens in between the two, what is *evasive*, in the transition that eludes being assigned. At the same time, we can measure its result: not having been able (or known how) to give consistency to this *between* of life, they could only promote into the 'beyond', *meta*: what, in the *Theaetetus*, Plato had already called 'true life', the *alethes bios* ἀληθὴς βίος – *vera vita*, as Augustine called it – founded in Being and freeing itself at once from *becoming* and *ambiguity*. Not knowing how to think about the 'between', *metaxu*, they had to think about the *meta* of 'meta-physics'. This is where they felt comfortable and upon which it was possible to construct. Didn't everything else, including the renowned 'ascetic' values that have so often been denounced, count only as a consequence?

Yet one formula from the *Zhuangzi* is enough to warn us against this mirage of the rest-state, one that is to be attained in the 'beyond', as well as of the marked extremity. It shelters us from the overly brutal light that would pour out from the antipodes. Discreetly, it moves us forwards from this groove and keeps us in a *between* that has no end. 'To pour without ever filling, to draw without ever exhausting', says one conceptual character to another, 'Obscure Authenticity' (if this evasivity of the fundamental can still be translated) to 'Fertile Wind' (*Zhuangzi*, ch. 12). Since the *tao* is 'without demarcation', what detaches itself, that emerges and 'shines', is not the *tao*. In the same way, 'the word that singles out does not achieve anything'. In other words, what can most easily be singled out is also what is most arbitrary. The *tao*, the 'way', on the contrary, expresses this *between* which cannot be determined from either side, but constantly allows through: it is where we can therefore 'evolve' at leisure. It is when we neither pour until filling nor draw until exhausting – neither saturating nor depriving, withdrawing at the same time from these extreme and dramatic states of (painful) lack and from (boring) fulfilment. *To go forwards* (*yóu* 遊) is the verb that means precisely, through effacing the extremities and without assuming any beginning or end, any departure or destination, *variation in the between*, without fixation or focus, renewing itself by alternation and not extinguishing itself. The Sage 'goes forwards' in the *tao*, it is said, 'like fish in the water'.

If we pursue this three-way exchange from this point, allowing this other voice, that of the Taoist thinker, into the extended and unfinished dialogue between Socrates and Callicles (one of the fiercest of the Greek stage), simply by the counterbalance of his formula, this other voice unravels this alternative and takes apart – or rather *loosens* – this antagonism of the cask that permanently releases us from desire because it is full to the brim *or* the cask that continually renews it because it is full of holes. To pour, but without filling; to draw, but without exhausting: by the regulating alternation produced by the sentence, one verb responding to the other and both staying away from the extremity, this formula is enough to make the logic of the transition understandable – isn't the latter already, more elementarily, that of *respiration*, which is what maintains life? For isn't respiration what effectively stays within the *between* of activity and the tension that regenerates due to its continual exchange, one state already calling on the other one and staying away from untenable and disjunctive states, from complete emptiness and complete fullness? The breath, to which Chinese thought has given priority, offers the most resolute argument against the blockage occurring in one or other of contrary positions, consuming and all-consuming agitation, or inert rest – Greek philosophy, from the perspective of divergence, having given priority to thinking about visual perception but not respiration (because it is too anchored in what is vital and isn't cerebral enough?), distinguishes–assigns and constructs the object.

Let's not give in to the fascination with the extremity, says the Taoist, as though it is what can ultimately reveal the truth (or, if it remains interdependent with the extreme, let us challenge truth). In other words, let's not naïvely think that, by *touching the extremity*, we will be able to know something. It is a matter neither of what is empty making appeal to a relentless pouring out, nor of the full that rests as though we were dead. Let's avoid the critical stage, on both sides, and treat the 'reserve' or the retreat with care – the grounds without ground of the *tao*. By keeping a distance from the extreme, by not slipping into one or the other determination, and equally without 'leaving' or 'sticking' – *bù jí bù lí* 不即不离, as the Chinese so marvellously (and simply) says – in other words, also without either 'sinking into' or depriving oneself, but by illuminating this *between* of activity, you will avoid hypostasising either of what rise up as alternatives: neither the greedy hunger of desire (Callicles) nor the satiety of rest (Socrates); you will escape the suffering of destitution as well as the disgust of fulfilment.

2 This will make it entirely unnecessary to fear finally reversing the perspective under this oblique encouragement (invitation); it will be unnecessary to fear going back to biases that have perhaps been too hastily sealed off by philosophy. Indeed, let's not consider the *between* as what, left without concept and being restricted to separating the extremes, would only be of value as an interval that is easy for thought to straddle and acknowledge from the outset as less intense. Let's not see it as this relative that its indetermination consequently condemns as less 'existence', while the two extremities, that alone are determined (as *eidé*), would touch the absolute. Let's rather take the two borders that have been left as dotted lines, whose radicality we know is so easy to accentuate, as just a support for this *between* in which everything finally happens, starting with this continual transition that is the respiration of life. Life and death, striking us by their occurrence, 'exist', in truth, only to reveal this present and borderless *between*, which *alone exists*. Yet, would it be too much to advance the idea that the reversal valorising this discreet *between*, to the detriment of the dramatic bluster of extremities, silently indicates to us one of the great contemporary ideological mutations: a new value of 'holding between' or of between-your (maintenance of the world,[1] of the word or of health)? Overall, it would be understood that clarity doesn't come with the passage to the extreme (or that clarity needs to be 'blunted', as the *Laozi*, § 4, advises); that truth is not concealed in the extremity – at the *end* – as though it had to be pursued in its entrenchment. And this is undoubtedly what would distance us above all from metaphysics and its 'beyond', the *meta*, bearing on accentuation through surpassing.

It is true that the theoretical fertility of this 'beyond' has been achieved by deploying an operative plan of thought. In promoting the unity of the intelligible or of the concept (*kite main idean* κατὰ μίαν ἰδέαν, as Plato said) beyond the diversity of what is perceptible, or the perfection of a model conceived in the absolute beyond the groping of experience, this other level, projected outside of the world, *ektos tou kosmou* ἐκτὸς τοῦ κόσμου, has allowed an engagement with a capacity of abstraction that assures the mind's initiative has given it a decisive power all over the world that, through science, has in return been shown to be immense: a knowledge has emerged from it in Europe which, over the course of a few centuries, via technology, has changed the planet. Moreover (more involved), Plato knew how, by connecting it onto the force of *erôs*, to make this *ideal* beyond an ideal, one firmly fixed to the deepest desire and mobilising our wishes: just as this ideal has been the driving force of science (and of classical physics), so it has been the driving force of ethics and of politics. It has especially endorsed the thought of Revolution, as the summit of the theoretical and of progress. One would therefore need to be blind, with a blindness which is only the reversal of the past position, not to recognise what this cutting that has separated a 'beyond' from what would immediately lapse into what is 'within' (and, consequently, the *fertility* that comes from dualism) has released and made *possible*. That this cutting may have represented an assault, and even that we have barely begun to count the cost that it might have constituted for *living*, doesn't at all detract from its validity. 'Validity' here partialises its truth. As we distance ourselves from it upon leaving Europe, the time has also come to discern what dividing the world in two in such a way – far from being a banal necessity encountered by any mind in its development, and no matter how inventive it has been – contains that is necessarily arbitrary (or that it is one *possibility* among others), and that we can (and must) henceforth intersect its possibilities with others that haven't been noticed by it. This is where the thought of the *between* appears to me to serve as a unifying term. In consequence, it offers up a mirror in which this thought of the *beyond* will be able to reflect on what it hasn't thought about.

'Between', 'beyond': we shouldn't in fact neglect this conceptual strength of prepositions. Ahead of notions – that end in results and which stabilise – are those that *construct* in thought. In Greek, the 'with a view to what' expresses the aim, or the 'by which' expresses the cause, functionally structuring thought before abstract terms give a settled [*étale*] representation of it. Yet, if the prepositional range is a good deal less in Chinese than in our languages (hence also that Chinese thought-language constructs less), the 'between' enjoys a privileged function in it that is justified by its writing: the two halves of a door facing one another, forming a polarity 門, between which a moonbeam slips away 月 (in an earlier writing, that of the sun 日). This is what the ideogram *jian* offers seeing (and thinking): instead of the door being opaque and blocking out, some in-between remains which indefinitely lets through – the wind, life and the light. Wouldn't even what we call, perhaps too categorically, the world be 'between Heaven and earth' *tiān dì zhī jiān* 天地之間, says the *Laozi* (§ 5), 'comparable to a great bellows'? 'Empty, it is not flat': this emptiness is not a lack; and 'the more we press it, the more it stands out' – the *between* (of the partition of the bellows) is that of activity. Or again, as we are aware, the Chinese painter doesn't paint a given state but a 'between there is and there is not'.

It is still necessary to distinguish what this preposition of 'between', becoming a proposition for thought, can articulate about the diverse, and in consequence signify in a different way. For when such a 'between', *metaxu*, is intercalated, in the heart of Greek thought, it is principally to serve as an *intermediary*: between ignorance and knowledge, such is the 'between' of 'opinion', *doxa*, in Plato; or else between mankind and the gods, such is the intermediary function of Love, *érôs*, as it links them with one another, as in to be 'demonic', in the *Symposium* (or such is the 'between' of the hypostasis, with the soul serving as an intermediary to rise up to God, in Plotinus). From a logical point of view, this 'between' is rightly excluded as a third and middle term between contradictions, Aristotle suggests, thereby walling opposites up in their ontological separation and in principle forbidding any ambiguity. Or, when this 'between' nevertheless has to intervene in order to allow one to think about change in the imperfect world of 'physics', this intermediary 'is necessarily composed only of its contraries': it still doesn't have an *en-soi*, any existence, or its own nature.

The proof of this lies in the fact that Aristotle does not know how to think about the median note in music, or grey among colours (see *Physics*, V, 224 b). This median note 'is low-pitched in relation to the high, and high-pitched in relation to the low', he goes on to say, without being able to conceive of such a 'between' of the transition and the passage. In the same way, grey 'is black in relation to white and white in relation to black'. If change therefore proceeds from the 'between' or from the intermediary, it is because this in itself, in a minor mode, nevertheless extends the status of the extreme serving once again as the contrary of one or the other opposition. Or, as Aristotle sums this up: 'this intermediary is in some way the extremes' (*to metaxu ta akra*), so defining it as well and taking over from one or the other of them. For Aristotle, 'Grey' is therefore not grey, that is to say a colour where one, turning into the other, is neither one nor the other of them: a colour in which black and white, being mingled with one another, lose their boundaries and are neither severable nor characterisable – it is 'blurred', as Verlaine said. But it is alternately – but imperturbably – 'white in relation to black and black in relation to white'. The intermediary is a middle term, therefore equally a term, just as much a *terminus*. It interrupts change in mid-stream and decomposes it by setting itself up as a point both of arrival and departure of the latter, but doesn't allow a better grasp of how the transition operates through it.

3 It will therefore be necessary to explore this other vocation of the *between*, when it is not reduced to the status of an intermediary or degree, between the most and the least, but is deployed as the *letting pass through*. In Chinese thought, what we call (as we reify it) the 'real' being envisaged in terms of breath, flow and respiration (to translate *qi* 气 as 'energy' is still too Greek), the 'between' is – or rather 'serves' ('is worth') as – [that from which / by which any advent proceeds and is deployed. This is the way *by which*, in the

well-known passage in the *Zhuangzi* (ch. 3), the knife of Ding the butcher penetrates 'between the joints', 节者有閒, to separate the flesh of the ox to be cut open: not meeting with any obstacle, or therefore with any resistance in this 'between' of the interstice, this knife which has no thickness cannot wear out and remains as keen as when it was sharpened. Yet it is said that the same thing goes for our capacity to 'nourish' the life within us (the meaning of 'to nourish' here not being restricted to the body – or, more ideally, to the soul). If such a circulation is being thoroughly maintained in the 'between' of our physical actualisation (*xing* 形: let's avoid calling it separately the 'body'), irrigating it by passing through it from the interior, without encountering any obstacle or anything that obstructs its passage, without the 'way' being barred, which begins with respiration ('the human commonly breathes through his throat, the wise man through his heels', we read in the *Zhuangzi*), our vitality will remain alert and cannot be exhausted (the Chinese theme of 'long life' in loco of immortality).

In passing from the knife to the brush, isn't this also what the painter says – or rather does – in order to express vitality physically? 'Contemplating the painting of a literati', said Su Dongpo,[2] 'is comparable to examining a noble horse'. But what does it mean to paint or inspect a horse? Do we know how to reach the flow and force it bears internally? The artisans of the brush only attain the external attributes and only create a picturesque scene from it 'with the riding-whip, the pelt, the manger and the fodder': its surge [*essor*] is entirely lost and we soon grow weary of it. For if, remaining with this image of the horse, it should *effectively* 'not consist in its riding-whip and pelt' or any such attributes, at the same time, 'if there is no riding-whip or pelt, there's no horse at all': the tangible – what is physical and concrete – is needed so that what constitutes the impulsiveness of the steed passes through and animates it – since such a spirit is attained neither *in* the perceptible, which is limited by its concretion, nor in some 'beyond' that effaces its visibility. What therefore to paint? Or rather should the response be once again to withdraw from that too-reifying 'which' and substitute 'transition' for it? The response is sufficient to disontologise it (Fang Xun[3]): what we understand by the impetuous impulse animating the steed 'lies completely in the between' – between these external attributes – 'including the riding-crop and the pelt'. Yet, let's remind ourselves that the painters of our modernity, long before the philosophers, also practised this disontologisation in Europe. Braque, once again, said: 'what is between the apple and the plate can also be painted', and even 'this "in-between" seems to me as essential as what they call the "object"'.

The virtue of the 'between' and the 'through' is that they don't postpone – as the *beyond* does – neither containing nor limiting, as all concrete assignment does. It means to stay *evasive*, and hence in infinite unfolding, but without departing from the perceptible or abandoning the phenomenality of things. It means, in disappropriating the physical and the perceptible, in freeing them from their compartmentalised demarcations, to restore their circulation and allow them to emanate, instead of leaving them to stall. Therefore, it means opening them out onto a surpassing that would not be an abandonment. Landscape painters in China have been particularly responsive to this, or rather this is why from very early on they have privileged the landscape so much in painting. If they promoted landscape painting and made it into an art of living a millennium before European painting, it is because they realised that the landscape is not 'part of the land' that nature presents to an 'observer', such a subject posing it in front of the observer as an 'ob-ject', according to our ordinary definition – at least, according to that given by the dictionary – but as the place of activation of the *between* which, through its capacity to pass through and unfold, overcomes its limitation of place and becomes a 'world' in which we can endlessly 'develop', untrammelled and receptive.

The Chinese painter therefore tells us that a landscape 'is' not *in* one or another element, and as such offering itself to be viewed, but is 'between'. Consequently, it eludes the monopoly of sight, even of a panorama, and is promoted as a place in which *to live*. The characteristic of the landscape, in other words, is to *open up the between* among the elements which are no longer just components but become *correlants* – according to the logic of correlation as Chinese thought developed it in thinking through pairing: there is a 'landscape', rather than simply a 'land' standing out topographically, when *inter*-action occurs in it that brings into tension factors which, by the various plays of their polarity, become vectors of intensity. By naming what we call landscape 'mountain(s)–water(s)', *shān-shuǐ* 山水, the Chinese think about what makes the landscape in this *between-factors* (between-vectors) of 'mountain' and 'water': *between* the High of the mountain and the Low of the water, the stabilising effect of the one and flowing effect of the other, or *between* the compact form of the one and the formless transparency of the other, or what we see massively in front of us (the 'mountain') and what we hear trickling from all sides ('water'). Yet, from what opens and operates between these capacities, which are activated while being opposed, something infinite or 'unfathomable', or what could be called – but without allowing such a 'freeing' to slip into dualism – a 'spirit' of the landscape extricates itself evasively: widening out and decanting from the materiality of the perceptible, but still without leaving it.

Whether the 'between' is the source, perhaps the only one, of what is inexhaustible, rather than what one is tempted to *transfer* into the 'beyond', or, differently from what the terms mark out, separated and limited by their properties and qualities, this *between* that lets through is at the start of an unfinished unfolding, and reveals, more crucially still, the possibilities of *intimacy* developing *between* subjects. We need to enquire into why intimacy, which begins *between* subjects, is the only thing *within them* that doesn't dry up: why it alone, by eluding the contradiction I started with, can counteract the logic of passion sinking into possession or desire which, once satisfied, becomes disappointing. This is what makes it different from love, which, as we are aware, enjoys celebrating the Other, adorning it with so many qualities which, as they touch their limits, are consequently inclined of themselves to go into reverse, causing this 'love', once it has been satisfied, to slip into indifference or rejection. In contrast, intimacy, beginning between subjects, is not attributable to one or to the other and its fate is not therefore linked to the quality of one or the other, a quality that is always threatened when there is no further possibility of going beyond it and reaching its extremity, in consequence causing it to become disappointing and dis-qualifying it. We no longer know, in this between that is opened up by intimacy, to whom of the two the intimacy is due – this question itself loses its meaning. But here intimacy constantly renews itself by its own means, over the course of days, and holds itself *between*, as a ground which moreover hasn't found a ground, of these 'nothings' of a word that no longer seeks to 'express' what indefinitely allows the silence to pass by.

How, then, does this 'between' of intimacy which hasn't yet been confined to intimacy and has not – even worse – been reversed into self-absorption come to be produced and take shape? Or what existence can it have when it is before all else without an essence? What does it mean to open up the 'between' between us by each of us undoing our subjective property and 'privacy'? This *between* which is woven from my hand placed on the nape of her neck – or from the reminder of past moments, or the idea of sharing a home and the whole mythology we have naïvely invented between us, which has ritually sealed the complicity – this active *between* brings into tension, by detaching the Other from other listless people, it elevates her into a pole of relationality – this *between* is one that is intensive. Instead of leaving each to their own devices, in what is determined as their character or qualities, this *between* of intimacy, lifting the frontier that exists between them, opens a field of shared intentionality and, as this between is no more mine than it is yours, it doesn't dry up due to the limitation of subjects, and its possibilities aren't extinguished: the *interior* is discovered in it from the 'beyond'. Thus, instead of letting the relation lapse into a state of being settled down (as is the lot of everything which, no longer lacking anything, has been satisfied), this *between* of intimacy maintains it in its *surge*. It is activated in or rather *from* this between which, not being hoarded from any side, eludes the possession – the adequacy – that sterilises.

Notes

1   This is a play on words impossible to replicate in English: ' "tenir l'entre" ou de l'entre-tien (entretien du monde…') [trans.].
2   Su Dongpo, better known as Su Shi (1037–1101), one of China's greatest poets and essayists. He was also an accomplished calligrapher and public official [trans.].
3   Fang Xun (1736–99), a poet, calligrapher and painter of landscapes [trans.].

XVIII

Surge (vs Settled)

1 If the thought of Being misses something of our experience, it is because in determining, assigning and conferring properties, it assumes an adequacy of self with self; or, more precisely, it assumes that this 'self' coincides with itself and its essence, and its characterisation comes from this. Yet doesn't this *coincidence* contradict what *living* in its own being is, but which isn't rightfully of 'being'? Or let's say that, if things coincide completely with themselves, which leaves them in their state of 'things', the characteristic of living is constantly to de-coincide with the self, which holds it in the tension of life. Already, what is being signalled towards when we speak in passing – admittedly in a trivial way, admittedly without thinking of stopping there – that the 'festival happens before the festival'? Doesn't this *trivial*, that we only note, reveal – doesn't it raise – something that the thought of Being has concealed and has even prevented us from thinking about? The idea that the festival is before the festival doesn't just mean that the anticipation is more beautiful than the reality, or that we live more fully in the imagination than we do when it becomes actual, and therefore that any festival would be disappointing in relation to what we had hoped for. We could assuredly not be satisfied with this, to remain in what is 'psychological'. If we pick up the thread of what appears in it in a commonplace way, wouldn't we discover a more radical *non-coincidence* in it, so weakening the determinant basis of the ontological? Yet it is from this alone that we are able to think what *living* is in principle – I'd prefer to say: in its surge or its outpouring.

The fact that the festival doesn't coincide with the 'festival', that it loses its way when it settles [*étale*], that, when we say 'it's festival time', it is already not absolutely the case, this is what, being more widely verified, still doesn't escape logic – at least, that of onto-logy. Not that it would be me, personally, who doesn't know how to be contemporaneous with the festival, but it is rather the festival which, when it faithfully produces all the signs of being a 'festival', cannot be contemporaneous with itself in its flowing out. If the 'festival' is therefore attested, whether it is recognised and praised as such or whether we constantly say 'it's festival time', it is because the *festival* already no longer exists. Because, when the *marks* (*Merkmal*, as logicians say) by which we define the 'festival' are realised, and occur in a positive sense, it already isn't absolutely the festival; it is sufficient to reveal that it eludes them, not in its 'essence', but in what I'd call its surge – the two terms finding themselves opposed to one another; that what is effective about it – both in terms of going and being active – evades this positivity and therefore becomes lost in its definition. From these tangible marks in which it settles and which determine it, the festival has already withdrawn.

Let's therefore be able to pause for a moment at this triviality, not scorning the banality. When someone is said to be 'virtuous', someone we recognise and henceforth describe in such terms, don't we also suspect that, in a certain way, this virtue *already* no longer exists? Even though all of the demands that constitute virtue are fulfilled – or, rather, because of this very fact – he no longer satisfies them? For instance, take these cautious inverted commas which take hold of such a qualifying term and are sufficient to express, by ostensibly detaching it from the speaker, that we don't want to be duped by this statement. 'Virtue', in being dissociated and assigned, which allows it to be acknowledged and by which it is defined, finds itself at the same time determined. This means that it is bounded, sealed, stiffened and stamped. It puts it on the way to being a stereotype: it is already *a convention*. From what it has that is applied, being meticulously verified from one act to the next, the fertile, overflowing, inspiring–insolent generosity, which *effectively* constitutes virtue, is withdrawn. Whoever is said to be 'virtuous' (about whom we imagine saying that he is 'virtuous'), as everyone apart from him knows, is merely someone in need of virtue: by becoming describable – and identifiable – this virtue loses its capacity.

According to what, having emerged from the tombs, today appears to be the most authentic version, we see the *Laozi* begin with these words (§ 38):

Superior virtue isn't virtuous,

which is why it has virtue;

inferior virtue doesn't leave virtue,

which is why it is without virtue.

Yet, if such a formulation takes us straightaway to the edge of contradiction, and even resolutely challenges the so-called principle of non-contradiction as the predicate twice turns against its subject – for all that, it still isn't a paradox, or an example of abstruse or mystical thought. But the capacity at work, we are forewarned from the start, is to be considered in a divergent way, indeed at the greatest distance from its tangible marks: it cannot be reduced to any characteristics or properties that serve to define it or that would constitute its essence and through which one sees it presented. Not that what makes 'virtue' suspect in this way would be the opposition between appearance and existence, or even that it can be accused of hypocrisy: the expected division into two is irrelevant. Far from the 'virtuous' person being suspected of being virtuous only in appearance, it's rather the inverse: the fact that he clings too closely and diligently to virtue (so that he doesn't 'leave' it), is riveted to it and attached so conscientiously to what is described as an ideal of virtue. This means he engages in acts of virtue that are too easily identifiable, and in consequence praiseworthy, but which lead him to miss what actually makes virtue an inexhaustible flow.

When a country fully displays its strength, or is even designated as the strongest, or in any case is recognised as being at the summit of its power, we know quite well that at its apogee this strength is *already* withering: the process of decline has been set in motion – History offers repeated testimony to this effect. There is a non contemporaneous quality between the marks attesting to the effect on the one hand and their source (what the *Laozi* calls the 'mother') on the other. For the manifestation in itself constitutes a result and is therefore already surpassed. Yet what is effective lies in *propensity* – while what allows itself to be recognised and identified as such (the 'such' of the essence, that the definition expresses), in its state of surge, as marked out and labelled, has discreetly started to reverse. This is the sense in which I understand this other formula from the *Laozi* (§ 2):

> Everyone knows the beautiful as beautiful,
>
> and it is already ugly;
>
> everyone knows the good as good,
>
> and it is already not good.

Not only is what is recognised as 'beautiful', or as 'good', and which serves as their definition, already on the way to its wasting away, but it is even against this that a new 'beautiful', new values, without being completely formulatable or identifiable, are in the process of being invented. All those who participate in the renewal of art or thought know this. It is to this that they owe the fact that, for a while longer, they will remain misunderstood or thwarted.

We also need to draw out the consequences that follow from this. If the manifest – settled – stage of culmination is already one that is withering, the one of effective plenitude at its source is logically deficient. The (prior) 'superior virtue', not yet offering marks of virtue, appears 'lacking', as the *Laozi* consequently recognised; it is said to be hollow 'like a valley' (§ 41). Or, 'great achievement is like a lack', 'great plenitude is like emptiness' (§ 45). Or 'great eloquence' is like 'stammering' (ibid.). Let's pause again on this 'like': far from announcing a voluntary illusion or the deceit of an appearance, this *like* shows how necessarily this fundamental capacity appears in a topsy-turvy way – 'between the lines' – when it emerges at the point of the tangible. But it is also why, it is added, 'being used, it isn't exhausted': as it has no desire to settle and establish itself, and remains in retreat, it equally doesn't allow itself to be consumed. We see the evidence in painting in the value of the sketch (but how long has it taken us in Europe correctly to recognise this?): that there may be, according to Baudelaire's words, paintings that are 'made', but not 'finished' (while unfortunately so many are 'finished', but not 'made' ...). For what the sketch reveals against the ontological tradition – whose watchword is that the more determined something is, the more it 'exists' – is that the work is all the more effective when it knows how to keep itself upstream, maintaining itself in process: that it takes its leave ahead of time in order to remain *at work*, that it is not completed so as not to become settled. 'To finish off' a painting, Picasso once said, is like finishing off a bull; it means to kill it.

'The great square has no angle(s)', the *Laozi* (§ 41) says provocatively (but should this indicate any 'provocation'?), so shattering the definition of it. Just as the 'virtue' that 'doesn't come out of virtue' is 'without virtue', so the square which doesn't come out of its determination as a square, which encloses itself in its definition as a square (is a 'squared-square'), is revealed to be cramped up, has become sterile, and no longer unfolds its 'extent' or 'grandeur' as a square. Indeed, what does 'great' mean here? Evidently it would not be a matter of size (in this respect, the *tao* can equally well be declared 'small'), but that this proposed qualification, 'square', instead of folding in upon its determination, of closing itself over its relevance, stays within its deployment, in flight [*essor*], in a *de*-determination which preserves its *receptivity*, keeps it back from being stuck to its definition as a 'square' and becoming *settled* there. 'Great', therefore, here means what does not let itself be riveted to its determination but, exceeding what encloses it in its ground, stops itself from being immobilised and from freezing – from fixing itself in an essence subject to knowledge, and getting bogged down in it. 'The great work avoids happening', the *Laozi* says next: the work is all the more affirmed at work – remaining *effective* – when it keeps itself from sinking into a complete determination; remaining upstream from a definitive actualisation, it preserves, in the very heart of its advent, that ground which it emerges from and which keeps it in a living state.

2 Settled is therefore what I would call this inverse moment of the surge, when everything has reached the end of its development, is obvious and *coincides*. It is the moment of definition and statement, the *logos* – does it therefore follow that it is truth? It is when everything is completely accessible, obvious and saturated, and yet because of this it no longer 'works'. It is the same when something is certainly *seen* on the canvas but no longer *appears*. This immobile face-to-face, offering no further indirectness or revealing anything to hold on to, becomes sterile: it is a 'finished' painting (one that is no longer *in process*). Slack water, the turn of the tide: it has stopped rising but hasn't yet descended – it is there, flatly in front of us, no longer moving or having any energy. A ship is settled in the same way when it is said to be becalmed, at a standstill, when it neither advances nor goes back – it remains 'as it is' and doesn't go any farther; nothing more happens. Everything remains in its *en-soi*, folded into its determination, completely patent, but having become unproductive. I shall therefore finally have to detach what I've started to call, by opposition, the *effective* from this prescriptive realm of the *determinative* (that of ontology) – therefore, to strain what we too easily (unitarily) call the 'reality' between one and the other.

Between, on the one hand, the capacity at work such that, in its surge, it overflows and unmakes any possible determination, and, on the other hand, the *settled quality* of determination, retracting these possibilities and codifying them, consequently serving definition as such, for henceforth it is completely encirclable and is therefore specifiable–identifiable. In this state of qualification, there only remains a parcelling up of particular determinates, that are completely 'settled' but which, in their meticulous labelling, are cut off from their intense ground, amputated from their emergence.

Since the particular quality of the statement, the *logos*, and above all of the principle of non-contradiction which is its first axiom, is to assign the characteristic that belongs to it to an object and to assume its properties (in other words, the determinations it 'properly' possesses and which form its 'being', thereby conveniently placing it on the path towards knowledge, and even opening a royal way to science), we can see how a thinking like that of the *Laozi* from the outset takes the opposite path. But what other path does it open up? For it isn't so much the 'flowing' character of things which goes against definition (according to the old Greek, 'Heraclitean', argument of 'mobilism'), or that would make us miss what is individual and changeable – both are ineffable, under the generality and stability (the two of them marching in step) that would lead language to plaster things over as it properly makes 'things'. No, it is rather the more fundamental fact that determination – any determination – grasps the settled and not the surge; that definition is situated down- and not up-stream, in the state of what is flat, sterile, and not of what is fertile. In the state of what is already completely developed and spread out, it is therefore already in the process of wilting and has already ceased to exist: true virtue couldn't care less about virtue, just as true eloquence couldn't care less about eloquence. Definition (codification) thus grasps the capacity of things although it is already *ebbing away*. Because they are *already* in the process of isolation and retraction, some parts of living can be perceived and analytically detached in properties or qualities. Definition, indeed, actually grasps 'being' in its coincidence, but not the process from which this capacity emerges. Hence, the source of the surge would always be *in retreat*, as the *Laozi* teaches.

3 Having turned against ontology, modern philosophy in Europe, and more specifically phenomenology, has some awareness of the tension between the not yet determinable surge and the settling of determination, or between the fertile advance of the indefinable and the codification of the definition. And this tension is even carried along, with respect to European rationalism, to the point of contradiction. Indeed, I believe it is lacerated along the lines of this cleavage. For it has done one of two things. Either it has conceived of thought as knowledge, knowledge being founded on adequacy (of determination) – in other words, the fact of *coinciding*, and, as such, has had 'evidence' as a touchstone. In this, *evidence* is really the only way of having the thing present to consciousness, in total coincidence, and not only

'presumed' or 'aimed at', because it corresponds to the complete covering of one by the other, the 'gaze of the mind' then reaching the 'thing itself' (Husserl starting off from the Cartesian *cogito* to found the apodicticity of science). 'Evident' means on the whole the fulfilment of the 'characteristic' and the determination, a term beyond which we are unable to go further and therefore in which no advance is possible – how then can one be sure in the mind of blocking any presence in this way, in perfect coincidence because it is completely isolatable? Or else thought is therefore thought against the grain, as *eluding the enclosing of this characteristic* (see Heidegger in *What is Metaphysics?*, in which the rupture with Husserl appears for the first time): if it is true that science itself, in its 'characteristic' determination, is only interested in being itself so as to coincide with it, from the 'nothing' that it doesn't want to know anything about, discovering in doing so that it is nevertheless reliant on this 'nothing' from which it turns away – already involved in it. It is therefore necessarily postponed, so it may take hold of itself, ahead of itself: steered to disengagement.

From this, it appears that even science would not be sufficiently in alignment with itself, or *doesn't coincide* with itself (that it is *zwiespältig*); that it can only enclose its characteristic ('being') by overflowing equally from it; that the ground therefore is never the ground, but opens on to an unfathomed 'without-ground', *Abgrund*, in which the Cartesian tree of philosophy takes root without thinking about it. It would similarly prove impossible to fix a radical point of departure, as much for Being as for thought, and we would find ourselves forced to go up ever higher towards the original – precisely towards this upstream, but escaping the understanding and even wherever there *actually are* opposites which coincide: where, when, as Heidegger said, we relegate nothingness, this fact means that we are still referencing it; where it is thus Being itself which, contradictorily, at the same time, 'denounces and hides' – 'harmonises and steals away'; where Being therefore cannot be revealed, in the settling of being, except by 'withdrawing' as Being, etc. Yet would there really be any choice in this alternative glimpsed between *coincidence* (claimed by 'science') and the *non-coincidence* (from which 'mystery' comes), or between the *evidence* of alignment and the *withdrawal* towards something more originating (*Evidenz /Entzug*)? In other words, do we need to 'resolve' this contradiction?

I'd prefer to believe it necessary to maintain the divergence between the two in order to *remain* within it. Indeed, what does 'to think' mean if not to work in this tension *between* one and the other? At the same time, it is to develop a logic of necessary alignment – in other words, of coincidence – therefore keeping legitimately to the evidence, without which thinking, without further relation to knowledge, loses its rigour. But this is equally without pausing at what we then too easily take for a 'ground', a reassuring ground (because it is one that is completely coincident) of knowledge, and opening oneself to the depth of the *without ground* which always goes beyond it, leading to 'reflection', in advance – the thought of *living* arises from this de-coincidence (and doesn't Husserl, again exploiting the fertility of the Cartesian *cogito*, go beyond the resource by inappropriately seeing it as 'experiential', *lebendig*, evidence of the 'I am'?). But, nevertheless, without consequently lapsing (precisely because one equally holds to the other demand, or rather that one remains in it – that of the evidence) into some complacency with respect to 'Mystery', becoming the abstruse, and from what he calls vaticination – Heidegger has not always escaped from this. 'To think' is to work jointly (contradictorily) between the two: *between* the determination of the characteristic and its own appeal to dispossession; *between* the evidence and the alignment of anxiety of that of which it is already the loss. This is why it is legitimate to think through the rigour of non-contradiction, but also the depth of ambiguity: to establish the vocation of science, determining the nature of *being*, but also to probe what, in *living*, logically escapes it.

In other words, it will ultimately be necessary to take the logic of *living* out from that of 'being' or onto-logy – I don't see how we can have access to thinking about living if we don't first adopt this suspicion, and this demand isn't taken into account in the first place. This is so because the one is exclusive of the other, even if my thinking occurs *between* the two. For the thought of *living* and the question of Being (in other words, taking the surge or that of *essence*, or more specifically non-coincidence and determination, into consideration) compete with one another; and the Greeks (although it is true this hasn't always been the case, as Heraclitus or the Stoics testify), from the moment their thinking occurred under the hegemony of the one, the 'question of being', have made us miss the other one.

If 'being' knows itself by coincidence, since it is what is settled, and since its determinative character delivers it as such to the definition of science, then *living*, in contrast and in order to be thought about (apprehended through *de-coincidence* in such a way that it can be married with its actual surge) will require that we elaborate a new logic from it.

4 Yet this ground without ground of withdrawal from which the *effective* assumes its surge, ahead of the determination, is *illuminated* by the *Laozi* (§ 41) in which it is seen as characteristic of the 'way', the *tao*, but in which there is no hint of any laceration or anticipation of a possible point of conflict:

The way withdraws: nameless,

only the way is apt to match and make happen.

So this Taoist thought of *non-coincidence*, which detaches the surge from the settled as (without being aware of it) it opens a breach in the determination of Being, offers at the same time an indirect approach by which to think about life. Or, more specifically, since the notion of 'life' will already be in a state of settling, to think about what *living* is in its surge rather than in its principle. For to live, in its surge, is nothing other than, de-coinciding with the self, to disengage the self, or to leave the self so as to become self. The characteristic of *living* in its intensity is that it cannot be confined in any property or, to express it differently, that it is always in a process of surpassing a 'self'. Coincidence with the self is death, or, more brutally, when one coincides completely with the self, one is dead – the limit of what is settled. This is actually what all thought of *living* has had to think about and it therefore equally applies to Christianity as it thinks about the 'living' God: no longer in a serene way this time, but dramatically, because it is in a direct break with the alignment of knowledge extolled by ontology. Its theoretical violence (its 'folly', *môria*, faced with the *sophia*) has been to seek to express *in Greek*, in an *anti-logos* logos, the fundamental impropriety which means that life is called upon to dissociate itself from itself in order to redefine itself in its other without ceasing to be in life: whoever is 'attached' to life 'loses' it (John, XII, 25); or it is necessary to renounce life to be able to deploy life (eternally).

For, as Hegel contemplated when thinking about 'life as a process' – in other words, in its 'in-quietude' or its 'un-rest' (*Unruhe*), the fundamental *impropriety* (or non-coincidence of self with self instead of coincidence with the self) by which alone the concept of 'life' can be animated, by which alone the concept of life can itself *live*, enclosing and stabilising it in the self and so making it an inert 'self', is actually most radically thought in the West in the Christian figure of God, in opposition to philosophy. All things considered, it is from this self alone that life (triumphing over the identity of essence that would fix it in itself) can find its concept. God (the Father) sends his son, claims (as the Master) to be a slave, and lives (as the Eternal one) through dying. God has to separate himself from himself and renounce his self, to pass into his other and go as far as to experience the contrary of the self, in order to become the 'living God' (as 'Mind'). This consequently amounts to recognising, in a conceptual rather than represented way, that the non-coincidence or 'inequality', *Ungleichheit*, of the self with its object 'is just as much the inequality of the substance with itself' (in the preface to the *Phenomenology*): this is what, as a self-negation of a 'self', makes it at the same time a mediation of the self to the self, promoting the self by dissociation from itself, and from this 'substance', that is otherwise inert, the 'subject' of a becoming is formed.

Yet wouldn't this capacity of the surge, from which comes what is *effective*, detaching itself from the determinative of the thing or from the 'substance', and in doing so actively maintaining itself in becoming, in other words in its process of emergence, be the source of any valorisation – what I think in its own way the *Laozi* began by posing? Would this not therefore be at the beginning of morality as well as of the aesthetic? Thereby separating what is prescriptive and codifying about it, what is set and stiff, from morality, wouldn't this capacity of the surge, withdrawing from what is settled and even being in conflict with it, be the fertile 'upstream', where all promotion originates? The *upstream* (of the surge) would thereby be substituted advantageously for what is 'superior' (hierarchical) about ordinary morality – which is why I'd speak of 'gaining access to' (the resource of *living*), which doesn't pre-suppose any meta-physical and ascetic dualism, and not of 'rising up' (for which all spiritualism has a taste: to the 'good', to the 'celestial', to the 'divine', etc.). And could there even be any other alternative, whether it would finally be a matter of the 'good' or the 'beautiful', if we stay with these categories that are already too *conclusive*, too *settled*, than these two rival possibilities: to *gain access* to the surge or to *fall back* into the settled, the surge that hasn't so far been recognised (or occurred), which holds in tension, or the settling which, at the same time that it establishes itself, is already on the wane?

There's life in surge, which is literally to live, opening possibilities not yet marked out in virtues as in faculties and consequently not getting stuck, and there's life that is settled, installing itself in its comfort because in alignment with itself and recognised in its quality, but at the same time it reifies itself by being retracted. 'Life as two' is settled in the 'state' of marriage, one that is reassuring and stabilised, and that yields to the 'gentle habit' (did Stendhal regret it?), in which we stay with the other primarily so as not to be alone, in which we keep each other company, and even where we are good together, this 'good' expressing an alignment and satisfaction that doesn't look any farther. Without analysing it, this is where the intimate is folded into intimacy, has lapsed into what is nothing more than a quality. Or else *living as two* is in surge: it constantly renews the encounter because it never takes it for granted, never believing that it is secured as it intersects the intimacy of sharing with the extimity of dispossession, and does so to render the Other in its radical strangeness – from which the infinity of complicity, as piercing as a source, is experienced. Living is then too intense, too ambiguous as well in its emergence, to be judged simply as a 'good' moment. A 'good moment' (like a 'beautiful painting') already belongs to the decline.

On the one hand, there are poets who are, strictly speaking, the singers of the surge, or who can be called the freshness of morning: René Char's *Matinaux*, 'I laugh at the blond waterfall … ' (Rimbaud) – but 'blond' doesn't here lapse into its colour; and there are all those who have put the settled description of things into alexandrines, each of which can be inspected and adequately expounded as is necessary. There are painters of the surge – the true painters, the only ones – including, of course, those from the age when the art of representation reigned supreme. For, while 'representing', the painter has already deviated from it; while depicting, he simply 'paints' and undoes what the painting has been 'depicting' (he *de*-depicts), lapsing into the emerging undercurrent [of] what has not yet become 'object' – such as we find in Chardin's still-lifes. Then so-called 'modern' painting has made an explicit claim for such a surge, declaring war on what is settled: Cézanne's apples are not left to be assigned as 'apples', as things, any more than the table is: they are grasped at an earlier moment, one that is ethical as much as aesthetic, a time that is upstream, that occurred before the 'lapse'. Or let's note that Kandinsky deliberately chose the pictural language of the surge while freeing himself from anything settled. Or, again, we know that, from the *settlement* of the 'land', where everything is there, flatly there, in its place and coinciding with itself, where everything is consequently rather bleak, the *landscape* detaches and promotes the surge, causing a whole world to emerge from this corner of nature. Once again, it is necessary to meet this surge head-on and confront it, to be genuinely contemporary without *postponing anything*.

XIX

Non-Postponement (vs Delaying Knowledge)

1 Coming face to face with the surge, so as to remain, so to speak, at its level, isn't to lose its abrupt emergence, isn't to *settle* it. To respond to its demand (for isn't this the only ethical demand, as everything else results from it?), to react to the fact that this *surge* comprises what is not yet arranged and specified and has sunk into the conventional, isn't to let it be diluted in a *postponement* that allows it to be tamed. It is not, in other words, to give it time to recover its specific and distinctive features that integrate and reassure, depriving it of what is prominent and assailing about it, and leaving it to 'decline'. Yet strategies of avoidance of the surge, all the enterprises that reduce its intensity, have become so familiar at the current time that we no longer notice them. They all the more effectively hide behind technical commodities. Those tourists who get out of their coach, take photos and then go back satisfied, are of this type. By putting what had attracted them 'into a box', while labelling it as being 'so beautiful!', as is so conventionally exclaimed, they have in fact got rid of it. Rather than letting themselves be seized – and deprived – by what they have alighted on, and which from all sides is suddenly extended to them, they hastily protect themselves, using tricks to fool themselves into thinking they are preserving this view, or it might just be this tree or the part of the roof caught by the light.

Photography has provided them with a propitious tool that allows them to evade what is *inappropriable* about the surge that has immediately and brutally summonsed them – even if they don't know by exactly what: it allows them to keep it at a distance, 'out of respect', to pass prudently to the side of it. To 'take' a photo (this 'take' should be understood in its elementary sense of hasty and even instantaneous capture) is like taking hold of a prop, or a handle, so as not to allow oneself to be 'shaken'. It's to avoid being present, here and now, *in the actual fact*, facing this corner of the world or this part of the roof. This intervention has given them a screen and allowed them to take cover, to interpose. Do they have any suspicion of this? Instead of dealing with what they have suddenly encountered that belongs to the surge, they have protected themselves – thanks to photographic reproduction – by allowing it to fall into what is settled in time and evenly divides it up. This is all done in good faith, of course. Because the ruse involved is too urgent, having too much of the quality of a stampede, for it to be analysed, or to give rise to any duplicity. They take the photo, they say, for remembrance, to keep it and once again to have the occasion to 'look at it' later. But the desire to keep or to conserve is to flee: it is to flee what has risen up as a surge, uncovering from the present, and in relation to which this exclamation of 'beautiful!' cast in passing by has already been turned into a folding screen.

In the same way, when listeners come in and set up their tape recorders on the desk, it is necessary to forewarn them: you are doing this to avoid *being present* and having to listen. You think you will be better able to make use of this talk (listen to it again later at leisure and so on), but in fact you are making a preliminary arrangement in such a way that you will never really listen to it: that you will never actually be *listening* at all. Not now, since you know you will be able to listen to it later at leisure, when you want to, *ad libitum*, as many times as you want: you can, therefore, be less attentive now and let your attention wander without remorse – you have put a security system in place. Not later, because if (when) you listen again, it will be in a way that has already formed a rut, that is settled, in relation to what you have anticipated or got used to, and to which you are at least a little immune and indifferent – whose effects you have taken the precaution of stifling. Words 'fly away', it's said, *verba volant* – they don't repeat themselves, but also become heightened by this foretold death. Yet, from these words, you have not confronted (or supported) the fact that they are really of the *instant*, and that, because of this, they involve 'instance', urgent solicitation and insistence, that cannot be reproduced and that will never again happen, and above all within yourself, activating a 'yourself' – in which they are, above all, precious.

Admittedly, it is not a matter of once more starting the everlasting trial of technology from another angle, but simply of dwelling on what everyone knows: that technology, by increasing presence, atrophies it; that, by extending its apparatus everywhere, it shelters and protects us. It protects us from the onslaught of the present or from what I shall call, in a less instrumental ('suspended') way, its constant 'assault'. It claims to be able to give us an ever greater mastery of 'time', as if time didn't find in its 'flight', which is incriminating, the very condition of its emergence. This allows us not only to go more quickly, but also to programme the future more rigorously as much as to conserve the past more completely, and especially to take revenge on the slenderness of the present by the simultaneity it has developed. But we all know that this is a false reign: that, by allowing us to do so many things at once (to walk at the same time as listen to music, answer the mobile phone, and so on), technology disengages us surreptitiously from an exacting present. It keeps us in a compressible blandness that no longer constitutes an encounter: *to surf* – the verb signals this proclaimed victory, works against the receptivity at which it claims to be aiming. For the present is based above all upon, and becomes salient because of, what is exclusive to it – this is already the difference between a recording to which we listen and the concert we attend. Yet this banal observation should make us uneasy; we need to emerge from its truism and probe it. For this *present* of the surge, at the same time as it is given to us in immediacy (and isn't it even the only thing that is immediate?), is what we nevertheless must conquer – and to which we have to *gain access*.

2 Heraclitus formulated it in a trenchant way: 'Lacking intelligence, they are as if deaf to what they have listened to; the saying bears witness to them: while present, they are absent' (fr. 34). Not that they might have listened without intelligence but that, while 'listening', they are nevertheless 'like the deaf', making them 'unintelligent'. Absent to what is their present, says Heraclitus, they don't *encounter*. They are actually there, physically present, but, as the saying goes, they have their minds elsewhere — in fact, nowhere at all: dispersed, dissipated, idle; 'not awakened', as Heraclitus puts it (fr. 89). For these 'many', who are 'not awakened', don't think about things 'as they stumble upon them', he further says, but 'they think they do' (fr. 17). 'Stumble upon', 'encounter' (*enkureîn*): there is what I stumble on, but that I am tempted not to take responsibility for in my 'thinking' (*phroneîn*), in other words that I risk not conceiving in the raw, sudden, confused – because appearing – 'as it is' [*tel quel*] of its surge. I let it fall back into this settling of acquired codifications, consequently projecting conventional images onto it, such that they sediment in the mind (as 'they seem [to be] to themselves', *heautoisi dokeousin*, as Heraclitus aptly said) – without allowing this surge of the present to burst in. Hence the presence–absence to which we are condemned, a presence but one diluted with absence, and with which *living* is threatened.

But, instead of being content with photographing the landscape (so as to neutralise it), we suddenly 'run into' some corner of it – for instance, encountering these three trees at a bend in the road, we confront, rather than mechanically sketch it: this is when a presence of the surge immediately opens up. Whether we allow this presence to occur through its own resolution or, as Heraclitus said, an 'awakening' operates in this *as-it-is* of the encounter: this *decision* is the 'present' of the surge, and this is a decision *not to postpone*. It is this decision not to dismiss (to a falsely fleeting later on) which alone opens up an actual present. Whether it is a question of the two Martinville church towers revealed in the setting sun at a bend in the road, or simply 'three trees' at the entrance to an alleyway, the discovery and shock are the same: a 'special pleasure' arises from what suddenly comes into our presence, as Proust tells us, returning all others to an equal chilliness – a 'pallor' – and throwing us into confusion. Finally, in this *as-it-is* of the encounter, within our mind we no longer substitute for it that 'standard convention' which we form day after day when making a sort of average of 'different faces that have pleased us' or 'pleasures we have known': in this way, we use the thread of years to weave a sort of personal *doxa*, or a parasitical 'thinking', that spreads over everything, as Heraclitus said. Under its shelter, we deaden the singular surge of *living*, and primarily of that time which will only ever be one time, which will never return. In short, the reverse of the Nietzschean eternal return is therefore also its equivalent, minus the mythology, this summoning also to be assumed and requiring the same 'confrontation'.

Even if, repeating the old gesture of metaphysics, he still wants, in order to 'follow this sudden impression to the end' (revelation always comes at

the 'end'), to seek out something that would be 'behind', *beyond* this movement of the road or of this clarity (something 'slips away' whose 'envelope'
it would be wise to open), this didn't prevent Proust from concluding about
what is most essential in each of these scenes: the effort to be made so as
to *gain access* to this present of the surge as well as for an 'intoxication' to
unfold. A 'painful obligation', as he recognised, but one that 'obeys an
enthusiasm'. The temptation really is to allow the immersive moment once
again to escape, so it can quickly be integrated at the same level as others,
and not to be satisfied with what has actually been seen. It is to allow these
two church towers to 'join with so many trees, roofs, fragrances, sounds, that
I had distinguished from others due to the obscure pleasure they had given
me and that I have never thought more about'. Moreover, one word (in the
mouth of Saint-Loup) expresses for him this postponing of being present
to later – in other words, this way of avoiding taking responsibility for what
suddenly, as it emerges, is devolved upon us: 'procrastination' – we put it
back 'until tomorrow' ... But it is obvious that to *postpone* this confrontation of the encounter is definitively to miss the possibility offered by the
present – a 'present', moreover, that is understood auspiciously in two ways,
both in French and in English: as the actual moment and as a gift.

This danger is so well known that it may pass unnoticed. To conjure the
present away belongs to all approaches as well as to every instant. Even if
this would only be now, when I read: when I read, the temptation to *postpone* comes from the fact that I can re-read. It is the same when I write, and
it lies in the fact that I can correct (the trouble with the computer is that
it makes correction so easy). I count on the fact that no sooner is the sentence completed than I can rewrite it, thereby allowing me a reduced and
weakened presence for what I achieve that makes me less vigilant. Or, once
again to set this shock of contraries in motion, I will say that, in reading at
this moment, but already trusting that I shall re-read, I am 'present–absent'.
In other words, I count on the fact that I can redo so as not to do it. The
fact that I can re-read means that I don't have to read. With the second time
delineated, the first time can be straddled, and neither 'time' actually happens. I am already awaiting the next sentence in order to relieve me of the
one before, and to pursue the reading in a continual slippage and avoidance
of what I have to confront. In this way, I elude the clash of the encounter,
that of the surge of meaning and the demand it makes: by *postponing* it, I
protect myself from a too violent disorientation and so begin to settle
myself. In other words, I elude exactly the present effort of taking responsibility for what rises up through the assurance I give myself of being better
able to take it on in a second effort – but to what extent does this really
dupe me? The 'I'll return to it' represents laziness.

3 What is the faculty (and is it actually a 'faculty'?) that must be demonstrated in order to respond to the demand of the present as it offers itself, and
is able to capture the *surge*? Is it just a matter of 'attention' re-configuring
the question of the time from the disposition of the subject-self 'stretching'

itself between the expectation of the future, the memory of the past and the *attentio* brought to the present as it inserts itself between them (according to its *distentio animi*), as Saint Augustine argued? But how can we be attentive to this present if it is just the point of passage – without extension – of what comes from the future to penetrate into the past? As analysed by Husserl when he used Augustine as a starting point, this *attention* actually receives an extension that overflows the isolated present that belongs to us when we listen to a melody and it distends of itself between a 'protension' towards sounds immediately to come and the 'retention' of sounds that have immediately flowed out (without which there's no 'melody'), but it then remains dependant on a 'temporal object' (*Zeitobjekt*: this musical air) which alone gives it something to attach itself to in unfolding its beginning and end. Without this 'objective' support, our attention loses all relation to things – in other words, its 'pertinence' – and therefore the present loses its consistency. Evidence of this loss is when Bergson, wanting to stretch out the capacity of attention indefinitely, envisaged it as an attention spanning an 'entire life', in its 'duration'. For want of this support from the temporal object, he then inevitably lapsed into bad lyricism (remember the final pages of Bergson's *The Creative Mind*), that of a freewheeling subjectivism ('everything' 'revives within' us and so on) that no longer has anything *actually* to engage with.

It therefore seems to me vain to require a present that would be given by *extension*, as an atavistic conception of philosophy would like, but that it should rather be envisaged as proceeding actively from a resolution, one that would render it *intensive*: I *open up* the present and make it emerge as soon as, by a decision (the one Proust invoked), I create an opposition to the temptation to *postpone*. This happens as soon as I cease to assume that what is coming may return, when I attach myself to its 'occurrence' alone (Montaigne's word) without seeking anything more for its before or after, and this not so much for its possible scarcity as for the possible surge that is contained within it, instead of settling in it. For the decision *not to postpone* depends on myself alone – in other words, on my own capacity to make a choice, and on my 'will', and from the outset it inscribes a difficulty: not to postpone erects a dam, in the haemorrhagic course of time, on the other side of which the present can accumulate. The present in the partitive sense cannot have consistency by itself, this much has been said, but it is constituted only – fully – from this *act* (of the decision) which renders it 'actual', from this tonic accentuation. I am speaking of 'the' present in the partitive sense – this partitive is promotional (expressing the modality of the sudden appearance or emergence, in other words, of the surge) – and not 'the' present as a time apart, according to its definition (conjugation), and that could be detached from the two others (from which the inextricable difficulties we are aware of then follow). Let's say that, as soon as I refuse to put off doing what I have decided upon, I anchor the partitive sense of *the* present and this present possesses the quantitative only by its *quality of surge* in the face of what is settled: it is maintained or has a 'now' only in the *as-it-is* of the encounter and the 'confrontation', according to the invaluable words of Heraclitus. Or let's say that, in the undefined flow of duration, the *aiôn* αἰών, only such a confrontation allows an emergence.

4 But can this satisfy us? Or might not this praise of the voluntary resolution, intransigent as it is, provoke in return an appeal to its contrary, to what is defined by *receptivity*? In other words, this demand for 'non-postponement' calls upon another one that appears to be its opposite, but is just as much its complement. A necessary complement: it is in the divergence that opens between them, and therefore during the day or the play which unfolds in it and unmakes what would otherwise hastily be considered to be a paradox, that we promote the resources of *living*. On the one side, I refuse to postpone, by which I don't claim to 'suspend' time in its 'flight', according to the poet's bombastic wish, but aim to make it emerge from the present: this refusal of a postponement dimmed by anticipation and counting on continuation makes it possible to gather the partitive 'occurrence', or moment, and to *invest* them instead of letting them continually escape. But, from another side, which, turning to the contradiction, will counterbalance it, opening a breach by which to live, I accept some 'deferment'. And I do even more than accept: counting on the deferred means I don't limit myself to my aim, I give 'time to time', knowing how to wait for a result, itself the fruit of an unfolding which doesn't belong to me. The resolute refusal of *postponing* is doubled with being receptive to *letting it happen*. Or, if I get rid of the impatience to gather, it's because, to be able to 'gather' (according to the well-known *carpe diem* which will remain a pious wish if its possibility isn't opened up), it is already necessary somewhere to have left a 'ripening' open.

To accede to the *deferred* therefore means that I treat the present moment as an investment (in the sense that it no longer is just strategic but is what the financiers mean when they speak of a 'return on the investment'). Or, better still, we might speak of a return of immanence: at the same time that I am confronting this time, this occasion that I want to be the only occasion, without my taking account of it I am already in the process of investing in a continuation that I do not know, and of accumulating. Then, one day, 'it happens', by way of result, 'all by itself', *sponte sua*. 'That' makes its opening, deploys its effect of itself: 'an encounter'. The subject is no longer 'me', including within myself, but the process that is engaged in. 'It happens', but what is 'it'? And what, also, is this 'happening'? Each time, as though it was the only time, I practise, I work on my scales, I do my utmost: to little effect and the fumblings of the effort and its clumsiness are still apparent. There's a delay and I cease to think about it. Then, one morning, opening the piano, I find myself amazingly at ease in playing the sonata, as though it had been given to me: what subterranean work has taken place over the course of the days, without my thinking about it – whose 'present' has arrived? Or I have difficulty in finding my words and ideas during the evening, getting nowhere. Yet when I awake next morning the page is written, imposing itself on me as if by an encounter and bursting in – as if it were dictated to me (it will be said that I am 'inspired').

Let's return to the example of reading, or rather recognise that there are *two* re-readings. When we read, we will refuse to postpone the present reading in a lazy way by immediately re-reading in order to make good this 'presence–absence' of diluted attention. But, time having passed, the book having been placed to one side and even forgotten, when one day we re-read it, we aren't just renewing the past reading and remembering it. This is because in *re-reading* we have profited in the shadow of the many connections that have escaped us, along with the decanting, one that finally imposes itself in a clear way, operating without interference – something that I could earlier only discern with difficulty. It is as if the reading of this text had constantly been proceeding in silence, extricated from what choked up or paralysed its approach, so that its significance could finally be revealed. A time of forgetfulness having passed (a false forgetting: the memory was silently operating), this time I discover it more fundamentally and radically than I could at first, grasping it more in its basis, and amazing myself at all the things I hadn't read in it. To re-read is then not a laziness but reveals a progress that is as unhoped-for as it is unnoticed.

This *laisser-faire* (the expectation that things will come to fruition) is more subtle than the art of doing (immediately, by exerting oneself): it is when the subject places the initiative between parentheses so as to allow the process that has been engaged in to operate in concert and over a longer period. For all that, this disengagement isn't a renunciation (nor does this withdrawal mean slipping into irresponsibility, or this non-activism a tipping over into passivity). The faculties provoked are put on the back burner so that – or, better (with less intentionality), in such a way that – the implied factors and conditions can be mobilised more widely and find a way through the difficulty encountered in partnership, in and through their evolution. Even though it would have been heroic to have confronted it at the time, to have done so would have served little effect. The duration unravels of itself. This implies giving credit to the virtue of the unfolding; and perhaps it explains why contemporary society is inclined to neglect such a value of the *deferred*. It doesn't appreciate the generous contribution of the delay, as it is always in a state of greater anticipation and consequently rushes towards its goals, so giving in to the fascination of the 'in real time' (which is provided by the technology of communication). Do we still know how to let things proceed discreetly – and silently?

I've spoken about how the refusal of one (the postponement) and the acquiescence to the other (the deferred) open up a space in which to manoeuvre and how, far from being entirely synonyms, *deferred* and *postponed* rather hollowed out a divergence between them in which one could think about how to live. In doing so, I was above all emphasising that to live is 'strategic' in the sense that it frees up an operational capacity which, thinking in accordance with the situation confronted, can exploit the one as well as the other – not to deal indirectly with the present encountered, at the same time as to let it bear fruit. This will lead us to maintain both at once: to respond to the *instance* of the present, the 'instant' that passes as a demand that rejects repetition–conservation but equally allows both the immanence to which it is committed and its capacity for giving birth to operate. Living unfolds jointly – contradictorily – *between* the two. Hence, the question that stands out as an alternative, and is each time given to decide, is this: am I avoiding it *or* letting it happen? Am I fleeing the confrontation with the encounter, and subsequently missing the *appearance* (*emergence*) of the present and the capacity it offers? Or is it that, while not postponing, neither do I force it: that I don't avoid but, letting it rest, ensure in some way that a deposit silently accumulates, whose result will be the 'enduring' present – Mallarmé's 'the virgin, the enduring and the beautiful today …,' in an unhoped-for way?

Since it doesn't conjugate, the Chinese language cannot mark different tenses, but it keeps the verbal function in the form that for us would be the infinitive. It also doesn't distinguish between active and passive voices and readily dispenses with stating a grammatical subject, keeping it implicit in the sentence. Because its master categories are also those of the 'course' and 'capacity' invested (*dao* and *de*), it is not surprising that it principally expresses the relation of condition to consequence (the 'root' and the 'branches', *ben -mo*) rather than the relations of means to end (the Greek *skopos* σκοπός), which are therefore not expressed or 'alluded to' so much. Chinese thought is especially at ease in evoking the operativity that develops of itself, proceeding in silence, and which we learn to arrange, harnessing it as a 'source', but still also without governing it and therefore drying it up. *Tao*, the 'way', expresses at once the self-deployment of this immanence and the art of making use of it, the process and the procedure – the *tao* of the world and 'my' *tao*. Thus, as we have seen, *letting the effect happen* is recommended (and on this all of the schools intermingle), confident that we are one with the propensity engaged upon and are 'wisely' acquiescent with this deferment – rather than disturbing the world due to our desire and impatience.

A text like the *Laozi* thus has little difficulty in thinking about what we call morality in terms of strategy: 'The Sage places himself behind' so that he might be 'carried forwards'. Not due to modesty or a vow of humility, but because, choosing to situate himself in vacancy, he calls upon the effect to realise himself fully (§ 7). This *deferment* is in itself the bearer of the effect. Rather than from the outset desiring to achieve the result by his actions, it's better discreetly to put in place a process which *of itself* will end in the result – such is the art of 'non-acting' (*wú wéi* 无为). In other words, instead of 'keeping control to the end', it's better to stop intervening as soon as possible so as to arrange the field for what is to come *sponte sua* from the effect which, proceeding from its own maturation and carried along by conditions, will be so much better implanted and more solid in consequence. For it will gradually be implicated in the situation in proportion to its development, and will no longer be forcing it. What we ordinarily take (subjectively) as the virtue of patience is ultimately only the benefit drawn from the *deferred* that one has left to work and whose 'resource' we thereby exploit. Just as the non-postponement is what resolutely allows the realisation of the resource of the present in its surge, so, by causing it to emerge from the undefined course of time, the deferred is a resource, but an inverse one, that leaves the concern to fecundate this present which offers itself to the *silent transformation*. The resource is on two sides and it allows a choice and a crossing over. Unlike the exclusive character of the truth, the characteristic of the *resource* is that it can be concurrent with another, even one arising from an opposing logic, at the same time as they equally co-exist, and that they can be drawn from jointly.

XX

Resource (vs Truth)

1 So long as we stay within (European) philosophy, the concept of truth has found and proved its validity. It is at once pertinent and sufficient. It is able to articulate the field of thought at the same time as it promotes philosophy in its development. On the one hand, the *stake* of truth allows positions to be configured and separated and it sets the scene for philosophy as well as organises its debate through the work of for and against, thesis and antithesis, argument and refutation. The 'criterion' of truth is sufficient to establish a cleavage between assertions that are revealed through their antagonism. At the same time, its 'cutting edge' draws thought out of obscurity and cuts a section out in order that it may be grasped. On the other hand, because it can never be satisfied – and because any affirmation of the truth, as a principle and by the very fact of its character of assertion, puts it in danger – the *quest* for the truth impels philosophy forwards without respite. Philosophy is embarked on a history thanks to this driving force of truth, whether the next figure of truth reverses the previous one or integrates it as it goes beyond it. At the same time as it constantly opposes itself, it never stops dissociating itself, since the truth holds it in a suspense from which its passion, at once its suffering and its jubilation, is formed – in contrast, 'wisdom' because it isn't structured by truth, is 'without history', and this is how it is measured.

Truth therefore had something about it that 'functioned well' in thought. 'Functioned' too well, perhaps? For haven't we now encountered the limit of this work of truth? As soon as we come out of European philosophy and its history, when we take leave of what Rimbaud described as 'Europe with its ancient parapets', this stake of the truth isn't contradicted but taken apart: we cannot propose that Chinese thought is 'more true' (or 'less true') than European thought. And once we emerge from the history of philosophy, as though we are speaking about a family history, what does this path of truth, which we have followed as thought's legitimate path, impel (or force) us to think, if it is suddenly lost or even blocked up? I don't even wonder whether such a statement is itself true, but whether it still means anything. Is putting these thoughts in relation to one another from the perspective of the truth the only way that is pertinent? When it comes to truth, what do we touch here from what arises as its border, from confines we did not suspect, but which reveal its biases under the supposed universality of its concept? But then doesn't not being able to *count on the truth* plunge us into some disarray? For if we want to find a substitute for it that would respond to the diversity of cultures that form the world, this will not have to be as a disguised substitute, or even a compromise formation, but as one that opens up a comprehensive point of view and in which the truth would now be able to find its place.

Instead of the concept of truth, I will substitute that of 'resource', which integrates it without making it obsolete. We can say that there is a *resource* of Chinese thought and language: for example, its correlative or matching capacity, the result of its paratactic structure, which allows it not to separate the 'one' from the 'other', no matter what they might be (*yin* and *yang*), but to hold them functionally coupled ('just' in Chinese, *duì* 对, meaning, as I've already said, 'matched'). We have noted several times the fertility of thinking about landscape, its complete polarity 'of mountains and waters'. In the same way and in *parallel*, there is a resource of European thought-language, and above all of its structuring capacity, and it is this tool that allows it to *construct* in thought, notably in terms of hypotheses and deduction. This begins with its panoply of prepositions and conjunctions, its morphological system of cases and conjugations, its complex system of modalities, and its syntaxes of principals and subordinates. We can see its fertility in the realm of logical elaboration as well as in the support given to the geometrification of science – and we know the power that this has.

2 But what value (or what weight) does this term 'resource' have, relative to truth? We will consider whether these concepts really belong to the same order or are of the same rank. Truth gleams in its dignity and impresses with its majesty. But to think about thought in terms of *resources* will for its part lead to its being conceived according to what it has that may be of possible use and effectiveness, in other words as a 'cut-out section' that allows the thinkable to emerge (or what I'm not afraid to call too prosaically its 'yield'), and the notion is adorned with no prestige. To think thought in terms of resources will lead to our probing what this thought illuminates and configures, carrying it to thought, at the same time that, through this very gesture, it leaves the *unconfigured* and the *unthought* to one side, alongside this trail. Disclosing certain coherences from the partiality that sets it to work, it leaves them at the same time in the shadow, one that it either hides or doesn't consider at all. Each thought follows its trail-vein, which it explores and exploits. It opens up and discovers what is fertile, but at the same time it closes down others without realising it – it covers them over, neglects them, for no other reason than that the coherence it promotes requires this exclusion in order for it to be able to express itself.

Yet I think this already contains enough for us to look again usefully at the history of philosophy itself, for which truth appeared to be the spur, and to illuminate it anew in an indirect way, one that is less polemical and perhaps also, as a result, less forced and less theatrical. Let's go back to its first branching-off, at least what has been discussed as such and that serves it as an originating 'scene'. I am enabled to cease considering the opposition between Plato and Aristotle from the point of view of their respective truths, each of them pursuing the other, but to do so from the point of view of what fresh fertility Aristotle revealed due to the *divergence* from Plato he opened up, and the benefit he took from it. This is why, still today, this 'still' not having run dry, I can draw from the source of the Platonic phrase and thought, making good use of what it releases in its operating capacity and modelling, and above all by the doubling of levels (which his illustrious status of the 'Idea' serves), from which alone his gesture of radicalisation is possible through abstraction, and which promotes Plato's theoretical audacity. In the same way, I can draw equally from the resource opened by Aristotle, that of differentiated analysis in experience, without cutting it off from the regime of opinion, thus reducing the rupture of the abstract, and proceeding to the inventory and logical formalisation of the various cases to be distinguished.

To substitute the concept of *resource* for that of *truth* is not therefore to abandon truth, but to maintain it precisely as a resource, and one of the most singular and fertile – the one that has allowed philosophy to prosper. We know that we need to be careful not to take one or the other side, to consider that if Aristotle is right and has established the truth then Plato must be wrong, and that Aristotle, 'a greater friend of the truth' than Plato, would have 'gone beyond' him – whether he excludes him or integrates him. But we also have to be careful of the opposite: of thinking that both are equally true, that each is right in his own way, and thereby tipping into syncretism or eclecticism. This would mean abandoning the 'cutting edge' of truth and so losing the singularity (to advance) that all thinking (or perhaps it is only a matter of philosophy?) still implies and the refutation needed to spur itself on. I'd rather choose to envisage how each, reconfiguring the 'rational' or the 'true' as he does in offensively developing his *logos*, opens up (and discovers) new possibilities in thought. This doesn't make the concept of truth obsolete, but on the contrary justifies it by making it an effective operator as a resource, and even a formidably powerful one, of a deployment of what is thinkable. For, on the one hand, the stake of truth remains pertinent and the critique that philosophy makes of the other is to be followed closely, in its innovating way of proceeding, and loses nothing of its sharpness (at the same time, it is well known that every later philosopher *never understands* the philosopher who came before him – a blindness that is needed if he is himself to become a philosopher by diverging). On the other hand, this contradictory work of the truth finds its full vocation only insofar as, through the effort of refutation, it allows other coherences, or what I would call other *possibilities* of thought, that had continued to be unperceived, to appear.

3 In order for these 'possibilities' of the mind to be heard as they develop into *resources*, it will also be necessary to reveal an extension to the notion of the 'possible' by bringing a new use – in other words, we wonder about the possibilities with which this advanced 'possible' is endowed. It will above

all be necessary to make good use of the aptitude that the 'possible' has to unblock contraries – as we already saw in Aristotle when he was confronted by the Megarians – but now by opening its vocation to the diversity of cultures: to make use of how the possible interposes between the true and the false at a logical level, distinguishing itself from the false in that it isn't contradictory, as between being and non-being at an ontological level, in this way preserving the contingency of what is only potential, whose only status is that of the 'prospective'. To treat the *possibilities* of thought between various cultures will thereby produce an *ideological unblocking*, the very one that the 'dialogue' to come calls for, if we retain this character of the *possible* that is at once non-exclusive and non-necessary. Indeed, these possibilities of the mind being competitive but not exclusive, making one coherence or another prevail, because they are contradictory only within the perspective of one or the other culture (an 'agile' subject, the one I call upon here from my wishes, will be able to navigate them), we will be in a more effective position to envisage their condition of *co-existence* without further entrenching them in a single history – like that of the 'necessary development of the human mind' which the Europe of the Enlightenment, still thinking it is the only reference point, made into its ultimate grand Narrative. In the same way, by promoting what is potential, and in consequence what is inventive, about this 'possible', we will better understand that each possibility of thought, due to the fact that it could equally well not exist, in itself constitutes an opening, a 'thrust', an advance (in respect of the unthought), for which in consequence we measure how much thought has risked, has dared – in it, how far it has ventured. Thought, assuming its conditionality, emerges from its banality, from its false necessity, along with its evidences and its boredom. This now appears to me to be the condition of its survival in a regime of worldwide standardisation.

Hence, we shall also have to remember and to take advantage of this other use that has developed from classical philosophy's 'possible', the Kantian one of *conditions of possibility*, retrospective this time before being prospective: in the sense in which Kant wondered how mathematics had become 'possible' as one day in Greece it found its way through a theoretical revolution that allowed it to detach itself from the mere perception, or even conception, of figures in order to construct them *a priori* in thought. Or how, at the beginning of modern times, physics had become 'possible' by submitting nature to experiments in which the mind takes the initiative, and which alone make it possible to reveal necessary laws. For the same question really has to be asked in following the surge of cultures: what decisive coherences have been discovered in them and rendered as 'possibilities' in such a way that inventiveness is each time released from them locally, opening a fresh source of intelligibility. But we shouldn't limit ourselves to the development of contiguous and adjoining disciplines as Kant did in ranging from mathematics and physics to the metaphysics that might have been expected. These possibilities of the mind, henceforth envisaged

145

on a world scale, introduce parallel developments that do not allow themselves to be put in order, through a joint belonging, under the same rationality. And, as we have seen, they don't even necessarily respond to the question of the 'truth' any longer.

In order to think about these possibilities of thought, it will therefore be necessary to promote the plural capacity of its substantive responding to the indefinite of its use ('a' possibility / 'some' possibilities) and immediately putting them on an equal footing. It will be conceived in the same way that each culture and each thought is only one possibility among others – European culture as much as any other. But, at the same time, we'll need to measure these possibilities in terms of the coherence they have revealed and consequently how productive or inventive they are. This means evaluating their capacity of divergence as well as their fertility: in this respect, they really are 'resources'. I shall therefore call *possibilities of thought* that in which what has thus been conceivable to humanity has been allocated over the course of its development, and which gives it an option so that 'each possibility is entitled to claim an existence commensurate with the perfection that it envelops', as Leibniz said in a rigorous way, measuring the possible against its 'suitability', or what I shall call its *coherence* (1991, § 54). But, instead of reducing the infinity of possibilities to a single existent, as in the mind of God making the world, it will on the contrary mean, in detecting and unfolding the divergences of thought encountered, letting their chance of all these possibilities run in parallel – concurrently – going back to the singularity of their source as in deploying their logical diversity: in a way that they are not allowed to be lost under such a forced assimilation – an easy assimilation – as that towards which world uniformity is currently leading us.

But would *possibility* amount to a *resource*, or to what extent do the two terms encompass one another? If possibility provides the resource with its logical status, what more does 're-source' express? For, if we don't want to miss this resource of the resource, we shall need more than an enquiry about the diversity of cultures conducted in an anthropological way: the philosophical stake is other than this and, whilst leaving Europe, is to envisage it from all sides and open more broadly the range and plurality of their possibilities and their purposes. This diversity should not be maintained on the basis of 'differences', in the way that anthropology does when it erects typologies, but rather through inventive *divergences*, which at the same time we shall treat as *resources* only if they are henceforth of value to the whole of humanity – which means: for every thinking subject at a transcultural and transhistorical level. In other words, it means elaborating them precisely on a conceptual, and not just contextual, level, so releasing their universality – which is what characterises the philosophical perspective and forms its vocation. To express this in an even more elementary way, there is 'resource' only if, from this possibility of thought, *any* subject today can make use of it, in both their intelligence and experience. Reactively, this will be further doubled from an advantage internal to philosophy itself. For, as soon as we release the divergence in thought as we envisage these possibilities in resources, instead of being satisfied with the calming of differences, thought will be restored to a state of tension. The conformism (atavism) with which it is always threatened, even if we know that philosophy is traditionally recognised as standing up to itself and being self-critical, will be undermined. Notwithstanding that it is continually trying hard to say 'no' to itself, is it able to emerge from these *folds* according to which it was formed and in which perhaps somewhere (does it know where and how?) it got stuck: that which constitutes its unthought? This 'fold' of truth is first and foremost what is culturally conditioned in its very definition in a way that, within itself, it barely suspects.

4 In this respect, if I return to its 'truth', ignoring its presuppositions, would it indeed be blind in relation to itself? If the basic definition of it is 'the alignment of the thing and the mind', the *adequatio rei et intellectus* of the scholastics (a formula that has since been tirelessly criticised, but how far does this go?), it is because its two terms have been assumed to be admitted before the relation between them has been taken into account. As they face one another, there is initially no 'thing', any more than there is a 'mind'; their overlaying of one another *then* gives rise to the truth. For the 'thing' doesn't exist as such, *a parte rei*, in the way that Descartes set out in the *Rules for the Direction of the Mind*, but is always *already constituted* by the implicit choices made by what the mind gives emphasis to. At the same time, there is no 'mind' of the other, *a parte intellectus*, as a sovereign faculty, a pure formal activity, as it would still be in Kantian understanding and his table of 'categories'. Wouldn't these actually be the 'base-concepts' of any human mind, and as such transcultural and transhistoric, as Kant wanted in going beyond Aristotle? Kant didn't suspect (any more than Aristotle did) that they are above all the products of language, of *a* language, and of a choice contained deep within thought. We can see this in his work in the category of 'substance' (of 'inherence') which clearly emerges from the choice of 'being' and ontology – in that it assumes *beneath* the sub-strata (sup-port, sub-ject, and so on) – or in that of 'causality' serving as a physical explanation but neglecting the implicating point of view of *propensity*, or even in that of 'existence' as it is opposed to 'non-existence', but without taking into account the possibility of the *elusive*, and so on.

All of our concepts 'have become', as Nietzsche recognised (or, he said, 'das Erkenntnisvermögen geworden ist'), and we cannot be unaware that they secretly in-form the 'thing' – that they, so to speak, 'breathe' into it in advance what it must be, before the mind that conceived them has been able to enter into alignment with this 'thing' and give rise to the 'truth'. Instead of there being an 'alignment' between the 'thing' and the 'mind', posed as initial terms, in their generality and enjoying an absolute validity, there is 'alignment' only between a certain 'thing' and a certain 'mind', both of which are culturally constituted – the thing already reflecting the mind even before they have entered into correspondence and could be able to coincide. This problem includes this very concept of a 'thing', a concept it never occurs to us to doubt, that we at least think we have well in hand, even if we do not yet know what it is, and which, as soon as we pass through China, surreptitiously (and strangely), slips between our fingers, the Chinese calling it 'east-west' (dōng-xī 东西), which means a tension between oppositions. The efficacy – that is, the resource – of this system, which gives prominence to the 'thing' on the one hand and the 'mind' on the other – in other words, opposite one another like two autonomous entities – has been revealed in the promotion of so-called 'objective' knowledge, thereby giving classical science in Europe a bed in which to rest. But we have to recognise the extent to which it also contains a singular choice and that it is consequently all the more fascinating for it not being 'discovered', as is ordinarily thought, but *invented*.

Heidegger really went back to a point before such a purview that brought the thing and its expression into concordance. Calling for a 'discovering' of Being, he illuminated its condition, the 'opening' of *Dasein*, *Offenheit*, thereby breaking the impermeability, or 'encapsulation', that such a relation supposed. He showed how this truth of enunciation is in consequence second in relation to the 'apparition' of being. He subsequently called for the 'freedom' of conduct, *Freiheit*, as a basis of the intrinsic possibility of this conformity, that which invites a 'letting being be what being is' – which, as we have seen, is very much in harmony with Chinese thinking about *receptivity*, which as I've said expresses this even better than by forcing our concept of 'freedom'. Even so, does it manage to dispel the biases that are still assumed in this 'open' relation in the *internal* constitution of one side and the other, even if they then vanish as 'sides'? Retroceding into the implied relation, it does no more than shake the intellectual presuppositions that have rightly been criticised (that of 'representation', *Vor-stellung*, leaving the thing to remain facing us as an ob-ject) in what is still a presupposition, but one that is more concealed, because it buries the content of what has been taken on culturally even more and is therefore more ideological (taken to the point of the mystical imaginary), and that he could only evoke as the 'ecstasy' of 'ex-isting'.

Even if we could free ourselves of this relation with the 'thing' and fold the 'mind' onto itself in order to find the criteria of truth in it alone – in other words, if we could think of the truth simply in accordance with the pertinence of the mind *harmonising with itself*, and not in conformity with its object, as Spinoza did – it would still be vain to believe that the mind can find in this alignment with itself the assured certitude of the truth ('By an adequate idea, I mean an idea which, in so far as it is considered in itself, without relation to the object, has all the properties or intrinsic marks of a true idea', *Ethics* II, definition IV, 2000: 113). Such an 'alignment' responds only at a surface level to its conditions of alignment, for such a mind – that is, the Spinozoist intellect – isn't driven by evidence alone, *alias* natural light, but is itself also culturally constituted: it is the product of a singular history of the intelligence, the sedimentation of an invented logic. It takes for granted the whole apparatus of the European thought-language, and above all that of its grammar (such as, first and foremost, notions of 'essence' and 'existence', 'cause' and 'effect', *en-soi* and *hors de soi*, 'subject' and 'predicate' and so on, from which Spinoza didn't free himself and whose bias he doesn't even suspect). Hence, to conclude that there is no truth for which one would be sure that it is 'revealed to itself', or that would be *index sui*, and that what one takes so conveniently for 'natural light', with which all mind would ideally be inhabited, always runs the risk of hiding some cultural unthought that we are powerless to suspect. This is because we are always already judging it *from within* a logic, that of a certain *possibility of the mind*, the one from which no sooner do we extract ourselves than it is no longer needed. And so it is *already*, and in an exemplary way, what classical reason was most attached to (and which Spinoza didn't dream of questioning): the principle of non-contradiction, which it posed as a first axiom and which is only relevant in the perspective that it has itself elaborated.

So we won't abandon 'truth', but rather transfer the concept in order to deploy its resource, overflowing its native constriction. This is why 'true' will henceforth mean what 'produces the effects of coherence', or 'is the source of intelligence', this intelligence being understood at once as a faculty to produce the intelligible (as such it is never fixed) and as an effective power, always particular because it is marked by locality, grasp or apprehension (as it is said, 'to have intelligence of'). I shall call 'true' what, in keeping with its biases, at once makes discovery possible and allows operation. Its negative is no longer what is false but what is unconceived or unenvisaged, that is both sterile (ineffective) and unthought. The true will therefore be conceived not in a referential way – since there would always be the fear that this would be unwittingly self-referential – but from the perspective of its *operativity*. What is true is what configures something thinkable and gains a hold over it – in other words, what is true is what promotes the intelligible and makes it serve and work. In a similar way to what I was calling a 'possibility' of thought, the true at the same time then illuminates its condition of possibility, by divergence from other possibilities, as well as its yield. It is measured against its fertility in this way, in other words by its heuristic as well as its pragmatic power – which it allows to be annexed under the *resource*. Rather than arising from a contradictory truth (even if this is the way they have had to work and be born), the great philosophies are themselves great operations or resources of thought – and even all the greater and heroic in that, at the same time as they stabilise a certain 'possible' conception of 'things', which they convincingly show should be adhered to, they are inventing tools that are already inclinations to enable a divergence from them (this shows the greatness of Kant).

5 Let's nevertheless also not forget what this empire of the true, this hege-monic 'quest' for the truth, has entailed by way of consequences in Euro-pean philosophy – its cost as well as its benefits. Because it has been through them that philosophy has acquired its consistency in relation to knowledge, because it has thus 'been directed' towards the truth, it has at the same time abandoned what I've started, along the way and by opposition, to call *living*, or has vehemently dropped it – 'sometimes I think, sometimes I see', Paul Valéry said, keeping them separate. When he was questioned about 'wisdom', Socrates was already the first to reply that wisdom 'is science' (or that 'science and wisdom are the same thing', *Theaetetus*, 145e): *sophia* σοφία is henceforth equivalent to an *episteme* ἐπιστήμη, and a turning point has been taken from which philosophy has not since emerged. It will now take responsibility for the question of living only secondarily, by way of consequence and through 'morality'. Or it transfers it to the sphere of the religious, which would be the only remaining place in which it could be deposited – or it would itself become religious in order to be approached (we find both ideas in Plato). This is why the weakening of religion in contemporary Europe meant that, in losing this support, the question of *living* could only sink into the inconsistency of what is currently called 'personal development' or, as I'd call it, the marketplace in happiness. I call it a 'market' because it is concerned with using its promotional force to sell injunctions to 'be happy' (and be 'positive') in the naïve hope that any-thing negative – what I'd call *neg-active* – can be forgotten. To all of those losing their grip in a Europe in a state of retractation, we conveniently praise a 'letting go' (along the lines of to 'be Zen'). Yet when it comes to philosophy, it must think about the condition of *living* but remain within the element of the concept in order to do so: it designs, raises idealities, but doesn't 'preach'.

Yet to develop thinking about the *resource* precisely makes it possible to take the question of *living* out of the ineptitude of this sort of sub-philosophy – inept because it is powerless to develop questions and concepts without being impelled towards the religious (towards the 'what do I have the right to hope for?'). For *resource* is understood as much from the perspective of living as from that of the possibilities of thought – including that of truth, or rather it makes them coincide and finally be reconciled, even though they are ordinarily placed sterilely at a distance and held separate from one another (this is its quality). 'Resource' thus means that *living* finds its capac-ity as a surge, not in some elsewhere or beyond which turns away from them or overflows them, but in what is unfolded of itself as a *possibility* that can be explored and exploited, or else that can be neglected or missed. This can occur through making an opening to the Other, detaching it from the anonymous other (as the unlimited quest can be pursued in 'intimacy'), or better still by deploying some such place encountered throughout the world in its multiple tensions, a land turning to 'landscape'. In other words, on each occasion discovering within it an *internal* concealed *infinity* which doesn't run dry: in short, a *resource* can be conceived as a *local harnessing of immanence*, and it is from such resources that 'living', emerging from the settling of 'life', is promoted and becomes *intensive*.

This means that 'resource' privileges no domain or quality. Extricating themselves from the settling of what remains *en-soi*, or that coincides flatly (and sterilely) with 'themselves', whether they are understood ontologically as an 'essence' or a 'property', these resources would describe themselves as so many emergences, or better still as *dehiscences* opening by themselves – from below the surface or the disappointing flatness of 'life' which passes like gloomy thought – and releasing their fertility to whoever can detect the fissure by which the surge can penetrate. Or else I'd describe them as pockets or cavities – but bottomless cavities into which living and thinking inexhaustibly withdraw, allowing the unfathomed 'without-ground' finally and suddenly to appear, instead of life flowing out or timorous thought continuing to be boring. They thus draw from one as well as from the other – thereby finding in them the resources of 'non-postponement' or just as much what is 'deferred'. For both are resources of a similar stature to what is at stake in making good use of one or another possibility. Or let's say that, if the resource is not assumed to be from a particular domain, and is not measured according to a certain criterion, it arises from the same requirement or ethic, which is the only one – that of not *passing to one side*. Expressed in a positive way, it is to dare to open up an *approach* to it.

Let us not lack (or miss) the resource of *intimacy*. If I return once again to the 'intimate', if the theme continues to haunt these pages, if I can't extricate myself from the inexhaustible surge it contains, it's because intimacy is a resource in an exemplary way – and isn't this what is most crucial to living? One day to be daring and cross the frontier within which the 'self' is still sheltered, coinciding with itself, in what constitutes its 'privacy' or, as might be said, its 'imperturbability': to dare to shatter this wall of habitus and convention, of prudence and precaution and of modesty and protection into which each person ordinarily withdraws and where they are their own master. A pact is then implicitly formed between one and the other, discovering a new *possible*, and even one that would never have been imagined: the 'quality' of each of the two will matter less – what love celebrates in a self-satisfied way – than the capacity they find *together* in order to risk what is 'intimate' between them. The resource of the intimate can be found when the relation engaged upon comes out of the balance of power with the other, and one even gives up any design on it: intimacy completely gratifies the subject due to the way it unmakes its position as a subject. If love is also intense due to its passion, love is still not a resource because it reduces the other from the start to an 'object' (of choice and investment: 'I love you'), even if this might be an ideal one: one will be more or less 'in love' depending on how strong and exclusive this investment is, but this intensity of love doesn't leave the sphere the self describes and therefore will be exhausted by its limit. On the other hand, the intimate is a resource because, as it makes (lets) the 'Other' be experienced in the 'deepest part of the self' (*intimus*), and even 'further within' the self (*interior intimo meo*), therefore, in activating this undivided *between* of the relationship, it draws on this ground without ground in that it de-insulates and creates a bond: that in which *living*, finding itself in what is no longer the comfort of a 'self', or the postponement into some 'beyond', but the infinity of *being-with* (with a 'you'), of being-*near to*, can rid itself of its enclosure and invent itself.

Or, if I never get tired of thinking from landscape, if I've been drawn to move back and forth through the way it promotes the surge and breaks with the settling of what is merely 'land', even if I've been inclined to force language just a little in daring this 'from' ('living *from* landscape', which I have recently used as the title of a book[1]), it is because this 'from' itself expresses the resource. What does this 'from' mean, that is more than a manner or means, and points to what is prior to them? We live 'from' – from love or from fresh water, they say, as well as from its work as from hope: this 'from' of the resource expresses the concrete as well as the abstract, which arises from thought as from what arises from what is physical. Or, in the case of landscape, it expresses how a dimension of 'mind' is released from its physicality, but without leaving this physicality and making it forgotten or, as philosophy too easily announces, 'going beyond it'. It rather undoes the opposition of the two and is what actually makes the 'resource' appear. *Resource* is therefore a concept of *de-exclusion*, perhaps the one that is best adapted to get away from the oppositions of ontology without losing its benefits. Indeed, the characteristic of resource is that it dissolves dualisms whilst informing itself about the conflicts they have raised – just as it integrates the question of the *truth*, whilst no longer setting itself up against *living*. The *resource* is a resource of living as well as of thinking; it doesn't separate them. From this resource of the resource, it will be possible to set off again, to take our ease in it, in order both to live and to think.

Note

1   The book is *Vivre de paysage ou L'impensé de la Raison*, 'Living from Landscape or the Unthought of Reason' [trans.].

Subject/Situation: On a Branching-off of Thought

Note of the Seminar 2013–2014

1 There can be little question that if there is a legitimate point of departure to begin with, if there is a statement which, withdrawing sufficiently into itself, offers a definitive basis for thought to emerge, it would be the 'I think therefore I am' of Descartes. And this is so in a unique way: it implies that I think due to the fact that I doubt and that I exist due to the fact that I think – everything else follows on from this. For some, ultimately requiring neither prior history nor justification, this might act as what is established and support all possible statements through its certainty alone. For others, directly drawn to its contrary – that of a doubt pushed as far as it can reasonably and even unreasonably be taken – constitutes a fixed, set and unquestionable point, in which any evidence will find its confirmation. Thought no longer starts with 'things' or the 'world' or 'God', for it sets itself up as the absolute point of departure of existence, dependent only on itself. With the *cogito*, philosophy definitively found the soil – or, to an even greater degree, the base – from which to raise a subject, which is the *ego*. We shall therefore never again emerge from this 'I think' that was set up as a great beginning. This 'I think' will become, under an operative angle, the act of pure, unitary and originating 'apperception' accompanying all of my representations and binding them together, and from which the consciousness of self and the possibility of knowledge proceed (according to Kant). It will also open up the possibility of a history from which this consciousness of self can raise itself through the internal movement engendered by its negation, from substance to Subject and attaining becoming (Hegel).

It amazes us when we repeat this following the defined course of philosophy. What are we to understand from it? We are surprised by one as much as by the other: whether this *cogito* might be credited with an absolute legitimacy and whether it might be considered a great beginning – Hegel says that Descartes is the *Anfänger* ('initiator'). It will initially seem astonishing that this Cartesian *cogito*, which has been credited with constituting a universal evidence at the same time as it legitimately emerged from within the language and thought of Descartes, itself widened the divergence in relation to such an external thought-language as that of the Chinese, and has proved to be – symptomatically, eminently and contradictorily – singular. What happens if I cannot say 'I exist' in Chinese (in the absolute sense of existence) or if I haven't semantically isolated a pure 'thinking' in it (at least before it was introduced by Westernisation)? Even today, we note that the beginning of the *Meditations* is still unread in China, may even still be universally unreadable – or in any case, not of much interest. But at the same time we can more easily see that, when it is viewed from China, the Cartesian *cogito*, far from appearing to be a radical beginning, a new raising of the curtain on the stage of the mind from which modern philosophy has unfolded, constitutes the materialisation of a long march of the 'West' whose heritage isn't limited to a few uncleansed remains of the scholastics: it has depended so much on its conditions of possibility that have effectively served it as its great relay. Seen from afar, the offshoots that have been taken and developed by European philosophy since the time of the Greeks represent nothing more than a glorious summit.

It isn't just the co-origination of the Other and the self that continues to be ignored within the fold of the *cogito*. This is what contemporary philosophy has since loudly demanded and without which it will not be able to confer a place for the Other except subsequently and secondarily, directly from the world and its plays of interdependency, nor attribute the Other with consciousness except by inference: without it, the other cannot consequently be recognised as 'Other'. But, from the outset, the Cartesian *cogito* also symbolises an evacuation which still hasn't troubled us and that I cannot even name or begin to approach in our language except by calling it a 'situation' – a starting point, a first approximation, that will need to be opened, corrected, taken away from its hinges and biases and tested so as to be promoted and deployed. And wouldn't there be a theoretical incompatibility between the two, at least initially? This would go to the point that the subject/situation might constitute a more elementary alternative whose conceptual divergences, as I shall show over the course of this essay, constitute in one way or another its arborescence, which thereby serves as the principal thread – which this time is historical – from which the earlier net is suspended.

2 When looking back at the Cartesian *cogito*, Nietzsche had, however, warned us about the abuse that is to be inferred in an 'I think', set out solemnly as a point of departure and principle. Only I myself have actual experience of this and this is solely from the phenomenal evidence that it 'comes to me from thought'. Nietzsche warned us about the illusion that consists in taking a pure 'it happens', *alles was geschiet*, for an activity, *ein Thun* – in other words, interpreting this fact as an 'act', and consequently setting this act out as the 'effect' of a 'cause', conferring upon it the status of the 'author', and even imbuing it with intentionality. From this, a creator God was born. This meant transforming the mere fact that thought comes to me as it comes, appearing–disappearing, detaching itself and linking up, intermittent and contingent, into a stable, isolable and definitive 'I think' – one as grandiose, as well as overrated and superfluous, as it is naïve. Yet this atavistic gesture is – as Nietzsche was able to identify – the very one of metaphysics. It consists in introducing an entity behind what is purely phenomenal, without suspecting the intrusion, which is to be set up in support of a substantive behind the verbal that would

subsist in itself, therefore as substantialised, supposedly underlying and promoted as a sub-ject and thereby taking us from 'thinking' to 'I think'. In this,
Nietzsche the philologist glimpsed in an inspired way, and from within European thought-language, the consequences inherent in its grammar, which is
exercised in a way that those who apply it are unaware of: such a promotion of the Subject proceeds from the predicative structure of our languages
rooted in a doubling-up, and above all it leads to a structural doubling of the
subject and an attribute like cause and effect. This is so even if such a 'subject'
would simply be the product of our syntax. Yet to glimpse, as Nietzsche did,
an operativity that has since then been left unassigned – being actualised but
not to the extent of being put into 'action', due to being allowed to be carved
out, detached and attributed, so that, as a result, the 'subject' comes situation-
ally apart – will at the same time get us closer to Chinese thought-language
and the difficulty we encounter in translating it into a European language.
But, equally, exploding as a flash, wasn't such a glimpse itself condemned to
remain isolated in the heart of European thought since it would otherwise
have to diverge from its own language?

Modern and contemporary thought in Europe, as it thinks in language, and
in its own language, is therefore still insufficiently wary about setting off
from the Cartesian 'I think' that was established as its first subject. It is still
insufficiently concerned with re-examining what it regards as the radicality
of the *cogito*'s starting point and so to return to some absolute intuition,
absolute Einsicht, prior to which it might not be possible to go back. This
would hence be to posit an antepredicative 'evidence' in which the subject
immediately apprehends itself, as a pure transcendental *ego*, understanding
itself in a perfect and immanent presence in the self, and as such as the only
possible basis of science (as Husserl says at the beginning of the *Cartesian
Meditations*). Or, if it finally starts from a situation – what Merleau-Ponty
calls 'an open situation' – which is always already given and, so as not to be
locked into Descartes' solipsism, recognises that the Subject belongs to its
world, it still doesn't hesitate about regressing from the 'realism' of things
to the 'thought' of them, or from the transcendence of these things to the
autonomy of this thought, since the affirmation of their existence 'is always
posited only from my thought'. In other words, it regresses from a consciousness of the Subject implicated in its world to the knowledge that it
takes for its own existence, 'not through statement or inference', but by
'direct contact with itself' (the *cogito* of the *Phenomenology of Perception*).
Sartre would sum this up in a few sweeping formulas, asserting that a truth
can only exist if there is an absolute truth at its point of departure that the
cogito alone gives to me, allowing me to grasp what I am without an intermediary so that consciousness attains itself whilst at the same time reaching
the Other (see *Existentialism is a Humanism*).

Even if contemporary philosophy no longer dares to take the experience
of the *cogito* for a unit of 'eternal' truth, as Husserl had done, it still continues to posit the 'I think' as an 'evidence' that instituted a first subject – and

it is this 'first' that matters. 'First' means that, even if it is finally recognised as 'situated', initially implicated in a world, this subject is posited at the start of its thinking, asserting its initiative. It is essentially the power of beginning, of being an *initium*, an absolute point of departure for consciousness, even before having affirmed its autonomy, which henceforth becomes easy to contest. To go back to the *cogito* would therefore be both to return to this possible position of exception, ahead of any constituted determination, the only one actually originating in an undercurrent common to opposites. During his polemic with Foucault, Derrida recognised a truth of the *cogito* from before the disjunction of reason and unreason, one which would be valid 'even if I were mad'. It is attained in its withdrawal, before the lapse into explanation and reasoning, marking the point – the 'tip' – of unbroachable certitude, when it excluded itself from all totalisation of what is thinkable by exceeding it and therefore escaping from any enclosure in a historically determined structure. And even if this first thought is considered to be unconscious, even if we now know that the subject is 'at home' in the field of the unconscious, Freud's approach is no less Cartesian, as it returns to a similar base of the subject of certitude, even if this subject is that of the signifier, as Lacan also said, since it perpetually draws an 'I am', from doubt itself and from its 'support' – but henceforth from a 'that thinks' which is no longer 'me' (see the *Four Concepts*).

3 There would indeed be no sense in hastily marking out these positions if there were no recognition of how the *cogito* tirelessly roots itself in them, if its many offspring cannot be seen in them, or if its 'evidence' contains no adherence. And this occurs no matter how exacting the process to which this *cogito* is then submitted might be, and no matter how much care is taken to ensure that its thinking doesn't collapse (leaving it to become essentialised), or however we broach it with whatever means each of us has at our disposal that could more effectively define its vocation, in this stature–posture of the subject. The impossibility – if impossibility there is – would therefore not so much be to 'think otherwise', according to the repeated wish of philosophers in Europe, this 'thinking' having already been effectively instrumentalised as, I'd say, to be *treated* differently. How to *begin* thinking otherwise? How could we emerge from this *fold* of the *cogito* and from what at the same time, in its 'I think', it leaves unthought? Or couldn't we perhaps simply 'begin', not begin by wondering how to begin, not turning the beginning into a question, or seeking an absolute at the start. We notice that Chinese thought-language has never thought – imagined – a *cogito*; it hasn't examined the possibility of a beginning, or thought from an unprecedented beginning. It hasn't begun by abstracting 'thought' as a pure activity from our lives. Nor, furthermore, has it detached and removed that point of emancipation of a 'subject' from the world. This means that it leads us back not to the *cogito* itself but to what is prior to the *cogito*, prior to its prior, prior to its beginning, and to us asking ourselves which branch it was descended from, and from what it springs up, to the point of making

so great an impact that, right from the time it first appeared, we have been unable to emerge from it. This also means that it will no longer be possible to consider an 'archaeology of the Subject' in exactly the same way, except from such an external angle and according to the perspective that has unfolded from its advent and from within its history. Its conditions of possibility, cultural as well as theoretical, are to reflect upon it through divergence, using what, in comparison with the Chinese side, could be called *its conditions of impossibility*.

It might, however, be thought that the Greeks and the Chinese were initially at one in their thinking: for them both, the thought of the world and its changes was not considered other than on the basis of its oppositions – hot–cold, high–low; isn't this elementary? Aristotle saw this as being a common denominator in the thinking that had come before him, and Chinese thought could happily be associated with him were it not that the branching-off had already started earlier. In China, these oppositions are factors or vectors of breath-energy (of *qi* 气), forming a polarity (the well-known *yin* and *yang*), and their interaction alone is sufficient, from which the process of things follows by correlation, while for Aristotle these oppositions are modes of 'being' by means of states or extremities of the in-between in which changes operate. This is why Aristotle was impelled to introduce a 'third term' in addition to these opposites – in other words, the 'sub-ject' (*hupokeimenon* ὑποκείμενον), designating what is 'underlying' the change and so in this way passes from one state to the other. This 'sub-ject', the sub-stratum, sup-port of change, is what 'remains beneath it' (*hupomenôn* ὑπὸ-μένων) and doesn't change (*Physics*, 190a). It will be said that this is the degree zero of the European subject since the fact that it is confined to physics means that it is without an ounce, or suspicion, of subjectivity. But the fate of the European subject is nevertheless then sealed, because this clarifies it as being homologous with the subject of the sentence, from the perspective of *logos*, therefore on a 'logical' level – or isn't it, rather, what leads to an assumption of the other? It is from this subject that everything else is affirmed by virtue of the predicate, but it is not itself affirmed by anything else and is not the predicate of another subject (*Metaphysics*, 1007b, 1017b, 1028b, etc.). Because the Chinese language doesn't conjugate, it has no need to promote and set up such a syntaxical subject.

It might be argued that Chinese and Stoic thought meet in many places: in the absolutisation of the figure of the Sage, in the consciousness of social duties, or in the appeal to conform to the order of the world. And, closer to the question of the Subject, in the moral distinction, introduced on both sides, between what depends on the self, for which one is responsible, and what doesn't depend on it. By separating thought from Being, in advocating the embrace of the opportunity of what thereby comes from the self, the *phusis*, in other words by authorising a transcendence which is only a totalisation of immanence, Stoicism definitely serves as a bridge to Chinese thought – perhaps as the first bridge. In any case, the missionaries in China, failing to convert people to the gospels, strategically linked themselves with Stoic positions. But Stoicism precisely moves away from this in that it established a total exteriority of things in regard to a 'self' which is cut off from it: 'things' 'don't achieve a soul', *ouk haptetai tes psuches* (Marcus-Aurelius, IV, 3; V, 19), not because they wouldn't be the cause of our representations, but because they don't 'touch' the upper part of the soul, its controlling part, *to hegemonikon*, which, in its 'internal discourse', is capable of abstracting any value judgement (the *hupolepsis* ὑπόληψις) and therefore of exempting from it, and, thereby, knowing how to 'circumscribe themselves' and to fix their boundaries, will then consequently be constituted as an impregnable 'acropolis', an inviolable retreat that nothing in the world can weaken. Yet, if we envisage the authority that constitutes this islet of personal freedom at the heart of the sequences that make up the world from the external constituted by Chinese thought, such a claim for autonomy will no longer be judged to be an integral and necessary aspect of morality – we find in China an eminently moral thinking, but one about which it is unapologetic. On the other hand, it does appear as a decisive moment in our production and promotion of the Subject, even if it isn't recognised as such.

What will actually bring out such an *exoptic*, as it can be instituted in China in reconsidering the 'West', whether in Aristotle or in the Stoics, is that the subject *is promoted* on the basis of how it *detaches itself* (from its situation): the *situational* is the background from which it is cut out, including in the heart of its own person, from which it raises itself by freeing itself from it. Unlike the Sophists for whom, according to what Aristotle said, nothing exists except everything that happens in an 'accidental' way (*to sumbebekos*), and who, satisfied with this pure phenomenality, are unconcerned about establishing a distinction between the Subject and the attribute, Aristotle lays claim to a separate status for the Subject in that it is essentially distinguishable from what is attributed to it, precisely by virtue of being situational or 'accidental'. Socrates doesn't reduce himself – or doesn't identify himself – with 'Socrates sitting down' (*Metaphysics*, 1007 b). Otherwise, to instruct Clinias is to kill him, since to get rid of the ignorant Clinias is also to get rid of Clinias. A subject therefore has to be assumed as underlying the situation that is constituted from the change of everything that happens to it and which is attributed to it predicatively in the expression. It underlies it but, as such, is categorically independent of it: it is by absolutely differentiating itself from this situation that affects it that it at once affirms, from one point of view as from the other, a logic and a physics in its ontologically separated status, as a core of 'being', or as an 'essence', in *ousia*.

Let us set out these concentric circles, as the Stoics described them and with which they surround the hegemonic part of the soul that is alone to be preserved (Marcus-Aurelius, XII, 3): the most external is what designates others; next comes that of the past and future, circumscribing the present; then that of the involuntary emotions; finally, closest, that of the swirling waves of events that form fate. Yet, it's from this whole situational tissue that the principle or 'internal guide' entirely withdrawn into itself is isolated, like Empedocles' sphere that is so smooth and polished that nothing external can adhere to it. The situational is what I systematically extract myself from in order to discover my initiative within myself: to strengthen and affirm, in whatever situation it might be, what my autonomy reveals. Therefore, far from being a banal detachment from the world judged to be just a little corrupting, since one is ready to participate in it, assuming its duties scrupulously, it is gaining access to what 'alone' is 'sovereignly yours', *monon kuriôs son*, that is the aim of such an entrenchment. If the subject hasn't yet explicitly found its concept here, it will nevertheless cut it out in this preliminary way from everything that isn't it, as well as digging out the peripheral trench that secures it, so that its possibility can fully emerge.

4 In the same way, Saint Augustine contributed a decisive moment in the advent of the subject although not so much due to the fact that he was the first to formulate the *cogito*: if someone 'doubts, it is because he is alive', *si dubitat, vivit*; he can doubt everything else, but not the activity of his mind (*De trinitate*, X, 10, 14). Or again, 'if I make a mistake, it's because I exist'; I am therefore absolutely 'certain' of the fact that I 'am' (*City of God*, XI, 26). The proof is given – if it is still necessary – that even the great Cartesian beginning isn't a beginning, or that it isn't the first beginning in thought. More important and determining, already more Cartesian than this argument alone, is that, under the facile covering of asceticism, the 'mind' (*mens*) finds itself by looking for itself from the injunction of having to be rescued from the perceptible. What is most precursory and prescriptive in dealing with the advent of the subject is the fact that Augustine appeals to the mind in striving to 'think' alone (*se cogitare*), and that he isolates himself in his thinking. The consequence is that the mind then knows that it is 'certain', finding and proving its certainty through its activity alone: that, by distinguishing itself from what it knows it is not, it is directly able to discover itself as being present to the self – the subject's bed has already been made.

Yet China rather marks this certainty that the self has about itself, which has evidently so resolutely sustained the advent of the subject in the newness of its relation to God, by leaving it to one side. A subject – an *I* – found its place in Europe by being able to say 'Thou': 'Thou are great, Lord...', *Magnus es domine* (the first words of the *Confessions* of Saint Augustine). From this, in the face of this all-powerful Thou that it erects, there emerges a continuous 'I' of a dialogue. A relation is engaged from this system which instantly forms a *tabula rasa* of anything situational, retaining only its face-to-face meeting, and establishing the subject and the personal pronoun, interpolating from its 'I', in partnership with the absolute. Man is of course 'miserable' and God in his 'mercy' overflows him infinitely. But, even so, the one can say 'Thou' to the other, from the outset, and under cover of his indignity, as previously of asceticism: by opening up a one-to-one dialogue with God, he establishes a tête-à-tête with him, or of one mind to another.

His 'I' is anchored from (in) this 'Thou'. The transcendence of God concedes and confers (transfers) his consistency to this 'I' that invoked him. This means that the subject is described – and supported – by the fact that God appears in him, according to this *in-vocare*, as inversely, and because the two are equal, because he already recognises himself in God so that he might thereby in-voke him. 'God' proves to be the support of this subject (which 'resides' within him), at the same time as this subject that expresses 'I', so welcoming God, discovers himself to be God's dwelling place (the 'house of my soul'). From this intersected structure ('What are you to me?' / 'What am I to you?'), each is placed in comparison with the other, and man sees himself raised by God into the subject of his own life, since he draws from him the condition of possibility of a Self placed in comparison with oneself. And that God ('Thou'), making me see my truth, is what means that within this me there is a possible truth.

Thus, from what we then also learn from this obscure history, but drawn patiently into the light by the great historians, from this fascinating history – no less complex than that, facing it, of the advent of the 'object' – this history of the way in which Augustinian thinking about the certainty of self intersects with the Aristotelian plan of the Subject (substance) and the accident (predicate), in such a way that our acts can be considered to be the attributes of a subject and that the certainty of the self becomes a 'subjective certainty', *certitudo subjectiva*, we shall nevertheless be unable to forget what Augustine opened most decisively in thinking about the Subject under this technical history of philosophy: the discovery of an inner self that is still more internal, or 'the most internal', *intimus* – in other words, the emergence of the 'intimate'. Or that God is said to be 'more internal than my intimate', *interior intimo meo*, reveals that the self, by becoming deeper, withdrawing itself more deeply into itself, from this innermost part of itself, it appeals to the Other and, as it opens itself to it, discovers itself in the inauguration and spawning of an existence. As a result, the physical and logical system of the Subject has mutated into an adventure of subjectivity which is no longer limited to a matter of sentiment or affect, or even of self-consciousness, but makes the Subject the summary of a fixed term, that of a singular continuation within the extant, whose narrative is the key (and the *Confessions* of Saint Augustine are its revelation): I am the subject of what I have, or rather of the fact that I am a possible *narrative*, that of a life which makes itself. Hence that, in its relation with God, this subject, in saying 'I', conceives of itself as the subject of its own history, as a subject of memory, and might even be able to get him to give up the most shameful and secret: 'Thanks to Thou, I can tell my own story … '.

5 Yet Chinese thought-language doesn't furnish any similar story of the advent of the subject. And this comes above all from the fact of the poverty, or non-development, of its pronominal system: since it doesn't conjugate, not only can the subject of the verb remain implicit in it (as in the case of the

infinitive in European languages) but also the indication of a self remains elementary, since it isn't necessarily declined according to persons. 'In the way of conducting oneself' (*xíng jǐ* 行己), says Confucius, 'show respect', or 'surmount oneself (to return to the rites)' is a basic motto of his teaching. Often this 'self' is understood in opposition to the other: 'study for yourself and not for others', or, in a more dense way, to 'assemble oneself' (to contain oneself, *zong ji*), not to let oneself go (on the death of the prince, *Analects*, XIV, 43). Otherwise, to accentuate the reflective character of a verbal action, one would say (substituting *zì* 自 for *jǐ* 己): 'examine oneself from within' (*nèi zì xǐng* 內自省) or 'accuse oneself' (*zì sòng* 自讼), 'ask a lot of yourself and little of others', or, more interestingly, 'deploy yourself' (*zì zhì* 自致, *Analects*, XIX, 17). The Chinese thus translated 'freedom', from the Western term, as 'of oneself', *zì yóu* 自由. Yet these uses are the most developed there is and Chinese thought-language barely goes beyond them. It is well aware of the category of the *individual* (*gě* 个, *sī* 私: individuation, unlike in India, is considered to be actual), or that of the *person*, *shēn* 身, whose notion has a high moral import ('to cultivate his person', *xiū shēn* 修身; 'amend one's person', *shàn shēn* 善身, etc.). It is even demanded that one be 'attentive to the self' when one is 'alone', in the withdrawal into one's heart to which others have no access (*shen qi du, Zhongyong*, § 1). But it isn't disengaged from support, whether 'physical' or 'logical', for the function of the 'subject'. The term itself doesn't exist but will be translated from the Western sense, just like that of the 'object'.

Hence, the ethical aspiration would not be 'autonomy', 'being (to) oneself one's (own) law', as it was for the Stoics. It would not be Freedom conceived, in the classical thought of Europe, as the primary property of a subject. It would rather be what is inverse to it, not its contrary properly speaking but its contradiction, which is what *receptivity* expresses. The characteristic of freedom is to transcend the situation, any situation, but receptivity is an opening to the situation, without a projection onto it that would shackle it – to the point that the consistency of a 'subject' comes undone in it. The catchword of the teaching of Confucius is 'when it is appropriate to take charge, he takes it; when it is appropriate to leave, he leaves it'. Everything depends on the situation that is encountered: it is by conforming to it, that is by moving away from any fundamental position given as a rule regarding it, that on each occasion he promotes morality. Wisdom consists in knowing how to put oneself in phase; its ethics proceeds from that point, not from rules, but from a continuous regulation. Thus, when it is said that the Master has no 'idea' (that he would put forward), 'necessity' (to which he would hold in advance), or 'position' (on which he would pause), nor any 'ego' (in which he would in the end get bogged down), this negative formulation is enough to express how much of an obstacle, when confronted with the renewal of the situation, the institution of a subject would constitute. But if all of these markers, or expected landmarks, that prop up an identity are withdrawn, then morality is able to respond to all of the possibilities of the situation, without letting any of them be lost – in other words, to unite with its universality, so as not to be drawn towards sinking not into 'error' (philosophy's obsession) but into *partiality*.

From what is said about some thinkers of antiquity who 'got wind of the *tao*', I will translate these formulas precisely for their resistance to translation. They are at the limit of what is translatable, not because their notions are abstruse, or even because their meaning is unclear, but simply because they aren't secured in the Subject. Or, rather, they systematically take apart the possibility of it (we find this in the *Zhuangzi*, ch. 33, when speaking about Shen Dao[1] and his consorts):

> Impartial and non-partisan,
>
> well-balanced and not having anything in particular,
>
> in a distinct way without [anything of a] principal,
>
> tending to things without duality,
>
> not being fond of cogitation,
>
> not striving to know,
>
> not selecting anything about things,
>
> still continuing with them ...

Without any grammatical subject being stated, without there therefore being a recognised function of an attribute, such formulary expressions unhitch the anchorage in a self, by dissipating its consistency and even, above all, its pertinence. Everything in it expresses, through a continual slippage, non-rupture with the world, non-excision in thought, non-choice among possibilities and the non-withdrawal of what is compossible. The term I have translated as 'principal' – but which is here withdrawn – is precisely the one that has served to translate the Western 'subject' into contemporary Chinese (*zhǔ tǐ* 主体), which can mean 'director' or 'principal', but also 'welcoming' like that accorded to a guest, the 'object' being what is 'welcomed' (*kè tǐ* 客体). 'Welcoming' / 'welcomed': we see how unwilling Chinese thought-language is to lend itself to rendering the idea of a founding excision between the 'subject' and the 'object' as the basis of the neutrality of knowledge.

For the principle, if that is what it is, is to 'keep all things equal'. As true as it is that the one cannot do what the other does, so vice versa: 'the Sky can cover, but not produce; the Earth can produce but not cover; the vast Way can embrace, but not distinguish'. By taking into account that all things and all beings have their intrinsic possibilities, but also their impossibilities, we realise that, by 'choosing', we cannot 'hold everything', therefore it is faulty; or that to 'instruct is not to achieve', and that the way is 'to abandon nothing'. This is why it is said that Shen Dao 'freed himself from knowledge' and 'renounced the self' (*qù jǐ* 去己). He appears either as 'fresh', 'light', 'alert' (responsive), like water or the wind with respect to things (*ling tai*), so as to conform to the regulatory coherence of the way, or, always 'changing', he doesn't assume responsibility, disdaining the so-called Sages, and letting himself go at will, unconstrained and without being bound by morality. He unites with the most varied situation 'in its turns and detours', by ridding himself of separations, and in this way he can survive by avoiding impediment. 'Urged on, he advances', 'drawn, he follows', 'like the wind, spinning round'; 'like the feather, whirling': remaining in 'completeness', he is 'without rejection' and without regret; he doesn't experience the ravages of 'establishing a self'. In what is *situational*, in short, he remains in a floating state without being firmly fixed. As regards non-construction or non-imposition, as to the image, as to the sentence as it is reeled off, is it possible to go further in the non-constitution of a *subject*?

It is reported that, when his wife died, the thinker Zhuangzi sat with legs apart, in the least ritual position, and sang while striking a bowl. Confronted by those who were indignant at such an attitude, he justified himself with this sentence which also goes to the limit of what is translatable and that I will try to render as closely as is possible (in other words, by adding as little as possible of what the European sentence *expects*: Zhuangzi, ch. 18, 'Supreme Joy'):

Mixed-indistinct: between (jiān 间),

modify [modification], from which there is breath-energy (qì 气),

breath-energy modifies (itself), from which there is form-which-activates itself (xing 形),

form activating itself, from which there is living (shēng 生),

today, a new modification, from which the end is dying (sǐ 死).

An early translator (Liou Kia-hwai, published by Gallimard) rendered it like this: 'Something receding and ungraspable is transformed into breath, the breath into form, form into life, and now we have life transforming itself into death.' We see that this translator was – or believed he was – constrained to add a subject, as indefinite as it was, a 'something' (*ti*, 'something'), a properly Aristotelian subject, one that is both 'physical', as support for the change, and 'logical', as the subject of the sentence around which everything else happens – so many 'modifications' – by virtue of the predicate and the 'accident'. Immediately unfolding from this (for us) is the question, which is metaphysical par excellence, from which Chinese thought-language, as it remains at pure phenomenal description, is excused – to which it doesn't, so to speak, 'confer a subject'. But where does this something come from? What is there in the beginning? We return to our inescapable question of the Commencement or first beginning ('Genesis', the *big bang*: is a creator God needed as a great Subject? – and so on). A later translator (Jean Lévi) reconstructed this statement even further by inserting – assuming – a personal subject, Zhuangzi's actual wife, as the subject of the sentence: 'And

163

then suddenly, pfft! Thanks to an ungraspable germ, she had the unbelievable luck to go from non-being to Being; and then suddenly, pfft! breath having left her, she then had the unbelievable luck to return to her primitive dwelling.' So here once again the translation, by introducing a subject, reintroduces at the same time a theory of causality, without there being anything corresponding to it in the Chinese text (*in loco* of procedural propensity: 'Thanks to an ungraspable germ'), a scene as well as a value judgement (the 'primitive dwelling', the 'unbelievable luck') and, in the in-between, the very terms of ontology: 'Being' and 'non-being'. A whole European syntaxical-theoretical apparatus intercalates and is even established and settled, ordered by such a return of the Subject – apparently without the slightest suspicion that an intrusion is being committed.

It's true that, since Michel Foucault in his final classes opened up a new genealogy for the hermeneutics of the subject and that he especially stressed the importance of the ancient recommendation of 'care of the self', *epimeleia heautou*, in the face of the 'Know thyself' he especially separated so-called Greek techniques of the 'transformation of self' from the Cartesian evidence that gave direct access to self-certainty and therefore to philosophical truth. We've seen in the reminder of these 'spiritual' exercises a new bridge – accessible without knowing too much about it, but operative – to the thought of the Far East. And, in fact, the Chinese thinkers did consider that a 'transformation', *huà* 化, was needed to rise to wisdom. But is this a transformation 'of the self'? Or even, is there still a 'self' when an actual transformation takes place? An expression from the *Mencius* evoking such a progressive and step-by-step transformation ends in this way: 'great and transforming that is what we call "Sage"' (*da er hua zhi zhi wei sheng*, VII, B, 25). In other words, the one who is raised from one state to the other doesn't stop at the culminating stage of – still partial – 'greatness' but goes beyond it by 'transforming that'. 'That', left indefinite, keeps the verb active, but it isn't reduced to a 'self', which would be too 'circumscribed' (to pick up the Stoic term) and restrictive. For the Sage 'makes the others happen' at the same time as he 'happens himself' – inseparably, it is ordinarily said – and thereby reaches the dimension of the 'unfathomable' in which he is confused with (in) the infinity of the process of the world (*shén* 神): the 'self' of a subject comes apart in this ascension.

There is, nevertheless, an aspect here by which these two thoughts of ethical transformation communicate with each other. This is the diligent work, the patient and everyday application and the discipline and repeated exercises that the Greeks called *askesis* and that the Chinese named *gōngfu* 功夫. And it is also true that the Chinese have dealt with a 'natural' knowledge that is immanent to the mind and unfolds as a kind of evidence of consciousness. But this evidence is, on the one hand, a moral evidence and could not serve as a criterion for a knowledge of truth in the theoretical and Cartesian sense that we have given it in Europe. And, on the other hand, even in a thinker like Wang Yangming, from the sixteenth century, who has in this respect been compared with Descartes, this immediate intuition of natural regulation (*tiān lǐ* 天 理) is only revealed at the level of the diversity of situations. For we know spontaneously what 'filial piety' is 'in the presence of one's father', 'what respect is due to the elder in the presence of one's elder brother', or, more generally, 'the reaction of humanity if it is faced with the unbearable that happens to others in the presence of a child in danger of falling into a well', and so on (*Yulu*, I, 8). As such situations are particular and aren't subsumed under any comprehensive category, and as, on the other hand, it is always in relation to a given situation that such a moral intuition is immediately revealed, as an innate knowledge (*liáng zhī* 良知), we understand that this moral thinking challenges any apparatus of rules and commandments that could conceal this diversity. There's no generalising and codifying intermediary that might be able to interpose between the immediate apprehension in the mind of the natural regulation and the diversity of cases encountered calling upon it, *hic et nunc*, to manifest itself. In China, it is from such a *typology of situations* (as we already see in Mencius) that the typology of virtues is conceived, and not from what would be the qualities or properties of a subject.

6 In presenting *subject* and *situation* as two rival concepts, as I am here inclined to do, it will be understood how that of the situation has remained underdeveloped in Europe under the ascendant reign of the subject. This is why the situation has not gained autonomy, but has remained under the domination of the other that has maintained it under its protection or within its sphere. If we return to the term itself, we can already measure what it implicitly imposes. For this term, in its basis, is only locative (situated 'in') at the same time as it is already attributive: the situation is only understood in relation to the subject that is *situated there* and which sovereignly transcends it. And when (in the seventeenth century) meaning is abstracted from it, the term which comments upon it, 'circumstance', does not come from this centring of the Subject, but on the contrary accentuates the purely environmental character (*circum*: 'around') of what the subject, for its part, thereby keeps strictly separated. Alone, such a particular idiom, 'to be in a situation of' (for example, in a situation of refusal) discreetly opens a breach in this citadel of the Subject, turns the situation, under its cover, into orders, and gives a glimpse of another possibility of the notion in which it is the situation itself that would be the source of the effect, revealing a *potential* of itself. Yet it is such a thread which will have to be drawn upon in order to gain a sense of the Chinese conception of what I have until now only been able to call thus, too economically, 'situation', and to begin to broaden it.

'Circum-stance' – let's pause on this word since situation, as the dictionary makes clear, is a 'set of circumstances'. According to the composition of this word, it is therefore something that 'occurs around' or 'surrounds'. Yet it is a European term: *peri-stasis* περί-στασις, in Greek; *Um-stand*, in German. But occurring 'around' what, if not the perspective that a subject projects of itself over the world, and 'around' which the 'situation' is envisaged?

Such is the last of the cases in Latin, the ablative, in which what isn't constructed from the statement in relation and determined reaction of an object, possession or attribution is crammed pell-mell into a single and last bundle. Yet language, in fact, thinks – it thinks, articulates and 'folds' thought up, prior to what we think. Isn't what is implied here the Stoic represention of an insularity of the subject in the midst of the world, taken out as it is into its autonomy, 'around' which there 'occur' – like waves continually renewing themselves, and pounding against the rock – the tumultuous eddies of 'circum-stances'? Due to the fact that it must rigorously 'circumscribe' itself so as to possess itself, it is against this that it also measures and can experience itself. Or, rather, didn't Stoicism only make use of this image, but an image that is a lot more than an image, since it fashions the way language has constructed its morphology? So, let's consider a language such as Chinese that is without morphology, and therefore without declension, and whose system of prepositions has remained rudimentary. What can still remain of this plan of a subject from the outset prescribing the situation and dominating its initiative, even when it must tragically succumb to it?

Has European thought ever emerged from this submission of the situation to the subject? Jean-Paul Sartre was the first person, or at least the one best known in Europe, to propose a concept of *situation*, but far from opening out the cultural biases implied in this representation, he did so in order to confirm and ratify them. Above all, he improved on the attributive character of the situation envisaged in the dependency of the subject, according simply to the perspective of its *pour soi*, by virtue of an aid, or rather a shackle: 'my position in the midst of the world is defined by the relation between the instrumental utility or adversity in the realities which surround me [...], this is what we mean by the situation' (Sartre, 1989: 548). Repeating the concentric circles of Stoicism in his own terms (for him: my place, my past, my surroundings, my fellows, my death), he doesn't leave behind this circularity of 'circum-stance'. Still less does he envisage that a situation might, he said, be 'considered from outside' – the formula, which is not made explicit, nevertheless reveals what thought from the outset formed an obstruction to and closed itself off against. And then, if the concept of the situation remains primordial as far as he is concerned, it is because he is the one who effects the mediation between the subject (*alias* its freedom) and the *given* (or between the 'pour soi' of the subject and the necessity to 'be-in- the-world', and so on) – in other words, its factuality.

The situation is the always-singular face that the contingency of things offers to my project so as to go beyond it by making it the 'aim', from which I promote myself precisely as a subject. Hence, the 'situation' outlines its 'limits' by its effect of concretion. The subject's choice and what it has to confront is determined from this. We have therefore not come out of the Western dramaturgy of a Subject with which everything begins. Or, rather, it's the 'situation' that henceforth serves it as its staging and theatre.

The fact that, in the summary of *Existentialism is a Humanism*, Sartre envisages the concept of situation directly after having reaffirmed the 'absolute truth' of the *cogito* as the only possible basis of thought is sufficient to show that, from one to the other, the logic is effectively that of a single block and a continuous thought.

7 Yet the most ancient book of China, the fundamental book of its thought, the *Oracle of Change*, the *Yi-jing* or *I Ching*, which in the beginning was not a book but an operative (manipulative) tool, conceived from a combination of superimposed lines and consisting of figures, radically modifies this approach, offering thought a new possibility. This system of hexagrams (sixty-four in total) allows us to examine many cases of the process of things, from which follows a *typology of situations* envisaged in their own structure and not dependent on a subject. For example, the hexagrams for Surge and Decline (11 and 12) don't deal with a subject experiencing a surge or a decline, but with what constitutes the very logic of a surge and a decline by illuminating their coherence. When factors are opposed but at the same time complementary (*yin* and *yang*), 'communicating' together and cooperating, a surge results from it. Three *yang* lines below, three *yin* lines above symbolically configure the situation amounting to prosperity: the *yang* propensity, which is that of Heaven, being to ascend, while that of the *yin*, the 'Earth', being to descend, these two factors and vectors of energy, established in relation to one another, meet at the height of their intensity, generating activation – a surge being verified as much in nature (the surge of spring: when the flow enters interaction) as in politics when the prince (*yang*) and the people (*yin*), instead of each remaining apart from one another, draw closer and collaborate. The hexagram of Decline is the opposite: the *yang*, in the upper part of the hexagram, is apt to withdraw into its height, while the *yin*, in the lower part of the hexagram, withdraws into its lowliness, and so the factors dissociate themselves: the flows retract in order to hibernate, or the prince withdraws to his palace, the people into their poverty. It is from this secession that the energy of the whole of reality goes into decline.

A second point of divergence from our conception of the situation perceived within the perspective of the subject will be inferred: the Chinese *Oracle of Change* considers what we call 'situation' not by way of *circumstances* that 'surround' this point of view of the subject, but from an internal *tension* occurring between factors as they enter into correlation. It is from this tension alone that a situation emerges by itself or, expressed differently – for we have to pause on this phenomenon and think about it – a situation is outlined as soon as the tension has been organised. Expressed differently again, a situation occurs and is configured from the *emergence of a polarity*, and this is true whatever its register. A polarity exists between the energies of *yin* and *yang* in nature, or between masculine and feminine, between government and governed, between parent and child, between adversary and associate, and so on, in the heart of society. If, in this way,

Chinese thought approaches what we call a situation, it is, in fact, because it has viewed the whole of reality in terms of opposed complementaries (in the form of *yin* and *yang*) engaging in an interaction (or, more precisely, an 'affective interaction' as the Chinese says: *xiàng gǎn* 相感): there is no Heaven or Earth considered apart from one another, as isolated instances, but it is from the relation and the exchange tying them together that the whole process of things proceeds.

The third divergence finally results from the preceding ones: a situation is always, from the outset, *in transformation* – and this is why the *Oracle of Change* is called a classic of change, *yi-jing*. It is a 'classic' not because it is enduring, but because it is always in process. Against what the other semantic component of 'circum-stance' assumes, in that it is not only 'around' but, moreover, that it 'stays' in a stable (*stare*) way, no bringing into tension could of itself be stable and precipitate an evolution. A situation doesn't belong to the register of Being, any more than it does to that of 'becoming', which is still referred to Being (becoming and processivity will have to be distinguished), which is where the difficulty of grasping it in European terms arises, but it is always in 'modification' (*biàn* 变). Thus, each hexagram of the *Oracle of Change* generally names a situation that is shown more precisely in its unfolding, from low to high, or from one stage to the next, from its first to its sixth line. For example, the characters for Surge and Decline have the same departure point (a conjectural entanglement, like 'tangled roots'); the second line of the Surge then brings into view a solid 'backing' from which one can 'completely embrace', and the third warns that the Surge is threatened before even reaching its highest point ('there is no flat ground which will not be followed by a slope'). While the fifth finally marks the point that culminates in ascension (the marriage of a 'young girl'), the sixth and last marks the exhaustion of the surge and its equalisation ('the high wall falls into a ditch'). Conversely, the upper lines of the Decline mark the gradual ending of the decline: a 'clarification' appears (fourth line); we then once again find something to 'hang on to' (fifth line); we then (finally) see ourselves passing from the obstruction of the decline to the 'joy' of prosperity (sixth line). At the same time as they are opposed, the two figures link up as they transform themselves. It will therefore be necessary to learn to detect how the decline is already at work at the time of the surge and how the factors of a renewal are already, in the half-light, being reconstituted at the time of the decline.

A new definition of the situation can thus be deduced from this notional triangle which no longer makes it simply a 'site': of a situation which might no longer be dominated by the subject (1), nor reduced to the circumstantial (2), nor left immobilised and fixed (3). To break free of this dependent concept that the 'situation' has continued to be in Europe, we shall thus think that a situation is by itself an implication of factors or instances entering into correlation (1), from which a tension unfolds (2), and from which an evolution follows (3). It is this bringing into tension that makes a situation emerge and that confers it with a unity ('a' situation) at the same time as any situation is oriented by its propensity, whose favourable or unfavourable direction ('magnificent' or 'fatal') remains to be detected. Hence, the *Oracle of Change* proposes one notion, 'moment-position', *shi-wèi* 时位, from which it will be worthwhile to erect a concept to conceive of a situation which is that of the processes themselves. Each line of each hexagram occupies a 'position' at the heart of the hexagram at the same time as it marks a 'moment' of its evolution. There are only *moments-situations* weaving the world, or the world is actually this 'totality' of what happens, forming a 'case' – or of which each occasion is a 'case': *alles, was der Fall ist*.

In relation to this, the *Oracle of Change*, by freeing the situational from the control of the subject, responds to its operatory vocation: scrutinising and detecting how the consultant, by manipulating it, can interfere at the heart of this play of factors, to collaborate with it and take advantage of it. This results in a function that is both ethical and strategic and reveals the situation no longer as a *limit* posed at the initiative of my freedom, as in Sartrian confrontation, but as a *resource* of a potential with which it is wise to learn to manoeuvre, by making it a partner: the art of operating *effectively* (by and in a process) is substituted for the 'engagement' (of the Subject). This occurs in such a way that no situation is actually negative: since, at the time of settling, I remain vigilant in relation to what already threatens it, and, during the time of decline, I remain confident in scrutinising how the decline is also drawn to transform itself, therefore of itself to decline, to be transformed into a new settling. But – here is the principal lesson (notably emphasised by Wang Fuzhi) – I can't decipher such indications of renewal from my past reading, which now becomes redundant, otherwise this renewal isn't new. The lesson is to be thought about: I must elaborate a new grid of reading to perceive the new. For I can't let my reading of the situation become fossilised any more than a situation can be fixed. If the penultimate hexagram of the book, where all the lines are in their place, where everything is in order (odd lines in odd places, even lines in even places and so on), is that of 'After the crossing', the final hexagram of the *Oracle of Change*, an inverse hexagram, in which no line is in its place, is that of 'Before the crossing': history is never ended, and I must realise the new coherence of what thereby continually makes its way afresh.

8 Hence the situation, as *moment-position*, is be to thought about not as what 'surrounds', in however tenuously 'stable' a way, the 'circum'-'stance', but as a *conjuncture*, in other words a conjunction of instances or factors exerting together a reciprocal 'encouragement' that is constantly being renewed and from which an evolution continually unfolds. Hence also that the *Oracle of Change*, whose primary rationale is divination, isn't devoted to forecasting or constructing hypotheses that would be projected onto the future, but represents a diagnostic, as an examination of the undertaking of the relation of forces and in which the transformation to come is always already 'primed' (the notion of *jī* 幾). The same thing applies in the specifically strategic literature of the 'Arts of War': the first operation recommended is,

as we have already learned, not *projection* (to construct a plan of operations expected), but *detection*, at once of evaluation and calculation (the ancient sense of jì 计). It is a matter of revealing, even in an embryonic state, the strong points and the weak points, the 'gaps' and the 'solid parts', between oneself and the adversary. According to the five basic factors (the 'way' or moral conditions, the 'sky' or climatic conditions, the 'earth' or topographic conditions, the quality of the command and finally that of the management and organisation), it is necessary to 'compare in such a way as to evaluate so as to scrutinise the disposition', *xiào zhī yǐ jì ér suǒ qí qíng* 校之以 计而索其 情. *Disposition* (a way of translating 情) is as valid from a subjective as from an objective point of view, concerned as much with the affective disposition as the disposition on the ground (*gin-qíng* 感情 and *qíng-kuang* 情况). This is actually the term to be promoted in order to think about the internal layout of factors and forces in presence that will have an effect on the results (and they are as much moral as they are military, psychological or physical), and not only in war, integrating in this way from the outset every point of view of the subject. In the same way, one of the basic notions of this *Art of War* (*xíng* 形, *Sunzi*, ch. 4) expresses the *configuration* as it is actualised (the term is verbal as well as nominal) and in which the 'potential' to be located is to be inscribed and invested.

What I have therefore been led to translate as 'the potential of situation' (*shi* 势) consequently reveals the notion of 'circum-stance' that is its exact inverse, or better still its contradiction. This can be verified in Clausewitz, who was the first – even if a late – great thinker about war in Europe and who, as one might expect, envisaged strategy not from an antagonistic disposition, but from the position of the subject, therefore in terms of a projected modelisation or design (an 'absolute', model, war, as opposed to a real war) – and he did so even to the point of noting in it the bankruptcy of any strategy (since war never happens on the ground as it had been planned). He conceived the circumstance precisely as what always threatens to thwart any plan that is conceived in advance and is only partly agreed upon. The circumstance, unforeseeable and undesignable as it is (the Austerlitz 'fog') is what, intervening between the plan and its realisation, deflects it and leads to its becoming bogged down. Such is the 'friction' (of circumstances) that shackles its application. The *potential of situation* is then the perfect reversal of this negative. Due to the fact that I am not designing, and therefore not projecting onto it – in other words, that I don't consider the situation according to the plan conceived from the initiative of a subject-self – I am all the better able constantly to detect in a direct way what, in the configuration as it is evolving, can be more and more advantageously exploited. This sentence from *Sunzi* should be closely read: 'evaluating the advantage in such a way as to adopt it, I create from it a potential of situation that will assist the external conditions' (计利以听, 乃为之势, 以佐其外, ch. 1). It is said in what follows that the potential of situation therefore comes from 'taking advantage of what is profitable in order to govern the change' (因利而制权). It is thus about detecting the favourable factors at the heart of the situation encountered, no matter how trivial they may be, and not by following what I have designed, that I learn how to let myself be carried along by these conveying factors, gradually inflecting this antagonistic disposition so that it becomes a favourable incline from which the effects will then powerfully rush down (ibid., ch. 5).

It is therefore not by chance that, from ancient times, China has conceived a strategic thinking of which we have no equivalent in Europe. As Clausewitz said, but only in recognising why strategy is doomed to fail, it is because war is a phenomenon that *lives and reacts*. In other words, war originally takes place between two, between the partner-adversary, one of whom (the adversary) isn't second in relation to the initiative of a subject. And war is always only the outcome, which is not able to deviate from the correlation at work in the configuration involved. Yet, by constructing a *plan* that is to be projected onto the situation, rather than by inflecting it in a procedural way so that the effect rushes down due to the *incline*, I am always taking the evolution of the adverse position into account only after the event and I am condemned not to be able to consider it other than 'circumstantially'. If China has therefore conceived a strategic thinking that is unique in the world, it is because war cannot be thought except in terms of polarity and China has conceived everything as a polarity in which one end doesn't come after the other, but is conceived from it. It was therefore at ease in thinking about the phenomenon and without being burdened with the point of view of the conceiving and desiring Subject, according to its classical determinations in Europe. This subject conceives 'with a view to what is best' (the imperative that is projected by understanding) and is then intent on following it through with an effort of will, and in spite of the 'friction' that is sustained by circumstances, so as to bring this ideal into reality. This 'bringing' assumes a heroic forcing and it is one that cannot avoid the fact that the outcome, even if we refine the calculation of probabilities, always ultimately arises from chance and luck, which Sunzi excluded and which are as fascinating as in a 'card game' (it was Clausewitz who made this association). If the conduct of war deconstructs the representation of the 'subject' and the 'circumstantial' which is its correlative in an exemplary way, by revealing them as being both abstract and arbitrary, it's therefore because it leads to thinking about the conditions of a mastery that might be of a different kind and in which the self must put itself in phase with what isn't the self instead of withdrawing from it. It is where the subject therefore remains in the hollow of the configuration of things, and dextrously winds itself into them, rather than imposing itself right from the start.

9 Even so, would nothing be gained by detaching this 'subject' from the play of continuous interactions forming the constantly evolving configuration of what we call the 'world', and by establishing this at the beginning, in a point of emergence, as an initial term? Or, what is that resource

which causes the subject to come forth when considering the one that constitutes what we in Europe have inadequately called 'situation'? Such a *subject* shouldn't be confused with the claims of the 'individual' when faced with the collective, this degree of *individuation* being more or less marked according to the time and place, but having today to demand more and more insistently such a place for the individual, in the shape of its enfranchisement, that it amputates its own possibilities as it disregards the Other (the noble Kierkegaardian or Nietzschean exigency having fallen in such a sad way into individualism). Nor should this subject-self be confused with the status of the 'person', a judicial, ethical or political status, the *person* being thereby presented as a source of indefeasible rights at the same time as having defined duties, from which follows the range of so many responsibilities to be recognised and assumed. The promotion of the subject responds to another demand and is to be re-thought separately – indeed, in a certain rupture with its past elaboration. It doesn't arise so much from the appropriation and circumscription of a 'self', as Stoicism would have it, nor from the affirmation of an identity, assuming some permanence to this self, 'under' the change, as Aristotle demanded. It doesn't even bear so much on how the beginning of thought's self-justification might be founded in a consciousness of self, as in the great act of the *cogito* testing its evidence. Having so constantly compared the 'subject' with the 'situation' – or the 'I' with its implication in the 'world' – makes it appear that its legitimation is of another order: that of an ex-istence that discovers itself in it, precisely due to its capacity to extract itself from it, and which finds expression in this power of confrontation.

As the European language most strongly makes it understood, the subject doesn't simply draw its legitimacy initially from the 'case' erected by language – the 'subject-case' – which the word makes emerge every time as a *position*. The fact that an 'I' gains expression opposite a 'you' (of the Other), or by reference to a 'him' (of the world), frees – or deploys – a 'subject', and any 'configuration', which is opposite to it, becomes secondary to it. The subject is thus what doesn't belong completely to the world while it isn't being authorised by anywhere else. It finds its niche in this play of dispositions or configurations that form the world. We finally realise – something that forms our modernity (because modernity really exists) – that this 'outside the world', *ektos tou kosmou*, of metaphysics doesn't come from 'beyond' or over there, in the place it had been hastily and conveniently lodged – or perhaps is so only in a symbolic way. In other words, that there is no transcendence of the Elsewhere. And, indeed, is any transcendence possible except in this 'I' which expresses itself? The subject opens the only legitimate transcendence, because it alone is effective, because it alone is active in the here and now. For once the subject says 'I', it right away opens up a weak point (creates a divergence) in the whole unlimited play of the world – while death is the cessation of this 'I', its resorption into silence, and a position of subject has vanished for ever. But each time that an 'I' is repeated in the world, without needing this to be that of an 'I think', or when this aims at knowledge, an initiative is taken, a fresh perspective emerges, a new pathway is revealed in existing, and the narrative of 'a life' (the generic title of the modern novel) can begin.

Note

1   Shen Dao (*c.* 350 – *c.* 275 BCE), a Legalist theoretician [trans.].

Afterword: From Divergence to the Common

To philosophise is to diverge

To diverge is not only to leave, to separate, to open up a withdrawal, to abandon the ways and themes of common conversation and even to become dissident. It is equally, in opening an elsewhere, to risk going where no path is marked out, where the ground has become uncertain, where the even and settled light, the light known by everyone, no longer penetrates as it did before. Can we hope to perceive something else from this withdrawal and through this retreat, according to a childhood dream that still persists, or at least to perceive in a different way? 'And I've sometimes seen what man thought he saw ... ' (Rimbaud) – it is certain, in any case, that here we will face a solitude it would be impossible to avoid. Not a casual and more or less anecdotal solitude, but a solitude that is inevitable and constitutive as a principle, which arises from what began one day through dissociation, by and in thought, and that will no longer be effaceable. Perhaps through this divergence we have even started to become inaudible, and we shall need to make a lot of effort afterwards to get back to ordinary language, to reconnect with the habitus and conventions and hope to make ourselves heard once again so that, by lavishing so many pledges of good will, it will be believed that we have cast away at least a little of its strangeness.

Is this the heart – the *factum* and even the *fatum* – of any path of thought, or is it really only the case for philosophy? What seems certain is that philosophy made this its first act, to establish it as its point of entry, and that it draws its will from this resolution. This is its threshold. Parmenides, the father of philosophy – or in any case the first to have been made a 'father' so that 'parricide' could then be committed by diverging from him – posited it expressly as a condition of departure and point of access. The path sought and into which one ventured, that of 'law and justice', was accused of being 'apart from people', 'off the beaten track', *ap' anthrôpon ektos patou*. The formula is even insistent in its intensification. It says both that one has to separate oneself from others and that one must emerge from the common rut, from the path that has already been cleared, from the *patos*. It is only by leaving this unreliable field of 'opinions', *doxai*, that we will be able to raise ourselves to the 'unshakeable heart of truth'. Or perhaps it will be necessary to go back still further into this genealogy of divergence from which the philosopher would come? Perhaps the first philosopher is actually Ulysses, the Ulysses of the *Odyssey* who, in his drifting, wandered from one unknown place to another, running from divergence to divergence, before 'returning'. He diverged from the very milieu of his companions while staying close to them: enjoining them to stop up their ears while attaching himself naked to the ship's mast to expose himself alone, wanting (or being able) only to be alone when the dangerous revelation came.

To diverge from the language and culture in which one was born, at one moment, in that place and surroundings, and in that context where one started to open one's eyes, to discover and learn and to form and constitute oneself into a 'subject', and to do so through a deliberate – or I'd say strategic – choice, as I did when going from Europe to China, is therefore, all in all, only to reiterate the very gesture of philosophy, its first act, but to do so afresh, by exacerbating its conditions so that in consequence there is nothing really anecdotal or 'exotic' about it. It is to retrace the steps of Ulysses, but by systematically making use of the possibilities and ambition of this divergence. It is, *de facto*, to emerge from the history of European philosophy, to extract oneself all at once from its debates and notions and to break with its filiation. But to what extent aren't we always beginning to philosophise in Europe by going back into the *history of the question*, carried along by something that isn't just etymology? Right from the start, it means breaking not only with its great philosophemes like 'being', 'God', 'Truth', 'Freedom' and so on, but also, more radically, with the language in which they have been articulated, extracted as one suddenly finds oneself from the Indo-European and its family atmosphere – from its family site. To diverge from European philosophy by way of the Chinese elsewhere – this *elsewhere* of language as also, for such a long time, of History, the two extremities of the great continent, China and Europe, having spent so long before meeting, at least as far as thought is concerned – is therefore to diverge from what has already been thought and sedimented in Europe (from which the bed of thought is formed, and which is therefore no longer being thought about; from what within it is so well assimilated, integrated and accredited that it makes us forget those choices that have been hidden away and the concealed biases, no matter what suspicions of philosophy have followed and have come to constitute 'evidence'), therefore that one no longer thinks about: that one no longer thinks of thinking about.

But if I say that such a choice of *divergence* (by way of China) only exemplifies the inveterate gesture of philosophy, it is really because this work is already valid, in itself, in all respects, as on any scale. It is what is at work within the very history of philosophy and that renews it: each philosopher becomes a real philosopher to the extent that he separates himself from those coming before him or, to make the point more precisely, *opens up* a *divergence* in relation to them. This is even what is already valued with respect to oneself: to philosophise is nothing but mercilessly to distance oneself from what has been one's own thinking, detaching oneself from what one has already thought to progress into what one's thinking *will become*. This work of separation has nothing in common with any itching of originality but is established well beforehand, as an act *of departure* from what will subsequently be fixed as a critical operation, devoted to refutation, by which every philosophy is designated, or by which it frees itself and institutes itself. Whether each philosopher, according to the well-known phrase, will 'say no' to the one who came before or, as has been said time and again since (see Foucault or Deleuze), that to philosophise is 'to think otherwise', this is merely the consequence of it.

If to philosophise therefore means primarily and repeatedly to inscribe a break, to introduce a distance, to provoke an effect of dissociation and to engage a dissidence, it is because such a break, by being widened (and the more it widens), opens up *fresh access to what is unthought*. But if I insist on this primary gesture, it is also because I am wondering whether it may today be under threat – or perhaps it is already out of date? Today, it is constantly announced that, thanks to the convenience of the Internet deploying its all-embracing network and connecting everyone in 'real time', and thus also because of the indefinite multiplication of data, intelligence has now become collective, in such a way that we will think 'together' and no longer as each one of us in our own way. Today when, even when it comes to research in the 'human sciences' (very inappropriately when it comes to philosophy), it is endlessly repeated that any work can only be conducted, and validated, within a team, and that the figure of the solitary seeker is to be condemned, I wonder if a thought *that diverges* will even be tolerated? Yet, at the same time, to protest against 'unique thought' has become an all-pervasive theme, itself repeated to the point of tedium ... But will we be able to take heed of this if we are no longer able to leave it, to begin a withdrawal, to abandon established questions (those that appear to be obvious), to dissociate ourselves; or, to put it in a positive way, if we do not know how to open up, to explore a way into, the place where the terrain is no longer recognised, whose path is no longer taken (and is the path even still there?), and where the common light no longer penetrates, if we do not know how one evening to leave, to leave alone (disengaged and disconnected), facing the solitude and moving away to *who knows where*? This is what to 'diverge' really means.

The well-known unknown

But what should that from which philosopy each time diverges as it finds a new departure generally be called? What must it tear itself away from because thought sinks in it from the outset? It could be called, following Hegel and Nietzsche, who treated it in unison, although each in their own way, the 'well-known'. We need to take apart this illusion: what is close at hand and familiar, Nietzsche said, gives the irresistible impression of being what is most easily accessible, although this well-known is only the reflection of those of our beliefs and mental habits that have become fixed. 'What they call the known' is the 'habitual', yet this habitual is what is precisely most difficult to know, in other words to *consider as a problem*: as an unknown, far away and external thing, and it is what needs to be discovered instead of being taken for granted. Or, as Hegel said, the well-known is precisely 'unknown because it is well-known', *weil es bekannt ist, nicht erkannt* (see the Preface to the *Phenomenology*). Actually, it is not even 'recognised', *er-kannt*, due to the fact that it thereby causes us from the start to tip into the security of what we think we know, without even beginning to think it: to think that there is something there to be thought. Similarly, seeing in it only a support to enable us to go further, we hasten to stride over it.

It is said, with a wisdom that is on the whole commonplace, that we should not simply be surprised by what no longer surprises us, which is also referred to as the familiar. But that thought, all thought, at the same time as it becomes implanted (by the very fact that it has become implanted), is deactivated. It gets bogged down in (or rather due to) the very thing that has instituted it: as soon as it has become our representation of things, Hegel said that the mind believes it has finished with it. Worse still, it believes, with no further distrust, that it can be used as a tool. This means that the mind henceforth treats what has 'immediately' come to be imposed on thought as common categories and that it suspects neither its genesis nor what it contains that is unthought. In passing, Hegel opened up from such categories a list of terms that had become static, those around which European thought then did no more than turn – but, as is said, 'turn in a circle' and, therefore, to do so rather in vain. These are the couplings of 'subject' and 'object', 'God' and 'nature', or 'understanding' when faced with 'sensibility', and so on. The discourse of philosophy is then able to come and go between these terms as often as it likes and without any longer knowing how to move them. They have become pillars between which the 'movement' of thought circulates, but it no longer shakes them and does no more than evolve at the level of their 'surface', *Oberfläche*, each person believing that he is then able on every occasion to verify them directly from their representation and apart from their relevance because he doesn't have any distance from which to question them.

Yet how can we hope to have control over this well-known unknown, which has become immoveable, since it is from this that we think? If European thought is fundamentally marked *at the intersection of these terms* – 'terms' also meaning a place to stop – what obliqueness, or rather what cunning, is to be found in order to start 'prising' ourselves away from them? To go to China, to find an elsewhere of thought, is a strategy the mind needs in order no longer to submit. For what we find there is a thought as elaborate as 'ours' (in Europe), but without there being any suspicion of influence or contamination between them: it is an *elsewhere* that doesn't belong to the system of alphabetical composition, and one whose writing responds to the other possibility, which is ideographic rather than phonetic.

It is an elsewhere which has not spoken about 'being' and has therefore not conceived of the 'question' of Being and has not had to posit (or prove) the existence of 'God', and which, without having disregarded the divine, has not had to 'deal with God', which has not made 'truth' the pledge and the criterion of thought, which has not developed a thinking about the subject whose first attribute would be freedom, and so on. This is the strategic choice that I made in finally trying to *diverge* myself from this well-known unknown. But what relation exists between all of these pillars we see of 'Being', 'God', 'Truth', 'Freedom', and what edifice do they support? Without our being aware of it, won't *all* of our thoughts be consigned to the same boat?

Divergence versus difference

Yet it will first of all be necessary, in order to approach the question, to set out a fundamental distinction, without which the undertaking would be futile – an undertaking which one suspects would immediately be exposed to both turmoil and criticisms from all of those who refuse to move even slightly from what is 'well known' in thinking. Indeed, it is the notion of difference that is ordinarily invoked between these two ways of thinking – that is the Chinese and the European. Will this be enough? Or won't it straightaway betray the oblique strategy that I've made a start in putting forward, due to the perspective it requires and notwithstanding the banality of its use? If I've spoken of 'diverging', it is because *divergence* isn't *difference*. What is the 'difference' between divergence and difference? Further on, I will put the 'divergence' between them to work. In order to make a start let's therefore say that, if divergence and difference both have separation in common, difference *marks a distinction*, while divergence *opens a distance*. Hence, difference is classificatory (in operating through resemblance and difference) at the same time as being identificatory. According to Aristotle, it is by going 'from difference to difference', and doing so as far as the final difference, that the essence (definition) of the thing is reached. In contrast, divergence is a figure. It isn't identificatory but exploratory, or I'll call it *heuristic*: the question is thus no longer what the thing 'is' in its singularity, due to its difference(s), but 'how far' the divergence takes it as it overflows the norm. Not being classificatory, the divergent is therefore a figure that produces not an arrangement, as difference does (difference is really the tool of typologies), but what I'd conversely say is a *disarrangement* (as the French say: to 'create a divergence', when speaking about language or behaviour). In this sense, divergence is opposed to what is expected, to what is ordinary and conventional – or let's now say to what is 'well known'.

From this, it will be deduced that, while difference serves *description*, proceeding through analysis (already the *diairesis tôn eidôn* διαίρεσις τῶν εἴδων of the Ancients), divergence initiates *prospection*. Divergence envisages – it 'sounds out' – the extent to which other paths can be opened up, and while a difference *determines itself* (which marks its limit), a divergence *explores*. Yet from this difference of operations, we can distinguish the advantage that can respectively be derived from them. The operation of difference, as it arises from a neighbouring genre in which it distinguishes one species among others, serves to *establish a characteristic* from this specificity, while that of divergence, through the evident distance, *holds in tension* what it has separated. But what does it mean to 'hold in tension'? In the case of difference, once it has been recognised, each of the terms that have been distinguished are enough, since they are and remain flatly in their place, wedded to their specificity, while in the case of divergence each of the separated terms remains open to the other through the distance – the gulf – that appears: instead of each of the separated terms remaining in their *en-soi*, finding their essence in it, as in difference, it is by measuring themselves against the other, by remaining, so to speak, (sus)pended from it, that the divergence is appreciated. It is *through* the other, in accordance with it, that this 'through' is grasped by a divergence that remains active.

This enables us to understand why the fate of difference is linked to thinking about *identity*. In fact, it arises from it in a double sense: when it began, it assumed a common genus, identified as such, whose specification it marks, and in its aim or its destination, upon its arrival, it leads to the isolation of an identity, fixing its essence as a thing – in other words, giving it its definition. That such a difference would henceforth be presented as initial, as linguistic minimalism has already done for some time now, and even that it no longer has to be coupled with resemblance (the linguistics of this, as we know, having nothing more to do), the fact remains that the determination of such a difference is still sustained, and both founded and justified, by a concern with *identification*. The fact that one element would no longer have existence except in the name of a difference, or that it would no longer be isolated from the property other than by the establishment of differences – and no longer the inverse, as the classical schema (of metaphysics) would have liked – doesn't preclude the fact that, in this structure or system, the relation of difference, henceforth placed *ab initio*, still has the function of characterising or specifying – it knows no other end than knowledge. Confronted with this, divergence allows us to emerge from this perspective based on identity. It reveals what I would describe in an overflowing of identity as 'fertility', which allows us to abandon the point of view of knowledge so as to be understood as a *resource* of thought.

The *fertility* that is uncovered by divergence is in fact twofold. First of all, the fact that the inclines of the divergence continue to be turned towards one another, being maintained in a reciprocal apprehension instead of each of them having withdrawn into their own specificity, means that they work *between themselves* as they find out about one another through each other. Since they do not find an essence in themselves, they contemplate each other only through their relation. In other words, if the divergence is working, or if it operates, it is in the distance it brings into focus and which resists any future closure: the divergence *opens a between* as it places what has been separated *in tension*. The divergence isn't analytical, as difference is, but, by widening (the more it widens), the divergence is an *intensive*. If difference also establishes a relation, then each of its terms goes on its way alone and it isn't aware of the fertility of this *between* which is what generates intensity. Divergence, on the other hand, releases possibilities about which one wonders, amazed and intrigued, how far they might go. They overflow from what was previously envisaged and even from what could be imagined. Pushing the boundary markings aside, they unbolt the known and conventional, and throw the 'well-known' into confusion. They push back the frontiers of the explored and identified, and in consequence of the resources to be prospected, open more widely the range of capacities. In what diverges, and the more it diverges, a confrontation of limits, and perhaps a setting free – or in other words, an adventure – are uncovered.

It will thus be understood that *divergence* and *difference* differ not by their object but by the perspective they assume or, I would say, by their ethic: difference demands care and rigour in its determination, while divergence calls for audacity in its exploration–exploitation. The one scrutinises, the other probes – even here, after having begun to show how they differ, I am setting the divergence between them to work. Thus, by virtue of difference, I can analyse some particular feature with a comparatist aim, from which I will make a criterion of classification in order to determine specificities. I can equally well turn the same feature to account by way of divergence – but the 'feature' has regrettably already slipped towards differential description – to envisage what fresh branching out it opens and therefore what possibilities are to be discovered in it, one effect of which (*the* effect) is to be drawn indefinitely. In both cases, it is the same 'fact': for example, the European language conjugates, the Chinese doesn't. But in one case I perceive a discriminating–identifying character from the angle of difference allowing the linguistic facts to be described and distributed into a system and then to arrange the languages as a family. In the other, I perceive under the angle of divergence a possibility that enables me continually to measure the resources it releases, regarding the possibility diverged (and reciprocally) in the conception-expression of thought. Thanks to this, I especially see that Chinese poetry can remain in an indefinite processual time without projecting a subject but by enhancing the correlative dimension of what is stated, and so on.

Let's therefore learn to suspect 'synonyms' like those of divergence and difference so as to see how they have oriented thought differently due to the implied perspective, and to such a point that they will finally need to be placed in opposition, being reversed so as to form them as *antonyms*. Let's therefore look again, as an example or a lesson to be learned, reading them on a broader scale, at the categories of 'evil' and 'negative' which I once examined and which are ordinarily designated as the same thing (suffering, death, war: 'misfortune'), but to reverse them into opposites. Evil – let's recall the theodicies – does this under the angle of interiority (of a subject) and the negative, conversely, under that of functionality (of the great process of things). Therefore *evil*, in forming a concept, does so under the angle of singularity (individual fate), exclusion (evil struggling with good), dramatic narration (this struggle entails a history), an enigmatic questioning (pointing to the tormenting 'why') and finally leading to protest (the complaint made to the rebellious Job), while the concept of the *negative* occurs under the angle of universality (comprehensive 'harmony'), integration ('everything is needed to make a world'), 'logical' description (explaining the 'how' of this syntax of 'everything') and finally touches on Stoic acceptance (by com-prehension of the fact that you can't have one without the other) and so on. According to one or the other point of view engaged and forming an option, under its apparent synonyms, without even having been measured, you seek a way out that will liberate us from evil in salvation (the Saint) *or* you attain wisdom by becoming 'comprehensive' (from the 'indissociability of the negative'). Yet 'point of view' here means a *tool* – a tool we have produced, not which relativises (relativising comes from comparing), but which operates behind the scenes and, without being perceived, opens a gap: according to how you make one or the other work, and doing so in its own terms, your life slips into the opposite, from one side or the other.

Yet the same thing can be said from the points of view of *divergence* and *difference*: difference, by determining, closes the horizon, ending at the final difference that forms the definition; on the other hand, divergence, through the tension making it work, opens out onto infinite possiblility. And so if we go back to the history of philosophy, I won't think about why Aristotle's thought *differs* from that of Plato (such a way of thinking, which catalogues the differences, as though they were items, is sterile in advance), but about where his thought *diverges* from that of Plato, to reveal, through this act of committed and never extinguished dissidence, a new means of access to what is unthought. If these two tools are therefore legitimate, each according to how it is used, it is because difference, by identifying, serves *knowing*, while divergence, overflowing identities, serves *thinking*. Yet to say that we know through difference but think through divergence is also to verify that, of these two activities of the mind, the first is logically transitive, assuming an object, while the second, through its native intransitivity (that of the 'I think', *cogito*), by taking apart the enclosure of any object, maintains thought as it proceeds. Or let's say that, if difference is a tool of science (I have indicated it for linguistics and will also verify it for anthropology), philosophy is devoted to proceeding through divergence so as always to push the limit of what is thinkable farther back, and to do so by diverging from what is *already thought*.

Defend the fertilities and not the identities of cultures

I hope already to have said enough about the divergence opened by *divergence*, and the disturbance this concept effects, to have sufficiently shown its advantages for it to be understood why I treat cultural diversity in terms of *divergence* and not of *difference*, and promote it as a principle. This is above all because the fate of difference is linked to identity, an old pairing for philosophy, and here this is at both ends, or by two means which equally form a barrier. If difference is understood in relation to a known genre within which it marks a specification, we will find it rather awkward in this case to specify this unitary term or this common – 'next' – genre from which the differences between cultures will arise. Will it be called 'Humankind' or 'human nature'? These are rags that no longer conceal anything and are at best based simply on convenient convention since one would really be perplexed at how to fix a credible content to them. What else can be projected as preceding cultural differences, from which they could then proceed in the same way that a fan is unfolded? Could we avoid turning them into ideological constructions without which these cultural differences would, however, be unable to find anything to rest on? Moreover, when we speak of them as 'common ground', as Jean-François Billeter did when he criticised me ('When we depart from common ground, differences appear by themselves …'), it is just another naïve way of naming this great X that he too cannot do without since it is enclosed (entangled) in this register of 'difference' from which he has no means of extricating himself.

What's more, if we sort things out with this antiquated, reassuring and consequently recurrent – even frightfully tenacious – representation of the first One and of monism, it can easily be seen that the characteristic of the cultural, at whatever level it is considered, is to be plural *at the same time* as singular, or, to express it in a contrary way, that we need to take apart its convenient, but indelibly mythological, representation according to which an initial cultural unity–identity would *then* be diversified, as if through a curse (the Tower of Babel), or at least by complication (as it proliferated). The diversity of languages, which is not at all a later phenomenon, proves this. I'd prefer to say that the characteristic of the cultural is to unfold in this tension – or divergence – between the plural and the unitary, that is taken in a double movement of hetero- and homogenisation, brought to the point of both merging and differentiatiating, and to disidentify and reidentify itself, to conform and resist – in short, that there is no dominant culture without there also being a dissident culture, and so on. Indeed, what is the origin of the 'cultural' if it doesn't arise precisely from this tension of the diverse putting it to work, and therefore also continually transmuting it?

Just as (common) cultural identity cannot therefore be presented as coming before difference, so it cannot be presented as coming after it (which would be specific). If the peculiarity of difference is that it results in a characteristic identity, forming its definition, this can only betray the very nature of the cultural which is incessantly in the process of transforming itself (as the Chinese term *wén-huà* 文化, 'culture–transformation', rightly says, forming a pair). Indeed, a culture which no longer transforms itself, which therefore allows itself to be identified in distinctive features, would be a dead culture (as we speak of a dead language) and would find its place only in a museum. We need therefore, once and for all, to rid ourselves of the idea that we can construct cultural 'identities' or 'characteristics', and that we can do so by means of 'differences'. We only have to look at Huntington's celebrated book (celebrated for its conformism) to see the danger – which is not only theoretical but also (primarily) political. Not only will exceptions always be found to these typological generalities that distribute cultures in the form of a table, but also it is even always the 'exceptional', what is out of the common (out of the frame) which, because it is singular (that is, it opens a divergence) and makes it work, is its most significant element, and therefore the most worthy of interest. Let's recall that, having once wanted to define a European cultural identity as an introduction to its constitution (is Europe 'Christian' or 'atheist'? – and so on), this (inevitably) *had to* fail. This is because the divergence and *tension between the two* (religion *and* secularity) are significant for Europe and have allowed it to advance. Therefore, we need to abandon this impossible characterisation. The failure to *create* Europe, as a logical result, followed on from this.

If the idea of cultural identity, including that of 'multiple' cultural identities which is currently being advanced to evade this difficulty, coupled as it is with difference, therefore represents an impasse (which is inherent to it), it doesn't mean we will be reduced to resignation or historical passivity. All that is necessary is to abandon this contaminating language of Being, on which the 'id' 'entity' rests, like the *idem* of the *entity*, and that still requires us to think in terms of stability (which is contradicted by cultural mutation) and homogeneity (according to the myth of a 'pure' culture) – which has still been insufficiently thought about and criticised. In other words, it will be wise to think of the cultural in terms not of differences (so defining an essence) but of divergences opening out onto so many *resources* – that is, in terms of *fertility*. Thus, I won't preserve a French or European cultural identity when it is understood in terms of belonging (as though I possess 'my' culture), but of 'French' or 'European' cultural fertilities – which means the ones that have unfolded in France or Europe, in one or another milieu (culture always developing within a certain 'milieu', as Nietzsche recognised), but are now available to all. I will return to this, and want all the more to preserve and deploy it since the two go actively hand in hand both to 'defend' and 'illustrate', according to the terms of use, what we must now resist about the absorbent flattening generated by global standardisation. And, closer to home, most of all to defend (illustrate) this resource of the diversity of languages (and this especially applies in Europe) whose *divergences* contribute to thinking.

183

In spite of the manifest fragility apparent within the idea of cultural identity, I believe that what has lent it a basis in a subterranean, but also disproportionate, way is attached to its equivocal nature and notably to what we are often led to confuse with the (psychological) principle of *identification* – and it has thrived from this amalgamation. Yet if identification can be legitimate as a process in the formation of the subject (the child grows up by identifying with its father), cultural identity for its part is excessively adorned with such a legitimacy that folds it into a supposedly stable collective belonging that is even affirmed as long-lasting ('identification'), and that is authorised by the recognition of differences from which a subject would be constituted and prevail, and which would characterise it. On the other hand, the concepts of *divergence* and *fertility*, opposed to those of *difference* and *identity*, free us in an advantageous way from asking ourselves the always suspect question about Origin, that of the 'next type', whether this is called 'human nature' or 'common ground', with which the discourse of Difference unfortunately has to burden itself in order to justify itself. A divergence can only be conceived in relation to what it diverges from, so its legitimacy is only attached to the tension of the opposition that opens it up and reveals it, without leading us to assume and identify a common antecedent. In the perspective for which I am arguing, the only question that remains relevant is the manner in which humans discover and think about themselves, beginning with all of the divergences that constitute cultural diversity in proportion to their history. This is what I have called human *self-reflection*, substituting it for 'knowledge about human nature' (where would that come from?), the only effective exploration by which to grasp what is 'human' – a term taken here in its literal sense, but in an indefinitely open way – in the multiplicity of its adventure, at the same time as what constitutes the community of its fate.

These concepts of divergence, resource and fertility keep us in the sole register of exploration and exploitation and so they don't lead us to assume a belonging or claim to be 'founded' in some ontology. Following this scouring, the only question that still remains is *to what extent* can these divergences open up and clear a path and be deployed, revealing fresh horizons and making new possibilities appear? To what extent can these resources or the fertilities that follow on from them prosper? They can also be left to reabsorb and waste away this faculty of divergence and adventure, so letting it fall into equalisation and collective levelling, that comfort of thought that is said to be 'unique' – the media which complain about it are all the proof we need. Such resources or fertilities can also be lost, neglected and left underdeveloped. As evidence, we might wonder whether the 'elegance' that was once deployed in France has been lost for ever? But at the same time as resources are neglected here, they can be redeployed elsewhere: it is hardly the natives who are today most worried about the French language. What also makes this concept of the *inventive* (prospective) *divergence releasing fertility* so valuable is that, in occuring locally (in the 'milieu'), but without being blocked into some form of belonging, it sticks solely to the capacity of effect – in other words, it is maintained by what is *effective*. Consequently, too, the characteristic of such a resource, as I have said, is that it is *receptive*: whoever activates it deploys it; it isn't so much 'exportable', as without ties. The 'French' or 'European' fecundities I would defend – to distinguish them from 'values' – are not concerned with adhesion but are just as much at the disposal of everyone, outside of France as well as outside of Europe. Even so, this doesn't decree them as universal, in the way that has so often been required of 'our' values. We don't have to 'extol' resources.

This enables us to see the aporia to which the cultural discourse of Difference is condemned, and consequently how it is trapped and therefore mired in an empty dilemma, that of the reflection called 'inter'-'cultural', without knowing how to assume an intensive 'between'. Either cultural difference is presented as second, with cultural identity in consequence being first, that of a 'human nature' or 'common ground', and we inevitably lapse into a *facile universalism*, one that would be unable to hide its ethnocentrism. This means that we have missed the opportunity or the resource constituted by cultural diversity and will have remained in its initial categories which we project onto the rest of the world as being self-evident, and therefore we don't start to take them apart and disturb ourselves. Or else, inversely, cultural difference is presented as first, and a cultural identity characteristic of each culture follows from it, as though it possessed a unitary character: we then lapse into a *lazy relativism* – in other words, 'culturalism'. Each culture is then enclosed in its bubble, forming a world, and it is essentialised through its differences. These two positions, one just as much as the other, are politically dangerous. This is because the first option can only engender a 'soft' intercultural and latent dialogue, in which the *dia* of dia-logue is blurred, distorted or deactivated, while the second exacerbates and hardens positions, rendering them antagonistic from the outset (the much-heralded 'culture clash'): at best, the dialogue is not latent but simulated. They are both equally sterile. In the first case, the encounter is artificial and doesn't have an effect; in the second, the very possibility of the encounter is straightaway withdrawn.

There is therefore an impasse on both sides. But are these really 'two' sides, or doesn't the reversal of one into the other keep us in a comparable immobility? In neither case has anything of the Other been encountered, nothing of one's own representations has moved – nothing has happened. We can't expect to be able to release the bolt from this system which has been blocked in its false alternative. No adjustments can be expected in its respect or compromises be sought. Or rather this, being tinkered with every day, advances nothing and *produces nothing*, as is constantly being noted: the 'dialogue' of cultures remains a public relations exercise in power shifts, a pretext for 'good will' if it doesn't disguise a Will to power. The need to break – or, I'd argue, to diverge from – these old moulds which keep us enclosed in Difference can therefore hardly be denied.

If at last we want to give the 'dialogue of cultures' its historic opportunity, it will need to be understood in a literal sense, in a strong sense, so as to recover the virtues in the two components of the word – that is, both the *dia* and the *logos* in the fertile tension occurring between them: this *dia* which precisely expresses the *divergence*, along with the possibility of a path through (and a dialogue is a lot richer, as we have known from the time of the Greeks, when a divergence is at stake) and this *logos* that expresses the only effective commonality, which is that of the *intelligible*. It is a commonality that is no longer projected from the start, that is neither hypothetical nor hypostased as is inevitably the case for any identity presented as a principle, as 'human nature' or 'common ground', but which is also to be produced and is itself alone in constituting the community of the human, is alone in being able to be put forward: to propose that *the commonality of what is human* is the *intelligible* consequently means that this commonality is not definitively given, nor is it completed, but that it arises from our responsibility to deploy it through the *dia-logue* of cultures.

Not to compare but to reflect

This is why I don't compare. To c*ompare* is to single out resemblances and differences and to arrange them according to the Same and the Other, to characterise one in relation to the other and establish their respective identities. Between cultures, either the accent is placed on resemblance and then lapses into the comfort of an indefinite assimilation, being unable to lead to anything but a tautology ('everything is in everything', 'man is man', and so on). Or else primacy is given to difference and cultural diversity that are then mutated into being rival entities: we speak of 'China' or the 'West', as though these are possible abstractions or great Subjects – what I'd call 'forming worlds', practically theoretical monsters.

I'm doing something else. Instead of comparing, I organise *interfaces* between Chinese and European thoughts such that, through divergence, one will be drawn to examine oneself in the other, and reciprocally (when I speak of 'Chinese thought' I simply mean thought expressed in the Chinese language, while 'European thought' is what is expressed in a European language). Before China and Europe historically began to encounter one another, this opposition wasn't given; it had to be constructed. 'Through divergence', or *via* divergence, consequently means that I have located – or detected – divergences between these two expressions of thought and set them to work, divergences such as those between one philosopher and another in the heart of the history of philosophy (this is even what forms it) and indeed at the heart of thought itself, the means by which thought is thought. But are these divergences all of the same nature? They are of such a nature, in this case, in accordance with the *given* exteriority of these thoughts (I haven't yet used the word 'alterity'), that each can themselves be grasped, in the encounter with the other, in what they don't know about themselves (what I'd call 'contemplating'), and can probe what they haven't thought about, hence stimulating (themselves in) thought. I thus speak of the 'unthought' to continue this starting point of the lexicon, in order to begin from what I think and in the same way from what I don't think: the buried biases of my thinking, conveyed as evidence (*alias* 'natural light'), and thus in the same way that I *cannot* think. But such an *unthought* isn't to be understood in a purely negative way: it is the condition of possibility of my thought at the same time as it is its limit. It is what it doesn't think about in and of itself (in both of these senses) at the same time as being the source of its fertility – in other words, the *fold* of its inventiveness.

The virtue of divergence is that it opens out a retreat in thinking, and this *retreat*, through the distance it establishes, is revelatory – above all of what is well-known unknown because it conceals its unthought. I will therefore propose this as a general rule that goes beyond the framework of cultural studies: the characteristic of the divergence, its fertility, is that it allows a movement back into thought by operating a disadhesion at the same time as it modifies the perspective, introducing a *shift*. But such a divergence is only effectively possible – and this is why the intercultural is instructive for philosophy on this point – upon the encounter with the other. In other words, one *doesn't invent* (doesn't imagine) the conditions of one's defamiliarisation: we only leave our language by learning another and we only leave our thinking by entering into that of another. We don't emerge from our thought all alone, *proprio motu*. We can 'doubt' as much as we want, and even practise a hyperbolic doubt just as Descartes did, but we still only doubt what we believe or 'see' as doubtful (for example, in the classical age, whether or not I have a 'soul' or whether God 'exists'). But we don't doubt what we aren't aware could be doubted, what – without our knowing – is essential to our thought, and that we can only perceive through divergence. From within our language, we don't know where the borders of our language are or how it 'bends' thought. From within our own language, we don't know what language we are speaking and that forms our thinking. From within our thought, we don't know how it is *already* configured.

What results, in return, from this effect of retreat, disadhesion and distance that are authorised by divergence is what I will call an effect of 'grasping', or 'seizing', what cannot be seized, and above all of what cannot be defined, or, if it can be from within one's language and thought in which the possessive, the 'one's', expresses not a belonging but a dependency, as I have said, it is only with a great deal more difficulty. This applies especially in relation to those notions and representations *in* which we think and whose contours we don't see since language forces us to inhabit them from within. This is the case first and foremost in what I started to form as Europe's symbolic quadrilateral (Being-God-Truth-Freedom) and which I have had a great deal of difficulty in undoing from within what has become

187

'Europe' and from my language and thought. For a distance from them – or, more accurately, an *indifference* (to be distinguished, of course, from a critique), to which I'll return – can't be invented. And yet, 'by passing through' a thought-language like that of the Chinese from the outside, they may be (re)outlined from a distance and they then appear as one configuration among other possibilities – in other words, this brings attention to the edges or borders so they may be cut out and, being detached from the ground of what is thinkable, can be 'approached'.

It needs to be added in relation to this *exoptic* that seeing from outside (as when returning from China to Europe), or from a distance, by taking a step back, isn't to see in a broad or rough way. It is to bring out more clearly, under the effect of the cutting out or 'encircling' that has become possible, what is so present, significant, diffuse and pervasive that, when we regard it from close up, we no longer *discern* it. Or, if I remain temporarily in this field of the visual, with perhaps a convenient even if not the most adequate representation, I will say that this milieu or bath into which language (every language) places us – and all of the unsuspected options it conveys – gains *relief* only through superimposition (of visions as well of conceptions). And if I add that a change of scenery can't be invented, it's because it is something quite different from writing the *Persian Letters* or 'spending time in China'. In the first case, the fictitious exteriority underlines and reveals, but it does so on the basis of what one already (re)cognises. It doesn't trouble us because it doesn't de-configure. But when one goes away from Europe to reside within Chinese thought-language one finds oneself immersed in what one doesn't expect, in a strangeness (and above all a destitution) from which one has great difficulty in returning, and from which one may not even ever return.

In short, it is a question, when passing through a China that has been selected as a place of possible exteriority, not of comparing, or even contrasting, but of organising, displaying or 'showing' (in the experimental sense), what becomes a device for *reflection*. I mean here 'reflection' in its literal as well as figurative sense, in its transitive as well as intransitive use, for it will be necessary to make this play of optics and perspectives serve an emancipated deployment of thought. Just as a mirror reflects an image, a 'thought-language' is reflected in the other as it intently looks at itself within what it doesn't perceive about itself and reveals, underlying the prejudice Descartes sought to chase away, what can be called its prenotioned (pre-categorised and pre-questioned) – in other words, its unthought. And when I then speak, being unable to dissociate the two terms of a thought-language, since Descartes did not realise that he was thinking in language, I don't assume that language determines thought, but I do consider that thought exploits the resources of its language – that is, its *fertilities*. Hence also that *reflection* is then understood in not knowing given objects (saying 'I reflect' as one says 'I think'): thought, effecting a return to itself in the encounter with the other, can reflect, in the gap in between-languages between-thoughts, in a suddenly clearer (less bogged-down) way, without it already needing to know 'about what' or to have formed a theme or question to which it would be attached, and then to dream about a new point of departure – farther back (more authentically Cartesian perhaps?) – in its 'meditation'.

From the anthropology of differences to a philosophy of divergence

The response to this will be that there is a discipline that has precisely made cultural diversity its vocation, which treats it with authority in terms of differences and resemblances, aiming to establish specificities and continually comparing, drawing up and tabulating systems from case studies by defining criteria and taxons and, by isolating elements, determining the stable forms of their combinations – in short, this discipline, which has found such conditions of possibility, is anthropology. It has, for more than a century, made its way and proved its validity. And it is true that it has succeeded in effecting a decentring of Western thought due to the fact that it no longer conceives of a starting point in its own – that is, the European – culture as anything but one possibility among others. It therefore has the merit, as it seeks to constitute itself as a science, of having elaborated its methods and constructed its methods. What need is there for another path?

Anthropology can certainly be reproached for having produced excessive generalities. When Philippe Descola, in what is nevertheless a very beautiful book, established that the opposition of 'interiority' and 'physicality' crosses all cultures equally, he certainly furnished a *commonality of the intelligible*, but is this what is most significant in relation to the Chinese culture that is my concern? It has rather conceived of the whole of reality – but this term is already a dreadful option – according to the coupling of 'physicality' and 'operativity', *tǐ*体 and *yòng*用, giving priority as it does so to the procedural character of what it has traditionally named the 'way', *tào*道. One might also wonder what escapes this tabulation which it is unable to explain due to the very fact that its taxonomic logic prefers structure to History: if one arranges Greek and Chinese cultures according to the same classification of 'analogism', as Descola does, it may then become difficult to know how to give a sufficient account of the reasons for which, from this common analogism, European culture alone gave birth to modern 'naturalism'. We shall also wonder about the means by which anthropology, as it grapples with cultures external to Europe, has known (been able) to unmake the categories of European thought, and how far it has gone. Has it so far projected (I leave the question unresolved) what its own theoretical expectation would be in its schematisation of modes of 'objectification' of the 'world'? Has it taken sufficient account of the divergence of languages? (Or does it still speak too simply in the folds of European thought-language?) In particular, if it now appears to be at ease in classifying its typologies of cultures taken from the four corners of the earth, whose implicit, but so very complex (so much more complex?), structure it reconstructs, this being the reason it is so appropriately forged, how – in other words, to what point of its own theoretical elaboration – does it integrate the cultures, 'for example' the Chinese, so deployed (as well as explained, textualised, monumentalised and so on)? There's a singularity in its recognition (and an abundance, in return, as to its minorities). But as far as I am concerned this isn't what is essential.

In my view, it is necessary to open another path, one that is philosophical, to take charge of cultural diversity – one that would be parallel to what anthropology offers yet without being in rivalry with it. This is because anthropology deliberately aims at knowledge. In comparing the incomparable, according to Marcel Detienne's excellent programmatic title (2008) – in other words, by working through resemblance and difference – by establishing its criteria from the outset as well as by constructing typologies, anthropology places itself straightaway under the vocation and authority of science, being above all devoted to determination. That's why it barely lingers on the experience of destitution that constitutes entry into another thought: it seeks rather to straddle it. Consequently, it doesn't devote itself to the disturbing effect of *divergence* and wants to see this as *difference*, in its resultant form or as a tabular 'display' that would henceforth find a place in its typology, which is itself constructed as a panoply. In contrast, a philosophical approach finds value in remaining on the threshold and exploring it, acknowledging a difficulty that defeats the idea of any knowledge, in this intent scrutiny of the other whose reciprocity – reactivity – in relation to itself it experiences for as long as it can: that's to say, in a concern, *Unruhe*, that maintains open reflection. Or rather, if the anthropologist places himself within this disturbance, accepting this insecurity which draws him less to *know* than to *think*, doesn't he become (or doesn't he remain) a philosopher?

What consequently openly separates the anthropological and philosophical projects when it comes to cultural diversity is that the first is drawn to conceive of a *finite number* of possibilities. Determining criteria of classification from which its taxonomic enterprise follows, anthropology elaborates a system of cases which can be infinitely complex, giving rise to excessively varied combinations, but that as a principle is nevertheless limited. The net it casts over the multiple ways of 'inhabiting the world', as shimmering and variegated as this diversity may be, is enclosed within a frame which, once fixed, is maintained by its parameters and cannot be unmade. This diversity is a diversification, these cases so many variations, because any exploration of the structure carries a logic of completion with it due to the template it uses. Philippe Descola (2005) makes this demarcation and surveying of forms of relation to the world in conjunction with their commensurability a key to his programme.

So, once we consider this diversity of cultures from the perspective of divergence rather than difference, of an exploratory disarrangement rather than a determining arrangement, this diversity of the cultural is not only in principle infinite but it also finds its vocation, even more, in this infinity. For the characteristic of 'divergence' is to allow itself neither norms nor bounds, that it works in every respect as on any scale, no matter how disruptive it is, and it undermines any enterprise of framing, homogenisation and ratification. Instead of letting itself settle down in a fixed scene, it constantly contradicts any taxonomic enterprise and overflows any assignment. If these divergences, as I pursue them between Chinese and European cultures, link and work in turn, at once weaving together and branching out, and going so far as to form coherences that can take the form of theoretical alternatives, then, far from knowing a limit, their proliferation will nonetheless be indefinitely amplified, serving as support for inquiry, and it is therefore as inexhaustible as are questions in philosophy.

The two enterprises must be separated as to their destination. Anthropology inventories the diversity of cultures and puts them in order so as to know the possibilities that belong to humanity as it has developed over the course of its history, and without leaving them to be further subsumed within a unitary schema or destiny, even if it might be that of 'man' as an absolutely first limit and that was believed to be isolatable. In so doing, it has the merit of breaking with the universality that was so often projected by Bossuet's religion as well as by classical philosophy, only accepting relative, indeed concurrent, categories and refusing any global Narrative. So the case I am pleading for a philosophical approach is for this very reason unable to renounce the exigency of the universal. This is so even when it sets itself the task, as it puts divergences to work, of *tearing apart* thought as much as it can, not only to extend the thinkable outside of the field that has been marked out, but even more so to stretch thought from within, in opening up a dissidence that causes it to react in order that it might be able to reactivate it, and to do so with a view to shaking up all normative thought, and even all conceptualisation that rests within its set purposes. It should, of course, be understood that it will no longer act from universality to the totalising – actually totalitarian – claims of 'universalism', which we hope is now dead, but from a universal that has a converse vocation, a universal that is in rebellion since it is never satisfied, but, on the contrary, is intent upon reopening all acquired totality and serving as a 'regulatory' – initiatory – idea (in the Kantian sense) so as to push back the horizon of demarcation and to deploy commonality ever more completely.

The question that philosophy now asks about the diversity of cultures is no longer that of their categorical distribution and possible ordering, but rather what the concurrent ways 'of inhabiting the world and giving meaning to it' are. This is to speak of it in the still properly European – not sufficiently extraverted – terms favoured by anthropologists, today enlightening the experience of *any* subject and promoting it as a subject. Can they therefore contribute to the edification as well as to the description of its existence? In other words, what *resources* do they constitute, precisely thanks to their divergences, that today would open up and deploy *my* intelligence of 'things' or of 'life'? At the same time that it ceaselessly draws out the distant and the heterogeneous, the properly absurd, the perspective would then be trans-cultural and trans-historical. Just as no philosopher would abandon engaging thinkers as distant as Plato and Nietzsche in dialogue when he has elaborated a theoretical plan that makes their encounter possible, it is now appropriate to respond to the expectation of our times by bringing Western and Chinese thinkers into a dialogue. But there can be no doubt that if the *indifference* that separates them is to be overcome, at least as far as the past is concerned, as much in language as in history, which is more difficult confidently to cross than 'difference' would lead us to believe, even more will conception and mediation – in other words, philosophical *elaboration* – be required.

To philosophise from outside

If, as a young Hellenist, I chose to leave Europe and go to China at a time when it was actually the least open to dialogue (it was at the extreme end of Maoism), it was precisely for the purpose of *diverging myself* and approaching philosophy from without (not to risk remaining confined within it). I no longer wanted to go back into the history of questions, or even to know what the questions were (would they still be matters of 'being', 'truth' and so on?). I also wanted to experience a suspension in thought (each person has his *epoché*, mine had to be every bit as existential), a *suspension* such that I no longer knew what resembles or doesn't resemble, what does or doesn't differ, what earlier landmarks suddenly waver to the point that I began to be amazed at what my language makes me say and think, so as no longer to be a prisoner (or perhaps a dupe?) of a game (or of an 'I') I had not chosen. We commonly say that we are the 'inheritors' of the Greeks in Europe (or that philosophy is 'a Greek thing', as has been tirelessly repeated since Hegel) – we offer it up as evidence to reassure ourselves by the filiation that it immediately gives us, but what do we really know about this? What do we know about it, given that we don't have sufficient perspective – and therefore also sufficient 'grasp' – to be able to probe it? In addition, to learn what was then still considered to be a 'rare language', a very closed, not to say frankly exotic, 'speciality' ('sinology'), was actually not to be able (or need) to specialise. It was – once again, but inevitably – to have a foolish need 'for everything' in this destitution (this 'everything' which would be the characteristic of philosophy: aesthetics, morality, politics and so on) to begin to 'orient' oneself within thought.

I smile a little when I think back to this choice made at the age of 20. The choice was to this extent constructed, justified, hyper-motivated (perhaps garrulously) at the same time as it was empty. I knew nothing about China, but that was precisely what tempted me: the effect of a *tabula rasa*, of a 'blank page' (but not one within History – I wasn't a 'Maoist'), the hope of a fresh departure – not to let oneself be 'trapped' was a catchphrase of the time. To attack philosophy from the reverse side or from the back, don't allow yourself to get caught in what might perhaps in itself be a rut or an 'atavism' (something Nietzsche's work warned me against). (Greek) philosophy claimed to think 'everything' through what it constructed from oppositions (already in Parmenides–Heraclitus: immobile Being in the face of 'everything flows', and so on), to deploy all of the possibilities of thought; but does it know *alongside* what it is passing, alongside what it passes without thinking about it? This occurs in such a way that all of its deployments to come would always be just 'unfoldings'… Was there a strategy able to provide a way out of it? I use the word 'strategy' and not method, because what is unthought in it cannot be attacked frontally, unlike a 'prejudice' which occurs in the terminal state of the judgement – otherwise it would already be being thought about. As I've said, it needs indirectness, obliqueness and detour, along with a looking-back (a looking back that doesn't come later, because that would mean not looking back at all: we specialise or 'sinise') – walk like a crab, I'm told: a constant coming and going.

In passing through China, there is a particular indirectness in returning to what has been one of the most outstanding operations of the thought of the 1960s and 1970s in France: the operation of 'cutting', set out as a first axiom (as Saint Paul already did …), between a Before and an After, at the heart of so-called Western thought from which 'Modernity' would proceed. This was a cut that we know, according to some thinkers (Koyré, Kojève, Barthes, Lacan …), is either absolutised or relativised, more historicised or structuralised, established in a more universal or local way, considered as 'major' or not, 'synchronous' or not, and so on (according to terms I have taken from Jean-Claude Milner). Either we make this with a single action between the ancient *episteme* and modern science, therefore from the learning that, close to being mathematicised, is a matter of exactitude and measure (from the 'finite world' to the 'infinite universe': its synthetic and symbolic name is Galileo), or, conversely, it is fragmented into multiple cuts whose arrangements are consequently complex and about which we are no longer even sure if they are homologous and coincident (where Foucault sets to work). But is this a question of a single heterogeneity existing between the 'discourses', of the only possible caesura that allows for a break in the continuous 'synonymy' by which thought occurs, always slipping homologically and no longer offering a hold from which to glimpse and separate (which is something quite different from refuting), now, and, in so doing even avoiding thinking – and something against which René Char and Foucault have called for a revolt?

Yet 'passing through China' – according to this leitmotiv henceforth forming a programme – was another way of bringing into focus a discontinuity from which to recover a hold over thought, to 'reflect on it', by putting it in tension with itself instead of abandoning it to the somnolence of synonyms, to the nullity of commonplaces brought by a universal that would lazily be given from the outset (and not something to be *produced* in the way I would call for) from an already formed (and uncritical) humanism that is constantly being repainted and refenced. But the 'cutting' wasn't really one, or in any case wasn't a break, but rather the effect of a parallelism between two ways of thinking that had developed over more than two millennia without their knowing or observing each other; today it is necessary to organise their encounter – putting them 'face to face' – finally to put them in each other's presence. Yet suddenly it's here that, under the effect of this encounter, indirectly through this heterotopia, the very notion of a 'cut', with which Europe has chosen to make its first articulation (according to its great myth of Revolution), around which it had believed until now it was able to coil itself so as then to unfold its 'meaning' more effectively, would at once lose its assurance, and that the contrary terms of 'tradition', spurned by Foucault, would strangely recover a justification. It is within a culture that one is attentive to its effects of rupture, that thought looks back with passion on its discontinuities so as to promote and invent itself. But from the outside, as from China looking back to Europe, these are really the effects of coherence (of what I was evoking symbolically by this initial preserve of Being, God, Truth, Freedom), of persistence and tenacity (not to be confused with an ahistoricity) which, concealed as they were beneath this rupturism, rose back up to the surface.

Consequently, the task is to organise this parallelism given in History in a theoretical relation that itself takes the form of a *possible alternative* in thought: to construct this influx of countless, unclassifiable and unintegratable divergences which begin to appear on reflection and branch out when, after coming from Europe, we begin to study Chinese thought in logic and discover that this is a non-logical logic – in other words, one that would no longer be preconducted by the *logos*. So as not to betray it from the outset in a European language, I'd start by calling non 'logical' logic, which may be contrasted with the *ontological* logic which came to us from the Greeks, a 'Taoist' *coherence* – according to the catchword, a unifying and crucible term of Chinese thought that is ordinarily left untranslated. 'Coherence', since I have posited a common principle of the intelligible and that this is the term I think most directly serves as a bridge between the two (*li* 理 in Chinese), from the start overflowing those of 'reason' and 'truth' that are too strongly marked in European thought's corner. This is a coherence that doesn't respond to the question of essence or that of 'what is it?' ('quiddity'), doesn't have to be reconstructed at an abstract level, or that of pattern or ideality (the *eidos*); and that is no longer being extended by finality (both an end and a goal, a *télos*, those of teleology, or of 'entelechy'), deduced and declining the consequences (the importance of *zé* 則 in its linking up with function), but without separating itself from the processual nature of things or having to construct a set of hypotheses and so on.

Yet how can such coherence be expressed other than by remaining within our terms (but in order to refuse them), other than by withdrawal, lack and negativity? A place will only gradually be found for coherence in our language and spirit by means of progressive accommodation, by surreptitiously and, step by step, cracking it so as to introduce it, patiently, tirelessly, by unwriting and rewriting, by deviating and reformulating, by nudging them so that they link up and do so through a slow acculturation.

But this will be without expectation of a flash of brilliance or of a forced entry, without immediately hoping for a great synthetic presentation, through a revelation, of 'what' the 'other' would be (of what Chinese thought would thus be when expressed in European terms). How could such a presentation be possible since my language would need to 'get used to it' – in other words, also *little by little* to divest itself, move everything out and rearrange things? In consequence, this could only be done by small moves and successive shifts letting something thread its way in from the outside and so beginning to open up, accommodate and amalgamate – that is, by a sequence of organised drifts that will gradually be able to *blend* my language, beginning with a process of decategorising and *unfolding* it. Failing this, it would risk turning this external thought into nothing but a *fac-simile* of ours and so stay within its comfort zone.

Can we *deconstruct* from within and how far can this go? Wouldn't 'deconstruction', if I keep to this historic term of contemporary philosophy, itself have gained something by seeking for this outside which is no longer that of the Hebrew thought that has traditionally served as a counter-point, or fold, within philosophy when it wanted to free itself from the Greeks, to undo its closure and externalise itself? If the conceptual apparatus according to which thought is ruled and which is finally being recognised as 'Western' is, from a 'historical' point of view, that of 'logocentrism', which also takes the form of 'phonocentrism', as Derrida was right to suspect, would it not be instructive to enquire more closely into what Chinese thought can uncover for us in reverse? Its writing is constituted in such a marked way as it diverged from orality (as the sinologist Léon Vandermeersch has convincingly shown), in which the notion of 'trace' also soon became significant, at once de-excluding and leading to a 'transformation' (*jì huà* 迹化), and so on. And, in fact, that the voice, such a subtle element of the logos, might have favoured a metaphysics of presence will be verified *a contrario* by how this chain of interdependent oppositions from which European onto-theology has prospered has come undone in China. In Chinese thought, in which no 'being' other than a predicative one is isolated, the gap between presence and absence not having been determined, the relation of representation has not developed very much (at the semiotic, aesthetic but also political level), the image is also spoken of as a phenomenon (the same term of *xiàng* 象), and even the opposition between essence and appearance has not served as a fold for thought. On the other hand, it leaves us in this amazement that we'll indefinitely need time to return to: how *could* a metaphysical thought therefore be *possible*? Isn't it the 'Greeks' who are strange?

Thinking with Chinese thought

Will something different be possible one day? Will we be able to write something more than a 'History of Chinese thought', as has been done over and again during this past century in imitation of the history of European philosophy? Will it be possible to do this without even wondering whether the method of historicity is the same on both sides, and without from the start borrowing Western philosophical categories that are now globalised ('metaphysics', 'aesthetics', 'ontology', etc.) in a non-critical way? Or else they are then compared: X and Y, Wang Yangming and Descartes. The 'differences' and 'resemblances' are tabulated from the start as one is subjected to the thought-language of the other, whether this is done in China or the West, as if language were transparent, as if the intervention of translation was neutral and did not relegate or add anything, and consequently without elaborating mediations, therefore also without constructing any relation to draw out a commonality of what is intelligible and that would allow for the possibility of dialogue. It will be understood that, as far as I am concerned – or rather according to what I have *done* – Chinese thought isn't just an immense but still insufficiently prospected territory of thought, providing a large drawer of index cards and erudition, but can also serve as a theoretical *operator*. This is what I call thinking *with* Chinese thought: keeping it company, an always active company, even when I don't mention it – in other words, to lavish its infinite resources in such a way as to lead me, or rather to provoke me, to think.

If we don't address this propedeutic questioning – or let's call it this initiating problematic – if we don't resolve to take account of these initial difficulties so as to think about how to construct the *possible* objects of a Sinological knowledge which would not just be based on erudition or repetition (of Chinese knowledge) under the illusion that these objects would be given in advance, if we don't consider the conditions of such a scrutiny before we start to 'compare', then we can increase indefinitely its information but will find ourselves always condemned, unknowingly, to forced assimilation, embarked upon an equivalence or *synonymy* between languages that is always too quickly accorded. We shall still be giving in to the ease of translating *fǎ* 法 as 'law', without wondering what a law is when it doesn't respond to any idea of justice and serves only as an oppressive apparatus aiming to maintain, among the so-called Chinese 'jurists' of Antiquity, an authoritarian – not to say totalitarian – order; or to translate *xìn* 信 by 'sincerity', without wondering what such sincerity can be when it means sticking to what one has said rather than saying what one thinks – in other words, conducting oneself in a reliable way. Or to translate one or another term (*zhì* 志, *yì* 意, …) by 'ideal', without questioning the conditions of possibility of such ideality in China since the dividing in two of the 'ideal' in relation to the 'real' isn't emphasised. Can we neglect so many *divergences* when they *contribute to thinking* – or rather compel it, in what I've been referring to as 'provoking' it. For more than a century, 'philosophy' has been translated into Chinese, and now in a fixed and canonical way, by something like 'clarity-application' ('study-imitation', *xué* 学), this last term being the first character of the *Analects* of Confucius and expressing the importance of walking in the steps of one's masters. From the very beginning, desire, or the insolent and impudent *Erôs*, is lost. In Greece, *eros* called for rupture and provoked the philosopher. In the Chinese term, his place is taken by a diligence which is inseparable from the ritual and internal investment that is required in order to conform with it – in other words, it is the exact opposite. Under the translation, in the shelter of established equivalence, the hidden mis-understanding remains intact. Is it even suspected?

Desire – this, of course, is where everything starts. A disagreement that has sometimes arisen between myself and sinologists is probably based (no reason why it should be hidden or kept among those things that aren't said) on the fact that we don't place our desire in the same spot. My desire 'for China' isn't due to admiration, fascination or any dream of assimilation or Sinisation – which I am happy to acknowledge as possible motivations – but a desire which, by *passing through China*, looks to it for support that would enable me to dissociate myself from my language and once more to begin again to philosophise in a plainer – and more radical? – way. We shouldn't in fact ignore our subjective forms of investment, any more than we should the difference in the *speed* with which we think and that causes us to dare, circulate and operate in thought in diverse ways – as they say, arguments about 'ideas', when they don't come about due to fear or the jealous and primary desire for elimination, relate above all to these divergences of *ethos*. Otherwise, at the risk of not understanding why we conceptualise – haven't I said so often enough? – we don't have to scorn history, or that philosophy, rather than making way for philology, on the contrary clarifies it.

To take *context* into account, as sinologists are right forcefully to demand, doesn't at all prevent promoting the *concept* – in other words, the very instrument of philosophy. To forge a concept *based on* Chinese thought (like those I have elaborated here: propensity, potential of the situation, receptivity and so on) is not at all to 'essentialise' Chinese thought. It isn't to neglect its historic transformation, or even to privilege the long term, but to undertake, from a certain coherence that one per-ceives as being at work in Chinese texts, to *form a concept* that can then assume its generality *for itself*. To 'essentialise' sterilises, but what I do in contrast is to *activate* such a coherence by reflecting on it. In order words, the generality I produce is appropriate to the concept becoming an instru-ment of 'reflection', in the two senses I earlier indicated, and not that of a 'Chinese thought' which would be identified with it and so become mummified. Instead of abandoning it to mere occurrence, leaving it bur-ied and confined to the narrowness of its reference, the captive of a single path, it is an abstraction which *promotes*, makes explicit, utilises this coherence and makes it work by deploying the possibilities and making it a tool of thought (of all thought).

Two things will also need to be distinguished. On the one hand, we have what would be an excessive generalisation made in ignorance of the distinctions between schools and options at the heart of Chinese thought. This still organises discussions according to certain periods of its history when it became philosophical (at Jixia, in antiquity, or during the Song era) without carrying out the work of refutation as the Greeks did in such an outstanding and principled way. On the other hand, there is what I understand by a 'ground of understanding' of thought. As Zhuangzi, one of the greatest thinkers in ancient China, stated: 'in any discussion, there is what is unquestioned' (or, in any *disputatio*, there is the undisputed, *zài biàn zhě yǒu bù biàn* 在辩者有不辩). Therefore, I shall call this unquestioned or undisputed – or, better, undisputable – the *ground of understanding*, at once ground and source, which is not properly unthought but remains implicit and a condition of any clarification, in what thinkers understand among themselves, without even analysing it, and from which they can discuss with and refute one another. These ground(s) of understanding hold true just as much on the Greek side (and for the whole development of European philosophy). They are what they share in confidence and adherence, what aren't questioned, even among sceptics, and above all they touch upon this element or common bath that the *logos* and its choice of truth has constituted (to doubt, denounce or abandon it isn't to cut oneself off from it), and that it will be all the easier to explore – from the outside and through divergence – for the fact that the Chinese thought has from the start led us out of it.

I also understand that an objection has been raised, and has even become increasingly proclaimed, against the enterprise on which I have embarked. It is argued that the time for such work has now passed. The page has been turned; the war, in other words, is over. There is no longer a 'Chinese' or a 'European' philosophy, due to the fact of the globalisation in which we are engaged, but we now have a common world philosophy which can be discussed at conferences and debates that occur today across the four corners of the globe and take place in the same language, or at least about the same questions and using the same planetary concepts. From now on, no matter where we come from, we find ourselves in the same modernity, and the language in which it is spoken is of no consequence: we now have to think that modernity. This is shown by the fact that cultural differences which up to the present gave consistency to the diversity of culture, differences that were very marked until recently, are gradually in the process of vanishing and even, through a sudden change of rhythm and scale, have recently broken down. And, as everyone knows, this is due to the fact that the globalisation of exchange has been completed and that technical standardisation, especially when it comes to communication, has ended up being planetised, carrying off the standardisation of ways of living, and *therefore* of thought, along with it. We now only have common global problems, which have become so much more crucial for their new scale (the 'planet', governance, globalisation and so on): philosophers of the world, unite in order to have your say!

Who doesn't remember precisely the boredom and long yawns that inexorably greet these forums with completely accredited, established and stamped notions, with questions that are now agreed to be *the* vital questions of the world? When a question is established and so easily distributed among the panel, it is already relinquished. And when I say it is 'boring', I'm not designating one rather depressing psychic state among others, but a demobilisation that descends over thought, leaving it with only the semblance of flight (as the university well knows). Consequently, there is nothing to stimulate one's desire, unless it be due to the narcissism of the same 'small differences' that minutely assert positions and are alone in provoking discussion. Yet wouldn't such *boredom* (of *issues* and *topics*) threaten the 'world' thinking 'to come' that you describe? Or we then clutch at the most recent novelty in thought, the latest authority, the 'scoop', the next thing (forming a happening: Walter Benjamin, deconstruction, Badiou and so on), but which, introduced as if into a market, soon becomes no more than a fashion and gets reabsorbed into the conventions unless precisely some *divergence*, appearing unhoped-for from somewhere, suddenly cuts into this lethargy to give a glimpse of a possible way out of the designated ground, a path which goes somewhere else, into the most shaded, tangled, unlocatable areas and along which we don't know where we are going – *Holzweg* – but along which thought is again brought into question (into *tension*).

I shall respond to all those whose discourse will lay claim to modernity by hypostasing or erecting it into a great historic subject, even when we are at a point when history is becoming unique, which means that, by doing this, they are also extolling a globality which, under this uniqueness and its apparent unanimity, is just as abstract. Indeed, if there is a European modernity, worked by its representation of the cut, itself developed under the tutelary myth of Revolution and generated by an increasingly sharper critical function, this cutting edge of the negative that for two centuries European thought has more and more radically turned against itself, which is what constitutes its historical singularity – such a modernity is then *exported to* (*imposed upon*) China (at the end of the nineteenth century, in the wake of the Opium wars, unequal treaties and concessions), theoretical globalisation thereby having started in an oppressed and dismembered China. There is, therefore, a Before and an After. Concerning this *before*, the relation of European and Chinese thought-languages is still to be constructed, the work is *to be done* – or in any case to be pursued. Otherwise, there would be a risk of maintaining a dangerous misunderstanding, a *forced synonymy*, between these heritages, that would still consider the thought of classical China, the one from before the encounter with the West, only through Western categorisations that were introduced after the event (with everything this 'after the event', *nachträglich*, suggests of reconfiguration). This had two consequences. On the Chinese side, it favoured culturalism and claims for a national 'essence' ('Sinicity') in reaction to this coating it sustained as soon as it (or any of the other cultures of the world) no longer recognised itself under these Western categories that have now become globalised. On the European side, it has favoured the reversal of the earlier ethnocentrism into a facile exoticism that assumes that 'Far Eastern' thought, which is no longer translated but misrepresented, would directly respond to our questions and in our language, and could of itself constitute a way out of what would be revealed, in comparison, to be our top-heavy dualisms – I'd especially designate the fantasies and trade in *Zen* and the 'happiness according to Confucius'.

On the other hand, and touching on the *after*, on the future of modernity–globality, can the scene that begins to appear really be the one that has been set out for us on a basis of questions and notions which would first of all be common (I insist on this 'first of all')? Would we finally arrive at this unrivalled – and universal – table of judgements and categories that Kant thought he could establish as he went beyond Aristotle, but which, considering it was also in his language (his Latin-German), he too was unable to reach? This is already to make the endurance of Babel and the diversity of languages into so many cheap goods. If (as long as) we do not converse in only one language, pidgin English or *globish*, if we still speak-think in Chinese or, to express this in a general way, in *more than one* language, we still won't speak (think) exactly the same thing *from the outset* – some divergence continues, not in a residual way, but as fertile and subversive. This is so even if one is bilingual (in this case, one self-translates). The diversity of languages will be maintained not in a secondary way, even if these divergences appear at first glance reduced, but principally and radically in the *tension* of the divergence that confers thinking.

We'll have to go back once again to this blade that lies between *divergence* and *difference* and make use of its sharp edge. If differences between cultures are today blurred, with the resemblances still crossing over due to world uniformisation, and if cultures are therefore impelled to lose some of the identitarian characteristics that were attributed to them too fixedly and in an essentialising way, and to do so in a way that I believe would be propitious, it is very different for divergence, whose destiny cannot be associated with this decline. For, since it is agile, *divergence*, at whatever level or in whatever way it occurs, opens a breach in the conformism or atavism of thought – and so why would we deprive ourselves of the resource that, as if through an indentation, indefinitely brings to the surface the divergences located between the language-thoughts throughout the world, those that reveal other possibilities and open up a *reflection* that won't close up again? Such divergences between languages are the only angle from which to begin to get a glimpse – which can only be oblique – of the means by which we think. They are therefore the levers by which to recover a surge in thinking by shaking off its lethargy and cracking open its complacent adhesions or its too swiftly acquired commonality. They offer a way of inscribing *resistance* towards the boredom of a consensus which, in not finding a way to confront itself, is prone towards becoming planetary and pandemic.

To promote commonality from divergences

It may seem that, if divergence is worked in thought, or if one starts by 'diverging' rather than by considering the divergence to be a cultural residue pleading to be absorbed, then humanity will appear to become dissociated: by its divergence, it would introduce a dissensus and form an obstacle to the common. Wouldn't the formula be dangerous, perilous and ideologically risky (or, more bluntly, reactionary?). Yet I maintain that precisely the opposite is the case. The common *is not the similar*. This has to be said and said again in this age of facile uniformisation and forced assimilation, and presented as a principle. Braque argued the case for art: 'Trouillebert resembles Corot, but they have nothing in common.' Let's recognise the radicalness of this formula and take it as a warning: not only is resemblance not an indication of commonality, but it presents an obstacle to it. Not only does it not favour it, but it checks its possibility. In resemblance, the common not only remains at the surface level, as a kind of veneer, and doesn't work, but this *similarity* also dispenses with enquiry into it by loosening and dissolving its demand (as a concept, resemblance is even more lazy and inert than difference). Yet this can be understood in the most general way, as well as at the political level. I shall therefore propose it as a statement of departure: it is only by making *divergences work* that we can *promote the common*.

Let's distinguish two forms of the common: the common that is given to us and in which we discover ourselves (what might be called 'natural': from the family to the 'nation' – in other words, what we accept by being 'born', in living and in the cosmos ...); and the common we produce, or promote, as properly cultural and political. As such, the *common* signifies the inclusive sharing of what is inside, but one that becomes exclusive when the limit of this inside turns back into a frontier and banishes what is outside of it (as in communautarianism[1]). Differently from the *universal*, which is prescriptive, implying a necessity as a matter of principle, an *a priori* or logical necessity, that of the universal of science which Kant claimed to transfer to ethics, the *common* is established (and recognises itself) in its first sense, and is chosen or promoted in the second sense. We see this in the common of the City, in which the Greeks really perceived the founding concept of the political. But how is this common produced? Not by similitude, for this would be only repetition and cloning, but precisely by divergence which, by beginning to open up reflexivity and making it work, leading both of the separate sides to overflow as they enter into tension with the other, produces or promotes the common. I say *by* divergence, for this 'by' expresses the path followed even more than the cause or the means – in other words, proceeding through divergences and going beyond them – but this doesn't equate with abandonment: the common doesn't leave divergences behind, nor does it abandon them as being expired. On the contrary, to the extent to which these divergences are active, the common is *intensive*. Otherwise, it is only a coating of platitudes, like our 'commonplaces'.

It will therefore be necessary to *gain access* to the common – the proof of this, and in an exemplary way, being the commonality of the concept. Yet this commonality of the concept will be all the richer (more fruitful and active) in no longer being – flatly and calmly – a generality, but will be seen to be stimulated, called upon and provoked, by this open divergence that is even becoming gaping. This common will no longer just be a matter of a recoating (subsumption) but, through the evident divergence, will be tightened like a bow stretched by its extremities. In my recent enquiry into landscape, I was impelled as a *resource* to make use of two great cultures of landscape in the world – the only two, those of the Chinese and of the European, which have developed independently of one another and were for such a long time unaware of each other's existence. By establishing them in a relation, I tried to produce a fresh concept of landscape. This was a concept that – through the widening divergence between them in this respect, which is no less than the one, to the point of forming an alternative, between opposing perspectives about *living* (in China) and *seeing* (in Europe) – became both a challenge and something like an injunction. There would really have to be a *commonality of the intelligible*, whether approached under the term of 'landscape', which is detached from the 'land', or what the Chinese still today call 'mountain(s)-water(s)', *shān- shuǐ* 山水, maintaining these as a correlated term. Therefore, instead of being content to think of each of these cultures of landscape separately, or as one of them covering over the other – the European prevailing over the Chinese due to the success of its conception of 'nature', that has become 'physical' – the concept of landscape, thereby placed in tension, commanded a reconfiguration that is all the more radical in that it needs to be open to this diversity, even to this opposition – but without breaking it.

A net of divergences: from the question of Being to the thought of living

But what form can this work in progress that has been initiated between the thought-languages of China and Europe take if any comprehensive introduction is distrusted when it is immediately seen to include one within the frameworks of the other and would from the outset miss the *between* of their divergence in which the common is promoted? Or what mode of deployment – dare I speak of progress? – would not immediately be susceptible to folding back into a *projected ideological construction*? Each opposition selectively organised here, each conceptual divergence set out, crossing one thread over the other, is simply a mesh. Yet a mesh is a loop which keeps any between from coming through; it is only an intersection whose logic is then strictly additive. One mesh calls for another in its wake; consistency results only from this sequence. A certain number of meshes are also needed to make a net, or let's say that, as I work, my successive essays simply constitute one chapter at a time. The word I use is *net* and not system.

A system assumes a closure and it imposes an internal organisation consisting of parts whose assembly is so well ordered, according to its Stoic concept, that no element within it is even slightly displaceable. In our modernity, and since German Romanticism and Nietzsche, the archipelago and the fragment – in other words, a dispersal of impossible totality – have been preferred to this. Yet a net doesn't depend upon one or another logic; it increases indefinitely, going from one mesh to the next, solely from the intersections that it operates and re-operates by passing through and prolonging. A net only exists through its texture and the network that it gradually causes to appear, and yet doesn't depend on a structure. Conceptual divergences follow one another, link up with one another, respond to one another and communicate together, but they raise no architecture; still less can they represent worlds.

And yet what is a net for? Like the fisherman's net, it is used to catch, and what I have proposed to catch, by weaving this problematic net stretched between the thought-languages of China and Europe, is their *unthought*. But a net consequently has another use. By catching and containing, it assumes a shape that corresponds with what is collected in it – it holds together as it configures itself. It is left to move in a flexible way because it is spaced out, meshed and pierced; it doesn't enclose but envelops, remaining light, like a hairnet as it holds hair together. Yet what this net woven from conceptual divergences gradually and progressively configures keeps together, mesh by mesh, in a reticulated way – in the way that this gathering, one without any frame, retains its flexibility and receptivity – and is revealed after the event to be a way out of the 'question of Being', a clearing, or rather a disengagement from 'ontology', both from the 'ontology of Being and of the subject'. This departure can be done only *on the way*, step by step, in proportion to this weaving and its progress. Can an effective way out of ontology only be organised by being *projected* and constructed – even by 'de-constructing' it?

We know that this departure from ontology, which from Heidegger to Levinas and Derrida has been one of the great vocations of philosophy in the twentieth century, is always threatened with contradiction: we might be doing everything to get out of the question of Being, but as we do so we are still in the language of 'being'. In other words, we continue to speak the language of ontology at the very moment we are challenging it most firmly, or we continue to speak the language of 'presence' at the very moment we claim to be deconstructing it irreparably (remember Derrida to Levinas in 'Violence and Metaphysics' in Derrida, 1978: 79–153, and Levinas to Derrida in return in 'Wholly Otherwise'; see Levinas, 1996: 55–62). For in what other language could it actually be expressed while remaining in Europe? Or how to 'come out' if one can't *go in*? – to enter an elsewhere that is neither preconceived nor premeditated? Isn't the Judaic elsewhere itself too inscribed in Europe, equally forming Europe, to be an elsewhere to the extent of being troubling or *defamiliarising*? But also in the encounter with Chinese thought-language, this departure from ontology can then only be done by small shifts, as I have warned, in a way that is already first of all local, through successive divergences, mesh by mesh; by translation, de-translation and re-translation; de- and re-categorisation – in other words, by progressive, patient and modest accommodation, by 'weaving' and without some trumpeted Revelation.

Yet, what will we *already* have entered if we emerge from the question of Being? This emergence from ontology is not discovered all at once, but mesh by mesh, by passing from one divergence to the next, through successive attempts, and is, if considered universally and retrospectively, by a turning-back, a way out of the 'question of Being', the *Seinsfrage*, that is *at the same time* an entry into the thought of *living*. The question of 'being' or the thought of 'living' is the principal articulation, or generic alternative, that will enable us to perceive this net, in filigree, mesh by mesh. But isn't 'living' itself too elementary and indefinite to allow us to think in this way with respect to Being, or how to approach it? In order to elaborate the question and make a start, let's say that if 'to exist' is an originating term of theology and belongs to metaphysics, according to that initial interrogation that projects us out of the world, then the question is raised: 'Why do I exist?' And if, on the other hand, 'life' or 'living' above all reflect the biological – in other words, only its metabolic renewal – *living* will start to be defined and limited so that it won't slip into the one any more than it will be reduced to the other. Hence that *living*, between the two, is fundamentally an ethical category – or I would even say that it is strategic before being ethical. The question is to *attain* living, or, as I said earlier, to gain access to the common. Or, as everyone in Europe recalls in their own way, but as an injunction or a pious wish, not fully but implicitly, indirectly, as an aside and without being able to make it the very object of one's thinking: 'Don't forget to live!' said Goethe (*Gedenke zu leben*); or 'we must try to live' (the last strophe of Valéry's 'Cimetière marin'); or 'Learn finally to live' (Derrida's last interview). But what does it mean to gain access to 'living'? And why is it always kept until the end?

This does not mean that, by entering into one thought, we are abandoning the other one. What does 'coming out of' actually mean? It isn't to flee; nor is it a renunciation. What I understand by a passing through China is contrary to a certain messianic conception according to which the way out of ontology would be the object of an expectation and a hope that would mark such an emergence from the 'question of being' as a liberation. This question of Being, from its determination of the truth as well as its consequent erection of an ideality, has notably opened up the possibility of both an unparalleled scientific development and an ethical and political construction. In particular, in touching upon the question of Being, can we abandon its force of enigma and invention? Or let's consider things reciprocally: Chinese thought, as it comes out of its 'Taoist' thinking upon meeting the ontological thinking of Europe, also experienced a liberation (and, above all, a release from its 'royal way' – in other words, in fact, from its autocratic regulation). It is therefore not a matter of abandoning one way of thinking for another, or of arranging one way of thinking under the other, any more than it is of putting the European under the Chinese, through a reversal of past alienation – in other words, by converting to one or the other side – but of envisaging these ways of thinking in terms of their respective resources, or of what I'd call their fertility.

When I try to develop the coherences of Chinese thought (and I must do so with all the more commitment in relation to a Western public which, in a general way, doesn't know it – or if it does, it is only at second or third hand – in other words, according to an uncontrolled *doxa* that inclines towards fantasising), it is really the opposite of exoticism. This means that, notwithstanding the illusion generated, it is not a matter of rejecting or devaluing European coherences reshaped in relation through this open alternative. It is rather a matter of rediscovering them from the outside in their inventiveness so as to regain them at once in their singularity and in their possibilities. Indeed, nothing is more fraudulent than that false ideo-logical currency which, under the cover of Orientalism and the appeal to live, has caused its trade in happiness to prosper in the West in a way that constitutes only a flaccid thinking, and not at all an other or a counter-thought, still less another possibility of thinking. If, finally (just as from the outset), I recommend the form of 'divergence', of the tension it sets up and maintains and in which it keeps us engaged and functioning, but in a way that never ends and that doesn't give in to the facility of any conclusion or reconciliation, it is because it constantly puts reason back to work but without ever disqualifying it and so, by appealing to our freedom, it re-establishes *choice* in thinking.

Note

1   *Communautarisme*: this term is to an extent a French equivalent of 'identity politics', although with a stronger sense of identification, implying that one identifies more strongly with an immediate community than with the greater society, and often to the exclusion of other groups [trans.].

Bibliography

Aristotle (1984) *Complete Works of Aristotle*, edited and translated by Jonathan Barnes. Princeton, NJ: Princeton University Press.

Augustine, Saint, Bishop of Hippo (1962) *My Confessions*, translated by E. B. Pusey. London: Dent, Everyman Library.

Augustine, Saint, Bishop of Hippo (1998) *The City of God Against the Pagans*, edited and translated by R. W. Dyson. Cambridge: Cambridge University Press.

Augustine, Saint, Bishop of Hippo (2002) *On the Trinity*, edited by Gareth Matthews, translated by Stephen McKenna. Cambridge: Cambridge University Press.

Augustine, Saint, Bishop of Hippo (2017) *On Lying (De mendacio)*. CreateSpace Independent Publishing Platform.

Bergson, Henri (2010) *The Creative Mind: An Introduction to Metaphysics*. Mineola: Dover Publications.

Braudel, Fernand (1980) *On History*, translated by Sarah Matthews. Chicago: University of Chicago Press.

Chuang tzu (1968) *The Complete Works*, translated by Burton Watson. New York and London: Columbia University Press.

Cicero, Marcus Tullius (1985) *Tusculan Disputations*, edited with translation and notes by A. E. Douglas. Warminster: Aris & Phillips.

Clausewitz, Karl von (1976) *On War*, edited and translated by Michael Howard and Peter Paret. Princeton; Guildford : Princeton University Press.

Cleary, Thomas (ed. and trans.) (1992) *The Essential Tao*. Edison, NJ: Castle Books.

Confucius (1993) *The Analects*, translated with an introduction and notes by Raymond Dawson. Oxford and New York: Oxford University Press.

Derrida, Jacques (1978) *Writing and Difference*, translated with an introduction and additional notes by Alan Bass. Chicago: University of Chicago Press.

Derrida, Jacques (1981) 'Plato's Pharmacy', in *Dissemination*, translated with an introduction and additional notes by Barbara Johnson. London: Athlone, pp. 61–172.

Descartes, René (1957) *Rules for the Direction of the Mind*, reconstructed from notes taken by his pupils and edited by Errol E. Harris. London: Allen & Unwin.

Descartes, René (1996) *Meditations on First Philosophy: With Selections from the Objections and Replies*, edited and translated by John Cottingham with an introductory essay by Bernard Williams. Cambridge: Cambridge University Press.

Descola, Philippe (2005) *Par-delà nature et culture*. Paris: Éditions Gallimard.

Detienne, Marcel (1999) 'Le phalange: problèmes et controverses', in *Problèmes de la guerre en Grèce ancienne*, edited by Jean-Pierre Vernant. Paris: Seuil.

Detienne, Marcel (2002) *Comparer l'incomparable; Comparing the Incomparable*, trans. Janet Lloyd (Stanford University Press, 2008).

Detienne, Marcel and Vernant, Jean-Pierre (1978) *Cunning Intelligence in Greek Culture and Society*. Brighton: Harvester Press.

Douglas, Alfred (1971) *The Oracle of Change: How to Consult the I Ching*. Harmondsworth: Penguin Books.

Empedocles (1981) *The Extant Fragments*, edited with an introduction by M. R. Wright. New Haven, CT and London: Yale University Press.

Fang Xun (ed.) (1962) *Shanjing hualun*. Peking: Meishu Chubanshe.

Freud, Sigmund (1977) 'A Special Choice of Object Made by Men' [1910], in *On Sexuality*, The Pelican Freud Library, Vol. 7, compiled and edited by Angela Richards, translated by James Strachey. Harmondsworth: Penguin Books.

Freud, Sigmund (1979) 'The Rat Man' [1909], in *Case Histories II*, The Pelican Freud Library, Vol. 9, compiled and edited by Angela Richards, translated by James Strachey. Harmondsworth: Penguin Books.

Freud, Sigmund (1984) 'Repression' [1915], in *On Metapsychology: The History of Psychoanalysis*, The Pelican Freud Library, Vol. *11*, compiled and edited by Angela Richards, translated by James Strachey. Harmondsworth: Penguin Books.

Frontinus, Sextus Julius (1925) *Stratagems*, Loeb Classical Library, edited by Mary B. McElwain, translated by Charles Bennet. London: William Heinemann.

Gide, André (1952) *The Fruits of the Earth*, translated by Dorothy Bussy. London: Secker & Warburg.

Hegel, Georg Wilhelm Friedrich (1969) *Science of Logic*, translated by A. V. Miller. London: George Allen & Unwin.

Hegel, Georg Wilhelm Friedrich (1977) *Phenomenology of Spirit*, translated by A.V. Miller with analysis of the text and foreword by J. N. Findlay. Oxford: Clarendon Press.

Heidegger, Martin (1977) 'What is Metaphysics?', translated by David Krell, in *Basic Writings*. New York: Harper & Row.

Heidegger, Martin (2010) *Being and Time*; translated by Joan Stambaugh, revised and with a foreword by Dennis J. Schmidt. Albany, NY: State University of New York Press.

Heraclitus of Ephesus (1994) *Fragments*, translated by Dennis Sweet. Lanham, MD and London: University Press of America.

Heraclitus of Ephesus (2000) *Fragments*, edited and translated by Robin Waterfield, in *The First Philosophers: The Pre-Socratics and the Sophists*. Oxford: Oxford University Press.

Huntington, Samuel P. (1996) *The Clash of Civilizations and the Remaking of World Order*. New York: Simon & Schuster.

Husserl, Edmund (1991) *On the Phenomenology of the Consciousness of Internal Time (1893–1917)*, translated by John Barnett Brough. Dordrecht and Boston: Kluwer Academic Publishers.

I Ching, or, Book of Changes (1968), the Richard Wilhelm translation rendered into English by Cary F. Baynes. London: Routledge & Kegan Paul.

Kant, Immanuel (1969) *Foundations of the Metaphysics of Morals*, translated by Lewis White Beck, with critical essays edited by Robert Paul Wolff. New York: Macmillan; London: Collier Macmillan.

Lacan, Jacques (1979) *The Four Fundamental Concepts of Psycho-analysis*, translated by Alan Sheridan. Harmondsworth: Penguin.

Lao-Tzu (1992) *Te-tao ching*, translated with introduction and commentary by Robert G. Henricks. New York: Ballantine Books.

Leibniz, Gottfried Wilhelm (1991) *The Monadology*, translated by Nicholas Rescher. Pittsburgh, PA: University of Pittsburgh Press.

Levinas, Emmanuel (1996) *Proper Names*, translated by Michael B. Smith. Stanford: Stanford University Press.

Liang, Shih-Ch'iu (1949) *The Fine Art of Reviling*, translated by William B. Pettus. San Fransisco: Wallace Kibbee & Son.

Mallarmé, Stéphane (1956) 'Crisis in Poetry', in *Mallarmé: Selected Prose Poems, Essays & Letters*, translated by Bradford Cook. Baltimore, MD: The Johns Hopkins University Press.

Marcus Aurelius (1990) *The Meditations of Marcus Aurelius*, translated by A. S. L. Farquharson; and *A Selection from the Letters of Marcus and Fronto*, translated by R. B. Rutherford; with introduction and notes by R. B. Rutherford. Oxford and New York: Oxford University Press.

Mencius (1963) a new translation arranged and annotated for the general reader by W. A. C. H. Dobson. London: Oxford University Press.

Mencius (1998) translated by David Hinton. Washington, DC: Counterpoint.

Montaigne, Michel de (1987) *The Essays*, translated by M. A. Screech. Harmondsworth: Allen Lane, The Penguin Press.

Nietzsche, Friedrich (1961) *Thus Spoke Zarathustra*, translated by R. J. Hollingdale. Harmondsworth: Penguin.

Nietzsche, Friedrich (1968) *Beyond Good and Evil: Prelude to a Philosophy of the Future*, translated by Walter Kaufmann in *The Basic Writings of Nietzsche*. New York: The New Library.

Plato (1961) *The Collected Dialogues of Plato*, including the letters, edited by Edith Hamilton and Huntington Cairns. Princeton, NJ: Princeton University Press.

Polybius (1925) *The Histories*, translated by W. R. Paton. London: William Heinemann.

Proust, Marcel (1981) *In Search of Lost Time*, translated by C. K. Scott Moncrieff and Terence Kilmartin, revised by D. J. Enright. London: Chatto & Windus.

Rousseau, Jean-Jacques (1979) *Émile or On Education*, translated by Allan Bloom. Harmondsworth: Penguin Books.

Rousseau, Jean-Jacques (2000) *Confessions*, translated by Angela Scholar. Oxford: Oxford University Press.

Sartre, Jean-Paul (1989) *Being and Nothingness: An Essay in Phenomenological Ontology*, translated by Hazel E. Barnes. London: Methuen & Co. Ltd.

Spinoza, Baruch (2000) *Ethics*, translated by G. H. R. Parkinson. Oxford: Oxford University Press.

SunTzu (2005) *The Art of War*, translated by John Minford. London: Penguin.

Wang Fuzhi (1976) *Dutongjianlun*. Beijing: Zhong hua shuju.

Wang Guowei (1940) 'Lun xinxueyu de shuru' ['On the Introduction of Neologisms'], in *Haining Wang xiansheng yishu*. Shangwu.

Wittgenstein, Ludwig (1977) *Culture and Value: A Selection from the Posthumous Remains*, edited by Hendrik von Wright in collaboration with Heikki Nyman, translated by Peter Winch. Oxford: Blackwell.

Xenophon (1921) *Hellenica*, translated by Carleton L. Brownson. London: William Heinemann.

Xunzi (1988) *Complete Works* (2 vols), translated by John Knoblock. Stanford, CA: Stanford University Press.

Zhongyong (2001) *Focusing the Familiar: A Translation and Philosophical Interpretation of the Zhongyong*, annotated and translated by Roger T. Ames and David L. Hall. Honolulu: University of Hawaii Press; the Chinese text can be found at http://ctext.org/liji/zhong-yong (last accessed 20 June 2019).

Index